INNOCENTS ABROAD

Innocents Abroad

The story of British child evacuees in Australia, 1940–45

EDWARD STOKES

ALLEN & UNWIN

For George Woodger

This work was assisted by a writer's grant from
The Australia Council, the Federal Government's
arts funding and advisory body.

First published 1994
Allen & Unwin Pty Ltd
9 Atchison Street, St Leonards, NSW 2065 Australia

National Library of Australia
Cataloguing-in-Publication entry:
Stokes, Edward, 1948–   .
   Innocents abroad: the story of British child evacuees
   in Australia, 1940–45.

   Bibliography.
   ISBN 1 86373 529 1 (pb).
   ISBN 1 86373 657 3 (hb).

   1. World War, 1939–1945—Children—Great Britain.
   2. World War, 1939–1945—Children—Australia.
   3. World War, 1939–1945—Evacuation of Civilians—
   Great Britain.   4. World War, 1939–1945—Evacuation
   of Civilians—Australia.   I. Title.

940.53161

Set in Garamond by Graphicraft Typesetters Ltd, Hong Kong
Printed by South Wind Productions, Singapore

10   9   8   7   6   5   4   3   2   1

Contents

Preface

During 1990 I was asked to interview some Second World War evacuees for an Australian War Memorial oral history project. Fifty years earlier, as children, these people had been evacuated from Britain to Australia by the Children's Overseas Reception Board (CORB). Although fewer than six hundred children were sent to Australia their experiences raise issues of wide interest. In particular, they give insights into the significance of family bonds and into the perceptions, thoughts and feelings of children.

My first meetings with CORB evacuees suggested a wealth of memories. Their recollections revealed often poignant contrasts: of adventure and family separation, of love and abuse, of lifetime gains and losses. The saga interested me for two reasons.

Historically, the evacuees' experiences contrast life in Britain and life in Australia during the war years. Many of the people later settled in Australia. However, unlike some recently recorded Australian child migration schemes, the CORB evacuation is a story in which Australians, for the most part, can take pride.

The evacuees' recollections also touched me personally. Born in Australia, I grew up in Hong Kong and completed my education in Australia and Britain. I left home at the age of fifteen, with keen excitement but also with many backward glances to a close family. With roots in three places, and a family now divided between Britain and Australia, I know something of the mixed identity that the CORB evacuees describe.

The book relies primarily on the recollections of some fifty evacuees. My meetings with them were often happy and amusing, but other encounters were shadowed by the memory of wartime traumas. Even today these experiences rekindle deeply felt—and often rarely expressed—emotions. The evacuees' recollections are personal accounts of their formative years, recalled after half a century. As such, they are inevitably subjective, a strength not a weakness in a book of this nature. To provide an underlying objective framework, a questionnaire answered by one hundred evacuees was also employed. (Details concerning the oral history, the questionnaire and the evacuees who contributed appear at the back of the book.)

The book's themes are set in the context of the children's origins. The narrative recounts the war's beginnings, the children's evacuation to Australia, their five years there, and their postwar return to Britain. Wartime evacuation, as the accounts stress, is as much about journeys as about destinations. The evacuees' experiences during their voyages to Australia, as well as their lives there, affected and changed them. The balance of the book reflects this.

Many organisations and individuals have helped me. Above all, an Australia Council Literature Board Fellowship allowed me to work freely for a year. Without this generous support the book could not have been completed.

My 1990 CORB interviews for the Australian War Memorial's Keith Murdoch Sound Archive were commissioned by Australian Heritage Projects Ltd. The encouragement of Stephen Foster of Australian Heritage Projects Ltd is much appreciated. I also wish to thank Julie Gorrell and Roslyn Russell of the same organisation, and Harry Martin who recorded four of the War Memorial's CORB interviews. The War Memorial's permission to publish from the Keith Murdoch Sound Archive's CORB interviews was invaluable. Their later transcription of the British interviews was extremely helpful and generous. George Imashev and Bill Brassell at the War Memorial have been of great assistance. The Imperial War Museum, London, generously waived reproduction fees for numerous photographs from their collection, and I thank Jane Carmichael and Paul Kemp. (These and other photographs and documents are credited at the end of the book.)

Special thanks go to Olympus and R. Gunz Ltd. For some years Olympus and Gunz have given very generous support to my photography and writing—and Bob Pattie's encouragement is much appreciated. Staff at the National Library of Australia and at the *Australian Geographic* have also helped and encouraged my work. I thank especially John Thompson and Mark Cranfield at the Library, and Howard Whelan and Valerie Reed at 'AG'. Qantas Airways, and Mark Williams, helped with travel to and from Britain. I also wish to thank John Swire & Sons, who agreed to my postponing a Hong Kong project until after this book was completed.

For hospitality during a particularly nomadic year I thank: in Australia, Michael and Sue Scobie, Greg Jones, Wim and Barbara Boele, Peter and Jay Read, Ann Evers; in Britain, Michael and Margaret Fethney, Anne James and Jonathan Higgens; in Hong Kong, Gill Forestal; in Singapore, Peter and Julia Jolly—and 'the minnows'. George Woodger, Maurice and Margaret Finnis, Judith Stokes, Edith Marchant, John Stokes, Tom Goddard, Rachel Duncan and Madeleine Lynn helped in other ways.

The structure and style of the book have been greatly improved by Gwenneth Stokes, my mother, who interrupted her own writing to help with this text. Elizabeth Weiss' encouragement at Allen & Unwin is much appreciated, as are Lynne Frolich's and Devon Mills' later painstaking editing of the book. Barbara Mobbs, my anchor in Australia, encouraged and helped in countless ways.

My greatest debt is to the CORB evacuees who contributed. Their hospitality and willingness to help are gratefully acknowledged. Even more, I appreciate the trust they showed in a virtual stranger and their willingness to talk without reservation. A special debt is owed to those evacuees whose interviews or questionnaires brought back painful memories. The names of the contributors appear at the end of the book.

One 'CORB' deserves special thanks: Michael Fethney, whose book *The Absurd and the Brave* guided my first CORB interviews. He later gave me much encouragement and assistance. In 1992, while recalling his father's experiences in the trenches of 'the war to end all wars', Michael had this to say:

> In Sarajevo just over four hundred children have been evacuated this very day. Television showed scenes of children, some of them very young, clinging to their parents. One distraught mother was saying, 'We just don't know if we'll see them again'.

Edward Stokes
Oxford, 1993

Perhaps the only solidly real place we ever know is the place in which we spent our childhood and youth. It's there that there are genuinely real streets, squares, shops and houses, and their only fault is that they have a trick, like the queer cards that conjurers use, of appearing diminished every time we go back.

J.B. Priestley,
Postscripts 1940

To be torn up from the roots of home life, to be sent away from the family circle, in most instances for the first time in the child's life, was a painful event. This was no social experiment; it was a surgical rent only to be contemplated as a last resort . . . From the first day of September 1939, evacuation ceased to be a problem of administrative planning. It became instead a multitude of problems in human relationships.

R.M. Titmuss,
History of the Second World War 1950

Introduction

In June 1940 Britain stood almost alone against the might of Nazi Germany. The 'phoney war' was over, its sometimes comic aspects overtaken by impending disaster. Within a fortnight of the Allies' bitter-sweet evacuation from Dunkirk France was requesting an armistice. Meanwhile, Italy had entered the war on the German side. Newsreels graphically portrayed the ravages wrought by the Nazi forces in their advance across the Continent. German bombers were now flying over Britain itself: fears of imminent invasion were rife.

It was in that dark month that the British government established the Children's Overseas Reception Board (CORB), an organisation charged with evacuating children to the Dominions. Some wealthy parents had already sent their children to safety across the Atlantic. Partly to placate resentment at private evacuation, CORB was created to send the children of less well-off families overseas. Winston Churchill, by then Prime Minister, deplored the scheme's implied defeatism. Others warned that overseas evacuation posed dangers for family bonds. Within two weeks of CORB's establishment the scheme was closed: not defeated by lack of interest—but swamped by over 200 000 applications.

Between late July and early September 1940 some 3100 CORB evacuees sailed for Australia, Canada, New Zealand and South Africa. Then, on 17 September, while all the Australia-bound evacuees were at sea, the *City of Benares* was torpedoed. Seventy-seven CORB children were lost. Further overseas evacuation was deemed politically unacceptable. Future CORB sailings were cancelled, but the organisation retained responsibility for the evacuees already sent off.

This book tells the story of the CORB children evacuated to Australia. For these evacuees 'the war', though it began over fifty years ago, remains vivid. In place of bombs, they experienced the heartbreak—and adventure—of being wrenched from everything that was familiar: their families, their neighbourhoods, their country. However they fared, their formative wartime years spent in Australia are unforgettable.

Five hundred and seventy-seven children were en route to Australia when the *City of Benares* was sunk. They had left home at short notice amid the organised chaos of Britain's darkest hour. For some of the older children adventure beckoned. But most had never before left home; some were as young as five. Others—children who had

Tower Bridge and the Thames docks in flames, following the first mass daylight attack on London, 7 September 1940. The German bombing of London and other major British cities during the summer of 1940 was seen as the prelude to a full-scale invasion.

previously been sent for safety to rural areas in Britain—were being evacuated for a second time.

All the children bound for Australia sailed from Liverpool during August and September 1940. Before boarding their three ships they endured nightly bombing raids. Homesickness and seasickness made the early stages of their voyages bleak. However, most quickly adapted to shipboard life and incessant lifeboat drills. Tropical glare replaced leaden skies as the three ships steamed towards Australia. Anticipation and anxiety mingled in the children's thoughts as they approached their landfall. They yearned to be ashore, but for many 'their' ship had become home. What lay ahead?

The ships arrived separately in Australia in October and November 1940. Any doubts about the future were brushed aside in the enthusiastic welcome. 'Britain's Crown Jewels', the politicians chorused, had been entrusted to Australia.

The evacuees stayed with relatives or with foster parents. Most spent

Child evacuees leaving one of Britain's cities in 1940. The heartbreak and adventure of evacuation remain vivid for almost all evacuees—whether they were sent to rural areas of Britain or overseas to the Dominions.

the war in homes more affluent than their own. In general these children fared better than those evacuated within Britain itself, where class barriers often created deep tensions. In Australia far more of the evacuees were happy than were unhappy. But a few led joyless lives, enduring years of neglect and sometimes abuse. Most stayed with only one or two families throughout the war, but a handful led vagabond lives without any sustained relationships.

The majority of evacuees spent the war in suburban areas. Others went to live in the country. A few spent the war in the outback—mustering cattle, fighting bushfires, experiencing a life which the typical Australian child only read about.

Wherever they lived the evacuees almost all enjoyed Australia's space, its sparkling climate and the outdoor life. Today they vividly recall summer days on crystal beaches, verandah sleep-outs, plentiful food, strange birds and animals, warm-hearted people.

The CORB evacuees were isolated from the dangers and deprivations of war. Britain, bombed and rationed, seemed another world. The children were periodically reminded of what they had escaped by news reports and letters. Many felt disquiet, and sometimes guilt, when they heard of their parents' hardships. Even the Pacific War barely touched their own lives.

When they left Britain most of the children—and many parents—expected the war to be over within a year or so. As 1942 came and went parents agonised over whether they should have sent their children away. And for many evacuees anguish at the lost years of family life grew as the war dragged on. By 1945 a gulf of years and experiences separated children and parents.

For many of the evacuees the war's end was the culmination of their hopes. It meant a return voyage and long-awaited family reunions. But others felt torn. For them peace brought personal conflict, as a nagging question came into focus: 'To which family, and in which country, do I belong?'.

A few of the older evacuees never returned, but the majority sailed for Britain after the war. Homecomings were mixed. Most evacuees found postwar Britain bleak and depressing, though some settled relatively easily and enjoyed renewing their family life. But about half of those returning felt tense and distant. The parents of these children and young adults could barely comprehend the changes in their offspring, who themselves often felt a guilty disdain for their parents' seemingly narrow lives.

Most CORB evacuees initially made their homes in Britain; in many cases, however, only because of family ties. Some still yearn for Australia. Others, unhappy in Britain and missing Australia, emigrated in the late 1940s and early 1950s. In subsequent decades still others finally decided to follow their hearts, to leave Britain again and 'go home' to Australia. At least a third of the CORB evacuees live in Australia today.

The CORB legacy lingers on. Most of the evacuees have led ordinarily contented lives. However, even those who found kindness and love in Australia recall their wartime years with emotion, and often with silent tears. Many still bitterly regret the loss of intimacy with their parents. The small minority who endured abuse have mostly transcended their experiences, but some have remained scarred for life. Most say they would never have parted with their own children in similar circumstances.

One CORB evacuee—a boy who found great love in Australia and who lives today among the family that nurtured him during the war—still feels 'an emotional chill whenever I remember what I lost. Life was never the same again. The memory of those years will never leave me.'

At Home in Britain   1

We knew everybody in the street, and all the trades-people who used to come around . . .

SEPTEMBER 1940: Relentless bombing by the Luftwaffe was pounding London. Vapour trails by day and searchlights by night crisscrossed the sky. Fierce fires brought entire buildings crashing to the ground. 'If invasion is going to be tried at all, it does not seem that it can be long delayed', Winston Churchill declared. To this threat, and to the horrific destruction and death wrought by the Luftwaffe, Britain responded with stoic defiance. At Buckingham Palace the King practised pistol shooting.

Meanwhile, the three ships carrying 577 children evacuated from Britain were making their way towards Australia. The *Batory*, which had left first, was crossing the Indian Ocean. The *Nestor* was skirting Africa and the *Diomed*, the last of the three to leave, was pitching and rolling southwards through the Atlantic. The ships were voyaging across hostile seas. Completely cut off from their parents, the children sailed on towards safety in Australia—an unknown haven.

The lives of these children had been patterned by stability and continuity, their backgrounds firmly rooted in their families, neighbourhoods and regions. Only a handful had ever left Britain before. For almost all of them Australia was merely a distant country of the pink-mapped Empire, best known for its Aborigines, kangaroos and sheep—and diggers in slouch hats. The thought of going there was almost unimaginable.

Not all the CORB children came from loving homes, but most recall their family relationships as close. Only a few look back to childhoods marred by tension or lack of love.

Barbara Donald, from County Durham, was eleven in 1940. She came from a fairly typical family: 'We children always came first. The family home was filled with warmth and love, especially in the wintertime round the coal fires. Dad used to play the gramophone for us, or we used to just sit and chat and look at pictures in the fires.' Betty Deeley, a year older, grew up overlooking the Mersey. She recalls: 'We always listened to the news bulletins, and my father loved military music. We used to march about the house when that was on. My father would carry the poker over his shoulder, I'd have something, my brother would be behind and the Airedale came last.'

Phil Robinson, a fourteen-year-old from one of the better Birmingham suburbs, often went with his mother 'down to Dad's office to have afternoon tea and cakes in front of the gas fire. Over the fireplace was a portrait of my father's father who was one of the founding members of the business. I remember gazing up at this portrait with awe.'

For many of the children extended families added to their sense of belonging and continuity. As a small child Ruth Wilson had gone to stay at her grandmother's while her mother gave birth at home. 'My grandmother asked if I might stay and live with her, to have some young life', Ruth recalls. In 1940, ten years later, she was still there:

> We had our front room with a bay window, and you could sit there and look out and see the world going by. There was also the general living room, and there was a kitchen, which in those days was called the scullery, and off that was a big pantry under the stairs. Three bedrooms upstairs, and the toilet was outside and the laundry was in the back yard.
> We were a very close-knit family. In wintertime everything happened around the fireplace, an open fire with a hob where the kettle used to sing. All the brass was very highly polished, there were gas mantles over the fire and we would toast in front of it.

The CORB children were all born between 1925 and 1935. Many were from families with local roots stretching back over twenty years, some for generations. Over half the children came from cities, others lived in towns and villages. Virtually all had 'the feeling that you knew everybody'. As Barbara Donald recalls:

> We knew everybody in the street, and all the tradespeople who used to come around. If Mum was making a big pot of soup she would ask me to take some next door to elderly neighbours, and down the street. A friend of Mum's used to come and do the baking for us, cakes and buns, biscuits, all sorts of things. She used to hide us in corners and tell us not to tell the others that we had a lickey dish.

Isabella Wood's eleven years on Tyneside had been lived amongst 'the people around, and I missed them all when I had to leave'.

> The streets were cobbled. We had one beautiful park and we had a lovely beach, but the area where I lived was all industry, ship yards, coal mines and smoke. Later, when I grew up, I thought, 'How on earth did you live in a place like that?'.

The people in the north-east of England welcomed you with open arms. No matter how poor they were, you could have all that they had ... My brother slept in a put-you-up in the kitchen area because there was just one big bedroom for my parents, and one for me. My mother wanted to leave and get somewhere else. But my father thought it was better to be near his work, and he wouldn't leave his mother who lived next door.

The CORB children's families had almost all been affected by the 1930s Depression. The immediate prewar years had seen slightly better times, but poverty and slum conditions remained widespread. Britain's child mortality rate was high, and in 1936 free school lunches were introduced to combat hunger. Frugality, hand-me-down clothes and make-and-do repairs remained the norm. Woolworths still advertised itself as the 'nothing over sixpence' store. Virtually all the children's homes had a wireless, but only a very few had telephones.

Around Newcastle's mining villages, where Ted Flowers lived, 'bathrooms were comparatively uncommon'. Children like him, often grimy from shovelling coal into household bunkers 'to make a few sixpences', washed in fireside tubs. Middle class families mostly had the luxury of bathrooms. In Barbara Donald's home there was the joy of her father's left-over bath water 'smelling lovely with his bath salts'. Katharine Cuthbert fondly remembers a 'vast iron bath' which held three youngsters. Afterwards there was the pleasure of a motherly towelling: 'Under the window there was a raised seat, and in it the hot water tank. The tradition was that small children would be lifted out of the bath and sat or stood on the tank and dried.'

The children who lived in the newer suburbs saw less neighbourhood life than those in older, industrial areas. Walking from his suburban home to his father's office Phil Robinson often passed Birmingham's 'two-up, two-down terraces', where in tiny back courtyards 'children were always fighting and bickering and shouting'. The streets still had huge, hissing gas lamps suspended on wires. Itinerant workers still sometimes passed outside Phil's bedroom window:

> ... the organ grinder going past in the gas lamplight, with this little monkey on the top of his organ, the hot chestnut seller with his hot brazier on a cart selling hot chestnuts, and the lamplighter who came along with his ladder over his shoulder ...

Games, mostly played in streets and lanes, were part of the fabric of local life. Betty Deeley remembers living near Liverpool, in Warrington:

> We had football on the street, we had roller-skates, and we used to play hockey on roller-skates. One season you had whipping tops, another season you had marbles, another season it might

3

be hopscotch. We used to put on plays, and all the kids who played in the street would do a turn . . . And on May Day we used to have the maypole dance in the street.

Some of the CORB children could swim, but few were involved in organised sports. Many were familiar with country life: 'Two or three boys sitting up in an oak tree gnawing away at a turnip', was one of Ted Flowers' delights. Or, on summer evenings during the potato harvest, he and his mates from near Newcastle would go out and help themselves. 'We'd have a fire on the pit heap at the top of the street and roast these potatoes in their jackets, burnt black, mealy inside.' Boys from better-off families had Dinky toys, Meccano sets and wind-up Hornby trains. Bicycles were treasured, but far from universal, possessions.

Christmas was a time of simple pleasures, even for a doctor's daughter like Barbara Donald: 'We used to make all our own presents. We always knew we'd have an orange and apple, a shining new penny and a bag of chocolate pennies in our stockings.'

If the CORB children were tied to their localities by bonds of family and friendship, they were also held there by the exclusions of class. Half the children saw their parents as 'working class', the fathers ready to doff their caps to their betters. Another third had 'lower middle class' backgrounds, and the remainder regarded their families as belonging to the 'upper middle class'. The rigidities of British class-consciousness, and regional differences of accent and lifestyle, meant that for some children their backgrounds were both a haven and a cage: a comforting source of security—but a severe obstacle for those with aspirations 'above their station'.

Moving house, even between neighbourhoods of similar class, was difficult, as Betty Deeley discovered in 1938 when her family moved from Warrington's close-knit community to Birmingham. More challenging still was any shift into a 'better' area. Dorothy Loft grew up in Battersea, 'south of the Thames'. Her family later moved to Bromley, one of the newer suburbs on the outskirts of London:

It was a problem for me to move from a working class school into an upper class one . . . In Battersea, there was no awareness that there was something on the other side of the fence because all the children were the same. I had to have elocution lessons when I went to Bromley because I was south London—'ain't ya' and all that.

Moving 'down' the snakes-and-ladders of class could also be exclud-ing. Donald Mitchell was born in Manchester in 1927 and two years

Helen, Katharine and Bridget Cuthbert (*left to right*), and a playmate, photographed at Stirling, Scotland in 1939. The Cuthbert girls came from a close, middle-class family, as this cameo—complete with matching hats and coats—suggests.

later his parents moved to Colne, a Yorkshire mill town. Donald's father was a manager in a town of mill workers: 'We spoke more gently, so we were almost southerners in the eyes of local children'.

> We were somewhat mocked, and physically bullied from time to time. I didn't feel I really belonged there as a native, and I wasn't integrated in any deep way into the life of the town. You weren't considered a local unless your grandparents had lived there.

Before their evacuation to Australia many of the CORB children had never been more than a hundred kilometres from their homes. Some had never travelled more than fifty kilometres. About half, however, went away on annual holidays. These escapes, jaunts across a temporary no-man's land in the minefield of class, were the rare occasions when children experienced lives different from their own. Even then, East Enders who went hop picking in Kent spent their time with farm workers. Children from middle class homes were taken to the 'less vulgar' seaside

5

The Bullard family at the seaside in 1935, with Bob nestled beside his father. For typical British families, seaside holidays were the most common escape from daily life before the war.

resorts. And, as Phil Robinson's parents did, many found pleasure—and familiarity—in holidaying year after year at one place:

> Father was an ex-British Army officer. He was badly shot up in France, and he was very lucky to survive. He had somehow acquired an old Army bell tent. We used to take that down to the south coast at Dorset for year after year. We used to camp in a farmer's field. The milk used to come straight from the cow into a bucket, then back to the tent in a billycan. It had a beautiful scent to a kid who spent most of his life in Birmingham.

There were just the three of us, Mum and Dad and me. At night-time Mum always used to insist on having half an hour or whatever of what she used to call camp songs. We used to lie in bed there just singing these songs. 'Row, Row, Row the Boat', 'Ten Green Bottles' and all those songs.

The CORB children who were most aware of the wider world were those with relatives living overseas. In the years between the wars family relationships spread web-like across the Empire. Migration from Britain's overcrowded cities to the Dominions was long-standing. The First World War had also led to numerous marriages between Empire servicemen and British women.

Two-thirds of the children had relatives in Australia. Katharine Cuthbert, born in Scotland, had numerous aunts and uncles in Australia. Her parents, she recalls, projected the sense of a far-flung, yet unified, family. The Australian Cuthberts periodically visited Britain:

There was a very regular correspondence from the time my mother was separated from her sisters, when one married an Australian and she married a Scot. They wrote at least weekly, and so we were very familiar with their lives in Australia. We had this image of a lovely place with a very free sort of life.

Reg Loft, Dorothy's thirteen-year-old brother, had been born in Australia. Living in London in the 1930s he worshipped a man named Digger, 'bronzed with the typical Aussie face and body'. Reg 'adored Australians', especially when 'they marched during the Coronation with their slouch hats and feathers'. Newspaper photographs of the Australian troops celebrating the Coronation delighted him: 'Diggers opening the corrugated tops of bottles with their teeth and that type of thing. They came over as extremely strong men relative to Englishmen.'

Even fleeting visits by Australian relatives to the Old Country often left lasting impressions there. Michael Fethney grew up in Bradford where 'Australian merino fleeces came by the million'. He was fascinated by a forgotten uncle who suddenly appeared at the Fethney home: 'It transpired he had gone out to Australia aged twelve. His life in Australia seemed to be one big adventure, and all of it happening in sunlight—and occasional floods!' Charles Harold Fethney's yarns proved strong enough to entice Michael and his brother John to Australia in 1940. Phil Robinson's Uncle Len left equally striking images of his life in Queensland:

He had been absolutely adamant that he was going to farm his own land, so he went to Australia just before the First World War and began sugar-cane farming in Queensland. [His brothers] Uncle Norman and Uncle Cliff joined the Australian army when the First World War broke out. They were both wounded in

France, and finished up back in England convalescing in their own old family home.

Australians, with their light-hearted confidence and independence, seemed set apart from the rigidities that narrowed life in Britain. And Australia, these children gathered, was a place of sunshine, opportunity—and adventure!

For many families the First World War had left a legacy of lost and shattered lives—and deep-seated fears of the horrors of modern warfare. Over half of the CORB children's fathers had served in the war, and many still carried physical and psychological scars from it.

Michael Fethney, whose father had fought in France, was often drawn to the Roll of Honour at his parish church. It had over a hundred names. Even as a boy he sensed 'the utter desolation in the parish' that the list reflected. Michael was struck by the fact that 'near enough exactly half the names on that Roll of Honour were of men who'd been killed on 1st July 1916, the first day of the Battle of the Somme'. Other CORB children saw at first hand the lingering effects of war. Reg Harris, who grew up in South Wales, was one. His father had fought with the ANZACs:

> My father was gassed on his seventeenth birthday and it created quite a few problems as far as later being able to hold down a job. My mother was the caretaker, but my father did try a lot of small jobs: paperhanging, painting, things where he could get some work. But basically he was unemployed for many years.

Mary Clemes' father, an Australian Rhodes Scholar who settled in Britain, often talked about his wartime experiences. 'You couldn't call them happy memories', Mary recalls. 'But he seemed to think that there was a tremendous comradeship amongst the men in the First War.' David Massey, an eleven-year-old from Liverpool, remembers Christmases when his many uncles came to visit. 'The uncles and m'Dad used to talk about the First World War, about their stories of the trenches. We children [thought] it seemed glorious but to the poor men in the trenches it wasn't.'

In the late 1930s one inescapable matter intruded on the lives of British children: looming beyond the Channel was the possibility, soon the probability, of another war. Germany had become a fearfully armed colossus. Her armaments, especially air power, had outstripped Britain's.

Reg Loft recalls that, at meals, 'Dad would be saying, "What the hell are we doing not getting armed. We haven't got arms of any sort against

Anderson shelters being delivered to the London suburb of Muswell Hill, February 1938. The corrugated iron shelters, erected over holes dug into the ground, were to protect families from bomb blasts. Young children wondered what the strangely-shaped structures really 'meant'.

Germany." It was a worry which my father passed on to me.' Betty Deeley's father, a man of working class origins who read widely, was 'dreading the thought of another war':

> He was certain there would be war, and he was quite convinced that if a war did come all England would be badly bombed. But we didn't realise then to what extent he was thinking—such as sending us away from the bombing.

Michael Fethney's father 'had no doubt that we were going to have to stand up against Hitler. He was not going to be appeased.' The dictator's blustering, almost comic, malevolence created powerful images for children. Norman Townsend's father, another veteran, often tuned in to Radio Berlin. Thirteen-year-old Norman remembers hearing Hitler 'ranting and raving':

Hitler would shout and scream something, and the audience would applaud, a regimented applause, everybody clapping in unison. That was frightening, horrifying, that this huge crowd could be so regimented.

Paul Farquharson, aged twelve, recalls: 'There had to be complete silence while the nine o'clock news was on. My father and my elder brother discussed the news at great length. We were expecting war, I think everybody was expecting war.' Thinking back to the time immediately before the Munich crisis in September 1938, Paul says:

Slit trenches had been dug in the Ashford park, right across our football field. As a cub I helped with the sandbags, opening them up for the council workers who filled them. After Chamberlain came back from Munich they filled all the trenches in again.

Munich—Chamberlain's 'peace in our time'—foreshadowed the failure of appeasement. In February 1939 the battleship *Bismarck*, pride of the German fleet, was launched. In Britain, by then, factories were producing over 400 aircraft a month. Civil defence measures planned during the 1930s were being hastily implemented. Blast shelters—known as Anderson shelters—were delivered to homes in London and other 'target' cities. Posters and leaflets urged people to build air raid shelters, to hang blackout curtains. Trenches were dug, basements reinforced, and gas masks delivered to every adult and child. One eight-year-old remembers:

Phrases like ARP (air raid precautions) came into our lives and we were constantly being told: you must collect gas masks; you must think about having an Anderson shelter; you must think about putting tapes on your windows to stop them shattering in bomb bursts. All these things put the idea of war into young minds.

Isabella Woods, troubled by 'all the worried faces', came 'running in one night calling, "There's funny lights in the sky!"'—to be told they were searchlights. Joan Sharp, almost seven, ran out to see 'a big silvery-grey balloon with what looked like little tail wings'—a barrage balloon hovering over Lancashire's black landscape.

By the northern summer of 1939 war was virtually certain. Hitler's occupation of Czechoslovakia in March was the precursor of war. Then, in August, the Nazi–Soviet Pact was signed. Conscription had been introduced in Britain, and people were flocking to join the Territorial Army. Neville Chamberlain, the British Prime Minister, had pledged to defend Poland. Even youngsters sensed the changes shadowing their

'Dig for Victory' was to be a popular British wartime slogan. Even before the war, Mrs Prendergast had a crop of lettuce, beetroot and marrows atop her Anderson shelter—the only space for growing vegetables in her small Clapham backyard.

Following the Munich crisis of September 1938, as Europe drifted inexorably towards war, the British government urged families to protect their homes against bombing. Taping and boarding up windows were common precautions.

lives. Older children experienced excitement laced with foreboding as Europe drifted towards total war.

There was a pause. In 'a green and pleasant land' families holidayed together: around the coast, at resorts where piers glistened, and across the countryside near rustic villages. Outdated biplanes trailed lazy advertisements in the summer sky. Heather Staff's family, for the last time, went to a well-loved farm near Appleton-Wiske. 'It seemed sunny all the time', as Heather sees it now. 'Mornings milking the cows, going out picking mushrooms, visiting the village church . . .'

Far away, Australia had watched and waited. Now, on 1 September 1939, the *Sydney Morning Herald* editorialised: 'With the sword drawn from its scabbard, but still held only at guard, Europe awaits a decision for peace or war'.

Resigned rather than excited, most Australians accepted that their destiny was tied to Britain's. The imperial connection had been tested in the Boer War and in the trenches of the First World War. Australians would once again rally to the Empire's—and their own—defence. And their country would become a refuge for the CORB evacuees: an antipodean haven from the perils of the old world.

2 The War Begins

It was a whole different atmosphere when the war broke out. There wasn't that carefree feeling any more . . .

THE semblance of peace was shattered on 1 September 1939 when Germany invaded Poland. Britain mobilised its armed forces the same day. Two days later, at 11 a.m. on Sunday 3 September, Neville Chamberlain announced that Britain had declared war on Germany.

For Britain the Second World War began slowly. Eight months passed before Hitler's forces began a relentless advance towards the English Channel. The CORB children evacuated to Australia in 1940 took with them memories of the 'phoney war' and the dramatic escalation of the conflict in the spring and summer of 1940.

On the day war had been declared, 'everyone was indoors, ears to the wireless'. Pamela Palmer remembers:

> The announcement was no sooner over than the air raid sirens went. We'd already sandbagged the front of the house, the sticky paper was stuck onto the windows, and I had been given the job of filling some fire buckets with water. My mother had made a cupboard as a safe place for my younger sister and I.

The father of another of the girls 'went very white, I suppose thinking back to the last war when he was badly gassed'. And David Massey recalls that, after Chamberlain concluded,

> They played 'God Save the King'. My father walked to the window and stood for about an hour—just staring out. Then he came back and sat in his chair. And he said to my mother, 'I hope the poor devils don't have to go through what we went through in the First War'. There was total silence, total silence.

Braham Glass, a Jewish boy, had already been evacuated with his sister Essie from his East End home to the country. Braham was far from happy. His hosts had dragooned him into going to Sunday school, 'more or less into the enemy camp'. Chamberlain's news was relayed to the assembled children. 'I suppose I was a pessimist then, because I naturally assumed we were going to lose.' Braham was 'filled with terror because even then we knew what was happening to the Jews in Europe'.

Britain declared war on Germany on Sunday 3 September 1940, twenty-one years after 'the war to end all wars'. This photograph shows an ordinary London street—at an extraordinary, sombre moment.

For very young children the momentous news meant little. One simply recalls, 'My mother just got me out of the bath, dried me, got me dressed, and went running to find my father'.

Fact and fantasy blurred the horrors to come. Ken Dommerson realised his father and mother were 'stunned'. He was thirteen. 'I remember my first thought was: "I must dig an air raid shelter in the garden!" ' Paul Farquharson was with his family:

> We were still in the front room listening to the wireless when the air raid alarm went off. It turned out to be only an unidentified aircraft over the Channel, but we boys thought there

15

was something we ought to do. So we all went out and stuck our gas masks on, making ghastly noises which my mother objected to.

Children whose fathers had fought in the First World War understood the implications. Mary Clemes, aged thirteen, was on holiday in Cornwall. At Evensong that night, 'the minister preached a sermon on the text "He has changed sunset into sunrise". He was trying, I suppose, to give us some hope for the future in all that terrible blackness.'

Norman Townsend's home on the Isle of Wight lay across the Solent from the naval base at Portsmouth. Early on the morning of 3 September an army detachment 'established an anti-tank emplacement at the end of the street':

> My aunt was tearful because she remembered the First World War. But from a thirteen-year-old boy's point of view, to have the army right next door to us, to have an anti-tank gun parked virtually on our doorstep, was something a little exciting.

British Civil Defence reports prepared during the 1930s had all predicted immediate, relentless bombing by the Luftwaffe. These reports, which had created widespread fears, reflected the grim evidence of the Spanish Civil War and the Japanese atrocities in China. For every ton of explosives, one study suggested, 50 casualties would result. Another feared that saturation bombing of densely populated areas would kill 600 000 people in 60 days. The four key precautions aimed at minimising civilian casualties were blackout measures, the provision of gas masks, air raid shelters, and the evacuation of civilians from high-risk areas. Mary Clemes remembers:

> We didn't know whether we were going to have air raids immediately as they had in Czechoslovakia and Poland. We didn't know *what* was going to happen, I don't think anybody really did. I can't remember actual fear. It was just a question of girding up and making a lot of decisions. I know I had to be sent to another school, and we were preparing for evacuees and putting up the blackout. My father made wooden frames to fit all the biggest windows, and then my mother cut out the blackout material and we stuck it to the frames with drawing pins. These frames were put up as soon as it got to dusk every evening.

Gas masks were perhaps the war's most tangible intrusion on civilian life, and—especially for children—the most potent indication of the horrors of war. In 1938 the government, mindful of the gassing of troops in the First World War, had issued 44 000 000 rubberised masks

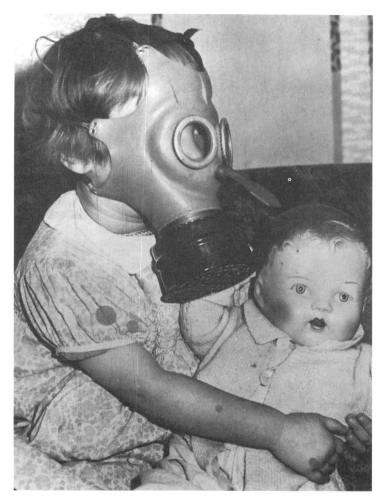

Gas masks issued to all adults and children were the war's most tangible intrusion into daily life. This photograph, of a small girl peering through her rubber mask, epitomises the grotesqueness of modern warfare: her doll appears more human than she. Masks such as this, specially made for toddlers, had 'red rubber and blue enamel'.

to every person over the age of five. Toddlers and infants later received special masks. Isabella Woods, on receiving hers, ran into the lavatory—aghast!

> My grandmother was banging on the door: 'If you don't put it on, I'm not putting mine on!' They had to get the air raid wardens to get me outside. It was a dreadful suffocating feeling, but I knew that I had to put it on otherwise Granny wouldn't put hers on.

By the time she left for Australia Isabella's gas mask had become 'part of me, just like my clothing'. These claustrophobic monstrosities, stored in small cardboard boxes, had to be taken everywhere. Mary Clemes had her gas mask 'slung on a cord over my shoulders'. But she

17

also had a school bag and a violin: 'So there was this violin case and the music case, all somehow attached to my bicycle'. Pamela Palmer remembers her mask's 'horrible rubbery smell'. She had to fight 'an almost irresistible urge to rip it off'. At school she once left her mask in a room being used for the top French class:

> I went in and said, 'Excuse me please, I've forgotten my gas mask'. The teacher rattled her cane: 'En francais, en francais!'. I thought, 'How do I ask for my gas mask in French?' I had to repeat it after her, in French, ten times.

But there were compensations, as Paul Farquharson discovered: 'If you held on to the rubber at the side and blew like [you would through] parchment, it made a rather rude blurting noise—bblurrp—which of course we did at school when we had gas mask drill!' Paul had also taken a lively interest in the family's air raid shelter:

> Reg and I dug a lot of holes in the yard but we never got down more than about a foot. Later the council came and dug in about three feet, put the Anderson shelter down, which was a corrugated iron, hoop-shaped device, and the earth they took out they threw over the top. This was supposedly a blast shelter. They had an emergency exit, so that if you couldn't get out the front you could pull a bit off the back.

Many families had installed their Anderson shelters—named after the Home Secretary—well before the war. Ruth Wilson's father, his shelter completed, conscientiously 'planted lettuces and vegetables on top of it'. Betty Deeley's father, a perfectionist, 'dug down to the regulation depth exactly'. Inside he put four bunk beds, a heater, emergency rations and water. 'If the sirens went', Betty remembers, 'we had a leather music case, and in it were all the necessary papers, birth certificates, wills, the insurance policies. Whoever ran out first picked up the panic bag.'

Heather Staff's uncle, on the other hand, had kept saying, 'There'll never be a war, you're wasting your time'.

> Of course when war was declared [my uncle and aunt] had no shelter and they had to spend the first six months of the war sleeping at our house ... We children used to pray there would be an air raid in the night so that we could go down to the shelter because it was lots of fun there. There were games and singsongs; there was cocoa to drink and biscuits to eat.

But others recoiled from 'the very dank, earthy smell' of most garden shelters.

18

Over 800 000 school children were evacuated from Britain's cities to country havens in September 1939 to escape the expected bombing. These girls' expressions suggest the gamut of emotions that evacuation created: excitement, bewilderment, anxiety, fear . . .

Far more ambitious than these measures—and potentially hazardous—was the mass evacuation of civilians. Civil Defence reports had all recommended the rapid removal from Britain's cities of as many people as possible. Evacuation was to be voluntary, but highly organised and disciplined. On 1 September 1939, on the eve of war, the government activated its evacuation programme.

The movement of people that followed was a logistical triumph. In four days over 1 400 000 evacuees, mostly children and young mothers, were taken to safe 'reception' areas in the country. By the end of September almost half London's children had been evacuated. The heavily populated cities had shed about a quarter of their total population: some 624 000 expectant mothers and mothers with young children, 825 000 school children and 113 000 teachers.

19

The personal results were far less successful. Parents had to choose rapidly between keeping their children, and perhaps exposing them to danger, or sending them to secret destinations and unknown homes. The children mostly left home relatively happily but, as countless groups trudged to railway stations, all one contemporary could hear was 'a kind of murmur because [the children] were too frightened to talk'.

About a third of the children sent to Australia in 1940 had been evacuated within Britain in September 1939. Michael Fethney, aged nine, was evacuated with his older sister:

> I don't think even the teachers knew what our destination was until we got there. We'd been told that our sandwiches were to last us possibly the entire day, and I remember being horrified when some of the kids began eating theirs straight away. I remember thinking, 'They might starve before we get there!'.

The sheer number of evacuees overwhelmed well-intentioned, but mostly inadequate, plans for their reception in towns and villages. Billeting, severely compromised by the shortage of available houses, often degenerated into a shameful lottery.

Ruth Wilson, a thirteen-year-old, was evacuated to a town in Yorkshire. Once there, she and her friends were 'marched down a hill from this school two-by-two in a crocodile'. Their hapless billeting officers 'knocked at the doors going down the street, and the people were asked how many they could accommodate . . . We were just counted out by heads: "You, you, you and you".' Braham Glass and his sister faced the invidious ordeal of being left in a room while locals selected the children they would take home:

> The prettiest girls went first, then girls on their own, and then sisters. Brothers and sisters were somewhat down the line. The ones who were selected last of all were the ugly kids, the fat kids, the kids with glasses . . . They were left standing there forlornly waiting to be chosen.

Ruth's and Braham's experiences were far from unusual. Ben Wicks, an evacuee who chronicled the saga, remembers 'strange, sad lines making their way through the village streets'. Later, in letters to him, other evacuees described how 'the humiliation of waiting to be picked . . . was seared into [their] minds with a branding iron'.

The 1939 evacuation was the greatest single relocation of people that Britain has ever seen. Hardly surprisingly, the evacuees swamped many country communities materially and psychologically. Some hosts encouraged enduring friendships, and many children blossomed as they discovered ways of life far removed from city existence. But there was also friction. Class attitudes were often to blame when evacuees and their hosts clashed. As the novelist Vera Brittain observed: 'the sorrowful truth [was] that one half of England did not know how the other half lived'.

For the CORB children later sent to Australia this first experience of evacuation provided an invaluable lesson: adapt or suffer. Sent to Colne, the Yorkshire mill town where Donald Mitchell had been ostracised, Michael Fethney found mill workers' children stamping into the school, 'marching through the playground with clogs on'. It was strange—and somehow menacing. More happily, his hosts introduced the sedate Fethney children to the beery delights of the working men's club. For Michael this was 'great stuff!':

> You know, tattie pie and smooshy peas and middle-aged women persuading me onto the dance floor and virtually carrying me around off my feet on their bosoms . . . It was probably one of the reasons my mother thought she ought to come and rescue us.

There were certainly many basically contented evacuees. But the large number of unhappy or deeply troubled children raised serious concerns. Homesickness, infrequent parental visits, mismatching of evacuees and hosts, downright nastiness, boarding costs and numerous related problems created significant doubts about the wisdom of evacuating children.

Early in 1940, with German bombing still posing no immediate threat, more and more children began drifting home. The British propaganda machine responded. One poster showed a child sitting peacefully beneath a tree with Hitler whispering to a bereft city mother: 'Take 'em back, take 'em back!'. The answer: 'LEAVE YOUR CHILDREN WHERE THEY ARE'. Nevertheless, early that year some 6000 children were wending their way homewards each week. 'The whole evacuation programme began to edge towards disaster', Ben Wicks wrote. Of the CORB children involved about half had returned home by the year's end—and almost all by March 1940. The difficulty of obtaining travel permits, trains crowded with troops, and petrol rationing made travelling irksome. But, without oceans to cross, returning home was never impossible.

Phyllis Ratcliffe was one of the future CORB children. Aged fourteen and very unhappy she finally ran away—'I grabbed my sister as she went to school and we somehow got back home to Leeds'. Derric Webster and his sister had been left with family friends in Cumbria, which 'turned out [to be] rather ill-advised. Our parents could tell from our letters that we weren't too happy. So they decided that as nothing was happening in the war to come and collect us. We were overjoyed to get back home!'

The expected devastation of Britain's cities had not occurred. Indeed,

21

Figures in the fields: evacuees from the cities have a novel arithmetic lesson as the harvest is brought in. The children, clustered before the black-board in this posed photograph, have apparently been told to 'concentrate'!

the neighbourhoods the evacuees returned to in early 1940 had changed only superficially since the war began.

The war itself remained peripheral and strangely distant, like the German reconnaissance planes—'silver pin-points almost, with little trails of smoke which you couldn't really relate to as being anything to be frightened of'. For Ken Dommerson, living in London, the reconnaissance flights were 'the closest we had come to war . . . At that stage there was no bombing where we were'. But even the tedium of this quiet war had its occasional excitement. Joan Sharp, the seven-year-old who had puzzled over barrage balloons, recalls how on hearing the air raid siren her family 'rushed down into the cellar':

We always had a flashlight handy, and we used to grab that, put our dressing gowns on and run down into the cellar. All was peaceful one night, when my grandmother said, 'I can hear a bomb falling . . .' It turned out to be the cat that had got underneath my dressing gown—purring like mad!

The 'phoney war' ended abruptly on 10 May 1940 when Hitler launched his Blitzkreig against the Low Countries. The Nazi advance, spearheaded by a formidable array of tanks, bombers and paratroopers, was relentless. Disaster followed disaster. Three days later, with the Allied defences crumbling, the new British Prime Minister Winston Churchill declared: 'I have nothing to offer but blood, toil, tears and sweat'. Waging war 'by sea, land and air', Churchill promised, Britain would secure victory. 'Victory at all costs, victory in spite of all terror, for without victory there is no survival.'

The onslaught highlighted the value of early—and orderly—civilian evacuation. Rotterdam was almost obliterated, and thousands killed, before the Germans occupied the Netherlands. Almost everywhere on the Continent fleeing civilians were indiscriminately bombed, strafed and machine-gunned by the Nazi forces. By late May Norway, Denmark, the Netherlands, Belgium and virtually all northern France were in enemy hands. The British Expeditionary Force, comprising almost all of the nation's combat-ready troops, was in desperate retreat—and, finally, almost trapped near Dunkirk. Miraculously, between 27 May and 4 June over 300 000 British and French troops were plucked from the Dunkirk beaches during Operation Dynamo. Over thirty Royal Navy destroyers were lost or severely damaged during the rescue.

The war had come suddenly and grimly to life. The heroism of the 'little boats' of Dunkirk fired Britain's war fervour—and fears. A National Day of Prayer was held. A prominent Foreign Office official wrote in his diary, 'I should count it a privilege to be dead if Hitler rules England'. Children were caught up in the excitement. Dunkirk was barely 60 kilometres from Dover: 'We could never actually see the coast of France', one child remembers, 'but when Dunkirk was on, the sky had a decided pink glow during the day and almost a bright red glow at night'. Norman Townsend remembers a friend being absent from school for a few days: 'When he came back he was rather loath to talk about where he'd been. It transpired that his father's boat had been commandeered—or he had volunteered—to help in the rescue.'

Many of the Dunkirk soldiers returned through Kent, where Joyce Briant lived. Her brother had been in France, and hoping to see him Joyce watched the countless troop trains passing through Ashford to London. 'The soldiers all looked very weary and tired. Some were French, you could tell by their helmets, but most of them were English. People were carting apples and cups of tea down to the trains.' Pamela Palmer discussed Dunkirk's implications with her friends on the way to

A trawler, crammed with troops fleeing to safety, steams out of Dunkirk. The collapse of the Allied forces in France during May 1940 left Britain open to invasion. The CORB evacuation, rapidly organised that June, was prompted by fears of invasion.

school near Harrow. 'Our school was one that could be commandeered at twenty-four hours notice. But it was an incredible thing: other than that life went on very much as before.' However, as older children knew, if Britain were invaded there would be chaos and carnage. Joyce recalls:

> The Pathe newsreels showed French people fleeing out of the towns, with their goods on carts and barrows and prams. They'd run off the roads into ditches to escape the German planes coming through and strafing them . . . We knew what was going on.

The scene was set for Operation Sea Lion, Hitler's invasion of Britain. The Luftwaffe, poised on French airfields near the coast, could now threaten any part of the British Isles. The German army was massing its ground forces. Ships, boats and barges were being prepared at the continental Channel ports. For the invasion to succeed the Luftwaffe had first to gain air supremacy. In early June the Luftwaffe flew its first large raid across the Channel. From then onwards its bombing missions escalated, hitting first the vital industrial cities and ports.

In Britain a curious calm prevailed. A ten-mile safety zone was established along the east coast. The Local Defence Volunteers (later the Home Guard) attracted some 250 000 people within a week. Concrete pillboxes were hastily built, beaches mined and surrounded with barbed wire, signposts removed, and churches instructed to ring their bells only to signal an invasion. Children were once again evacuated to the country. The War Office and Ministry of Home Security jointly published a two-page leaflet titled 'If the INVADER comes'. It detailed six 'rules' to help civilians avoid, and possibly weaken, the invading Germans. It ended: THINK BEFORE YOU ACT. BUT ALWAYS THINK OF YOUR COUNTRY BEFORE YOU THINK OF YOURSELF.

'Practically every night we had to troop down to the shelters, Mother, Dad, my brother, myself and the dog', Tony Houghton remembers of the summer of 1940, when German bombers heading for Liverpool tracked over nearby Warrington:

> We'd take our blankets with us and a flask of tea. We could hear the planes going over, and we knew they were Germans because of the sound of their engines. We took a light with us, but we had to keep it out so really all we did was sit and hope and wait. Coming out of the shelter I always went straight to the windows, to feel whether any of them had been broken.

The summer weather was blissful. The countryside was bright with flowers and traditional fairs still made their rounds. Near Tony's home 'a German plane came over very low, and [jettisoned] three bombs onto this fete. Six people, I think, were killed and some were blinded.' Further north, on Tyneside, Isabella Woods ran from planes strafing the shipyards near her home:

> There were so many air raids we were too tired to go to school. The Germans always came over about the same time. People would look at their clocks or watches and say: 'They'll be here soon. We'll be all right, we'll be all right'. There was a great spirit up in the north.

Germany stood triumphant from the North Sea to the Mediterranean, from the Danube to the English Channel. On 10 June 1940 Italy entered the war. Four days later the Nazis occupied Paris, and on 22 June French representatives signed an armistice. By then German troops were being issued with English phrase books.

Not since Napoleon's Grande Armeé threatened invasion in 1803–05 had Britain faced such peril. Now the 'Island Fortress' waited. Anti-aircraft batteries bristling around the coast stood ready, their barrels skywards. The Home Guard prepared to repel Hitler's divisions.

Children old enough to comprehend the dangers imagined the invasion. Mary Clemes remembers: 'We probably had all sorts of fantasies

The Luftwaffe began bombing Britain's cities in June 1940, and the raids rapidly escalate. For children, the bombing meant bedding down in Anderson shelters and other novelties. For women such as Mrs Shepherd, here reading a bedtime story to her seven children in a 'double Anderson' shelter, the bombing brought extra work and anxiety.

about it, but I don't think we really registered how terrible it would have been. I think we thought it would be quite an adventure, and what we would do, but we didn't have any conception of the horrors of it.' A few boys went further, exhilarated by the possibilities. Donald Mitchell, always fascinated by 'destructive films', had been marking a large map of Europe since the war began:

> I black-pencilled over the conquered areas, and I began to admire the marvellous efficiency of the Germans. The worse things got the more exciting it was. I was aware of what parachutists could do, and the thought of German parachutists landing anywhere near us was quite fascinating. My fantasies

were of desperate defences of the house as the Germans came up the street.

Norman Townsend, gazing at searchlights and bomb flashes stabbing the night sky over Portsmouth, had 'a feeling of excitement tinged with fear'. Not knowing what was going to happen next, he still believed that Britain would prevail:

> There might be an invasion, but it was only Germany that was going to invade us—and we were Britain. Therefore there was not a great threat. We would still beat them. The fact that we'd lost our army, we'd lost all of our armament and equipment in France was just by the way.

Such rock-like confidence, encouraged by Churchill's example and oratory, indeed existed. Others were less optimistic. And many, whatever their outward attitude, feared for their lives. As Reg Loft saw it:

> Dunkirk had fallen and France had thrown in the towel. They were saying over the radio for the ordinary people to arm themselves with garden forks and whatever to defend themselves against these Germans. It was only a matter of time before they landed on British soil and we had to fight. My father had a revolver and he was going to shoot my mother and us two children and then defend himself to the death. I think any mother and father would have to admit that if you were given the opportunity to get your children to safety you would grab it.

3 The Children's Overseas Reception Board

Everybody was frightened . . . You could smell it in the air.

IT was Britain's desperate situation in June 1940 that prompted the formation of the Children's Overseas Reception Board. None of the studies concerning civilian evacuation released in the 1930s had raised the possibility of sending people overseas. Now, with invasion seemingly imminent, politicians grasped at a straw.

The first moves to establish government-sponsored overseas evacuation were taken at the end of May, while the Dunkirk troops were being rescued. Details of the CORB scheme were finalised barely a fortnight later. But the genesis of CORB lay further back—and overseas in the Empire.

Early in 1939 the Dominions Office had received a letter from one of the colonies. A prominent resident of Southern Rhodesia wrote to propose the evacuation of children to the Empire in case of war. The letter was filed with the comment 'idea good-hearted but impracticable'. Later that year a Canadian women's organisation offered homes 'to take in the British population under sixteen and over sixty' if war was declared. Then, soon after war broke out, an offer came from Australia to take in 'orphans for the duration'.

The British government quietly rejected these proposals. Evacuation overseas, it was argued, might encourage panic and defeatism. Moreover, already buffeted by concerns over the evacuation of children within Britain, the government was unwilling to countenance sending evacuees overseas. In December 1939 the Dominions were advised: 'The question of evacuation is not really a pressing one here at the moment'. Hence, throughout the 'phoney war', a long and relatively safe lull when many thousands of children might have been sent overseas, evacuation to the Dominions was shelved officially.

Despite concerns about the welfare of children evacuated in 1939, more children—including these—were sent to the country in the summer of 1940. The government also allowed the evacuation of children to the Dominions to proceed.

In June 1940 Britain's dire situation prompted the government to reassess the option rapidly. Another factor forced the War Cabinet's hand: the increasing number of children being spirited across the Atlantic by affluent parents. By mid-1940 there was growing resentment, especially amongst the less well-off, at the spectacle of parents 'buying' their children's safety with trans-Atlantic tickets.

Two fundamental difficulties warned against the possibility of the government evacuating children overseas. First, the widespread expectation that many thousands of children could be shipped to safety was false. By mid-1940, some 11 000 children had been privately evacuated to Canada and the United States. However, given the drastically deteriorating war situation and the shortage of ships, it was unlikely—in fact inconceivable—that more than a fraction of that number could now quickly and safely be sent in their wake.

Second, war—as had recently been proved—is inherently unpredictable. If children were evacuated overseas, if the Allies then gained a strategic advantage but not final victory—what then? It would be unlikely that, once sent overseas, children could easily be brought home. They might well be stranded for years.

These cold facts were swept aside by the emotions that the likelihood of invasion engendered, and by a spate of generous pledges from Australia, Canada, New Zealand and South Africa. On 1 June *The Times* published the four Dominions' official offers to take evacuees, urging the home government to take up their 'generous offers of hospitality'.

In Australia Britain's peril awakened powerful imperial sentiments. Robert Menzies, the Prime Minister, had declared: 'So long as Great Britain is unconquered the world can be saved, and that Britain can or will be conquered is unthinkable'. In like spirit Senator Foll, the Minister for the Interior, spoke of evacuation of children to the Dominions as 'one of the most humanitarian [schemes] ever undertaken'. He himself promised that his own family would 'take two boys'. New Zealand, despite its small population, offered homes to 25 000 children.

To this volatile mix of fear, improbable expectations and altruism came Geoffrey Shakespeare. The Member of Parliament for Norwich since 1929, he was now—in Churchill's recently formed Cabinet—the Under Secretary of the Dominions Office. Shakespeare, aged 46, was energetic, efficient and compassionate—if also paternalistic. His time at Cambridge had been cut short by war in 1914. Later, fighting alongside the ANZACs at Gallipoli—'those tough, warm-hearted soldiers'—he developed a particular affection for Australians.

Shakespeare was instructed to handle the overseas evacuation issue in Parliament. An ardent supporter of the Empire, 'those expanding and exhilarating countries', he was to approach the question of overseas

Air raid wardens removing road signs during June 1940, to confuse and hinder the expected German invasion.

evacuation with unremitting energy and patriotic, indeed imperial, fervour. As Michael Fethney has observed, without his leadership the scheme would almost certainly never have gone ahead, 'so much did it owe to his personal and unswerving zeal'.

Only months before CORB's inception Shakespeare had questioned the wisdom of overseas evacuation. Apparently aware of the serious concerns being voiced in late 1939 concerning evacuation within Britain, he was to write that it had already 'gone to the limits of prudence in disrupting family life'. Moreover, he considered that sending children overseas 'would pander to the weaker elements in the community'.

By June 1940, however, Shakespeare saw matters differently. By then, he believed, evacuating children overseas was acceptable from the viewpoint of family relationships. Moreover, with the naval blockade of Britain already a fact, reducing the number of non-combatants would help shorten the war. 'If Britain was really to be a fortress, would it not be prudent to get rid of the weaker members of the fortress?' he later wrote.

Geoffrey Shakespeare chaired the government's hastily established interdepartmental committee assessing the issue. Its brief was to report on the feasibility of overseas evacuation for children. The committee considered both the logistics of sending children from Britain to the Dominions and the personal issues concerning their reception and welfare. Remarkably, however, the Admiralty was not consulted.

The committee first met on 7 June. Its report, ready about a week later, was a model of meticulous administrative thought. Overseas evacuation, the committee concluded, should proceed immediately. But the committee warned that, when it became known that Britain was prepared to 'ship off her children to the Dominions', the public might panic and swamp the scheme with impossible numbers of children. Inspired and shaped by Shakespeare's firm belief in overseas evacuation, the report glossed over this central issue. If the availability of shipping or questions of national morale made it impossible, or unwise, to evacuate very large numbers of children overseas—was the scheme anything more than a sop to the less privileged? Nor had the almost all-male committee squarely addressed the possible length of the war or the issue of family bonds and relationships.

Geoffrey Shakespeare presented the report to the War Cabinet on 17 June. They met in the underground, bombproof War Room at Westminster. Sentries lined the labyrinth of corridors leading to this nerve centre, a spartan room with massive girders supporting the ceiling. A large U-shaped desk occupied almost all the room. A 'Navy League Map of the British Empire' hung behind the Prime Minister's chair, the chart's shipping routes dark blue tentacles linking the pink Dominions.

Barely a fortnight after Dunkirk Churchill, with far more urgent matters intruding, sat silent in the smoke-filled room. Before the Cabinet had fully assessed the report on the proposed Children's Overseas Reception Board the discussion was interrupted. Churchill was handed a note: France, he grimly announced, was suing for peace. 'The stark magnitude of this momentous event', Shakespeare recorded, halted the CORB debate. As Churchill knew: 'The whole fury and might of the enemy must very soon be turned upon us. Hitler knows that he will have to break this island or lose the war.'

The Prime Minister's views on overseas evacuation, however, were already known. He condemned the defeatism that, to him, it implied. Relocating civilians within Britain to escape bombing was one matter; escaping to safe havens overseas another entirely. Indeed, Shakespeare was asked to intervene to dissuade a young Churchill relative from going privately across the Atlantic. He succeeded, thus averting a blow to national morale.

The War Cabinet of Winston Churchill's National Government. Churchill believed the CORB evacuation would damage national morale and was bitterly opposed to the scheme. *Front row, left to right* Ernest Bevin, Lord Beaverbrook, Anthony Eden, Clement Attlee, Winston Churchill, Sir John Anderson, Arthur Greenwood, Sir Kingsley Wood.

Shakespeare left the War Cabinet on 17 June uncertain whether or not it had approved the CORB scheme. In fact, this remains unclear today. However, it seems likely that—with the CORB discussion cut short by the news from France—the Cabinet Secretary later recorded a positive decision from his recollections of the Cabinet's views. Shakespeare, checking the minutes the next day, read that the War Cabinet 'agreed the scheme be announced in answer to a Parliamentary question the following Wednesday' and that 'the Committee report be published'. Shakespeare, clearly already personally committed to CORB, grasped the fait accompli.

On 19 June Clement Attlee, the senior Labour member of the National Government and Lord President of the Council, tabled the CORB report in the House of Commons. The government, he announced, had accepted the findings of the committee. A CORB organisation was to be set up immediately, with Geoffrey Shakespeare its first chairman.

In fact Shakespeare, his urge for 'vigour and action' matching the nation's mood, had already virtually established the CORB administration. Since 17 June there had been incessant activity at the premises he had found for the operation in Berkeley Square. A core staff of civil servants and others experienced in child welfare and administration had been rapidly appointed. The four Dominion High Commissioners had been brought in for consultations. And some thirty-five voluntary societies had agreed to assist by sitting on an Advisory Council. Two sub-committees were formed. One was to deal with land transport to the embarkation ports, embarkation, land and sea escorts, and medical staff. The other was to advise on finances, relations with the Dominions, and the children's reception overseas.

The original committee's proposals had been refined and CORB's objectives clarified. These were outlined in Circular 1515, written probably two days before Attlee officially announced the scheme. This circular, addressed to parents, was sent secretly to all Education Authorities on 17 June, to be sent on to the 'grant aid' schools attended by the children of the less well-off. It was also sent to the governing bodies of private schools.

Circular 1515 opened by summarising the Dominions' offers of homes. The Gestetnered form continued confidentially (how Geoffrey Shakespeare must have smiled!):

> A scheme for the evacuation of children overseas is at present under discussion with the Empire Governments and it is not possible to give final details. Meanwhile, the sooner the organisers are able to know the names of children who may be evacuated overseas, the sooner it will be possible to put the scheme into effect.

The key criteria for evacuation—'it was hoped'—would be: that children must be aged between five and fifteen; that they must still be attending school; that preference would be given to children from the more dangerous 'evacuation' areas; and that preference would be given to children from less affluent families. In the Dominions the children would stay with host families or, where possible, with relatives. Parents would be expected to make a modest contribution towards the cost of the voyage to the Dominions. The amount was set at six shillings per week, but parents whose incomes were above a certain level were to be independently assessed.

The notice included warnings that most parents apparently accepted. The children, it was stressed, were to be evacuated 'for the duration of the war'. They would only be returned home, the notice ended, 'as soon as possible after the war'.

It was assumed that the circular would reach parents on or about 20 June, the day the scheme was announced in the press and on radio. That same day, aware that some Cabinet colleagues were far from happy at the proposed evacuation, Geoffrey Shakespeare made a statement to the press. The government, he reiterated, had no intention of shipping large numbers of children overseas. Indeed, CORB's chairman stated:

Any idea of mass migration is absolutely contrary to the wishes of the governments concerned. For scores of thousands of children to be transferred in a few weeks, as suggested in some quarters, is outside the bounds of any practical scheme and would be an extremely dangerous process.

4 The Parents Respond

My parents took the view that, whatever happened to the rest of the family, one of us should be safe out in Australia.

THE public reaction to the CORB offer was totally unexpected. Fears of invasion, and the hope which overseas evacuation held out, led many thousands of parents to agree to part with their children—perhaps forever. Children's reactions varied. Some did not want to go, others could barely wait to be sent.

The response staggered even Geoffrey Shakespeare. It was, he later wrote, 'so instantaneous and overwhelming that it revealed a deep current of public apprehension'.

The scheme formally opened on Thursday 20 June 1940, the day it was announced in the press. By mid-morning some 3000 parents were queuing outside CORB's headquarters. The real level of anxiety emerged over the next days as parents' replies to Circular 1515 arrived at Berkeley Square. In barely two weeks the CORB staff was inundated with applications on behalf of 211 448 children, about half those who fulfilled the conditions of the circular.

Churchill was wrath. 'It is one thing to allow a limited number of children to be sent to North America, but the idea of a large scale evacuation stands on a different footing', he told the War Cabinet on 21 June. The War Cabinet, confused and indecisive, instructed Shakespeare to defuse the panic.

On Sunday 23 June CORB's chairman broadcast to the nation. Any notion of sending 'hundreds of thousands of children overseas in the space of a few weeks' was 'both dangerous and stupid', he stressed. Moreover, the scheme could only operate 'subject to the limitations of shipping and offers made by each Dominion'. But, hinting at adventure, Shakespeare continued:

> It is surely inspiring that lovers of freedom, far removed from the war zone, are so concerned about the safety of our children.

Barbed wire coils along the British coast, intended to obstruct a German invasion, October 1940. These sisters, equipped with a Mickey Mouse bucket and a bat—for French cricket?—seem perplexed at the seaside's transformation.

> Many parents will want to send their children to homes overseas
> . . . and this will be made possible under our scheme.

The final decision, of course, rested with parents. Shakespeare urged them to weigh carefully the dangers of air raids and possible invasion in Britain against the hazards of U-boats and surface attacks at sea. A father himself, he concluded:

> I know there will be much burning of the heart at the thought
> of parting, but parents will not allow themselves to be
> influenced by these considerations where the safety of their
> children is concerned. You will ask me, how long will the
> parting be? The answer is: our children will come back to us
> when we have secured the final victory, as inevitably we shall.

The overwhelming majority of parents who applied for their children to be evacuated did so because they feared an invasion. Pamela Palmer recalls: 'I was fourteen, and my parents thought I would be at a very vulnerable age if there had been an invasion'. In Heather Staff's case a cable from her father's cousin in Australia saying 'Home available for children if needed' made her parents decide that evacuation was 'a genuine possibility'. Some families had more reason than others to grasp the CORB offer. One girl's parents, who lived on the Thames estuary, feared they were

> . . . in a very vulnerable position, and that invasion was imminent. My parents felt they would regret having had the chance to send me away and not taking it. My father had been up to the War Office, and had seen documents suggesting that invasion was 'any minute now'.

About half the CORB children sent to Australia had already experienced local bombing raids. However, the threat of bombs was of less concern than invasion, mainly because bombing might be avoided by evacuation within Britain. But, near the coal fields and ports of South Wales, Reg Harris' parents were concerned that their four children might be 'maimed or injured . . . as the number of buildings getting blown up was increasing'.

Ted Flowers, the turnip-eating thirteen-year-old, recalls a poignant situation. He had resisted any thought of being sent to a strange home in the 1939 evacuation. But in the spring of 1940 his sister had died from consumption:

> I think the loss of my sister was a major factor in my parents' decision to send me. My brother was in Coastal Command, flying Avro Ansons over the Norwegian coast. I think my parents took the view that, whatever happened to the rest of the family, one of us should be safe out in Australia. I was asked if I'd like to go. I said yes. I think to some extent the excitement of the trip did a lot to blot out my sister's death.

Many parents were willing to evacuate their children only because they had relatives in Australia. David Cox, a seven-year-old from Essex, believes his mother 'in her heart of hearts probably wanted to say no'. His father and grandfather swayed the decision, but only because David and his nine-year-old brother Gerald were able to go to an aunt and uncle in Queensland. 'I don't think it would have been discussed at all if there hadn't been this strong family tie with Australia.'

One of the closest of the CORB 'Empire' families was the Cuthberts— of Stirling in Scotland and Sydney in New South Wales. They had maintained such a constant exchange of affectionate letters that

First things first: a boy adjusts the wheels on his cart after a German air raid. Whatever the war's dangers, for many children—especially boys—it also brought interest and excitement.

evacuating ten-year-old Helen and seven-year-old Katharine seemed not really to be changing families. Told of their parents' plans just after her mother gave birth to a baby sister, Katharine recalls:

> We had always thought of Australia as a marvellous place. Now we were to have the chance to go there. We knew that we were going to our aunt's, who we already knew, so our initial reaction was totally pleasurable.

The mutual support brothers and sisters could give one another was often the other decisive factor for parents. About half of the children evacuated to Australia went with one or more siblings. The Wastell parents sent all their four children, to escape the dangers of 'Bomb Alley' south of London. George was the eldest:

> In common with most fourteen-year-old boys at the time, I had no intention of 'running away'. But Dad made it clear that my job as the eldest was to look after the younger ones. If I refused then no one would go. I kept my resentment to myself.

39

David Massey had an older brother with a crippled leg. When the brother failed the medical test demanded by the Dominions, David was told: 'If Charlie can't go, you can't go'. But being very keen to go to Australia himself David objected strongly. 'I heard afterwards that my father had said, "If the bombing is going to be bad, perhaps, with David going to safety, if anything happens to the rest of us he can carry on the family name".'

Michael Storey, aged eight, remembers a 'rather cold unemotional father who ruled the roost'. He told his son that,

> I was going on a great adventure, to the other side of the world to live with someone they knew. I was stunned. But my father said, 'You do what you're told, it's the best, it's for you—so you're going to be brave, aren't you?'

Family tensions appear to have at least partly prompted the evacuation of a few of the children. Today, a small minority of evacuees believe that their departure reflected some lack of love. Parental rejection, perceived or real, was generally veiled with rationalisation. Phyllis Ratcliffe, the fourteen-year-old who had run away from the 1939 evacuation, remembers vaguely: 'My parents just told us we might be going to America on a trip'. Her sister, nine-year-old Anne, recalls being told they were going on a holiday. 'I was told I was going to a country where, because of [my] regular lung trouble, I would be healthier.'

The father of Braham Glass, the boy from a troubled East End family who had already experienced the 1939 evacuation, was appalled at the Nazis' persecution of Jews. He had now received 'one fateful letter' from a little-known Australian uncle of Braham's offering a home. Braham and his older sister Essie were to be evacuated again:

> We'll never know whether our parents really wanted to get rid of us or not. I think there was some of that in it, but by and large it was the fact that England could easily have lost the war and we could have ended up in a concentration camp.

Children's reactions to the news of CORB evacuation depended to some extent on how they were involved in the decision. Amongst the older children, those from families with dominant parents often accepted their evacuation as simply another edict. The urgency of the situation led other, usually more liberal, parents to consult their children only minimally. Some were probably too distraught to broach the matter until departure was imminent. Isabella Woods, for example, 'didn't know a thing about CORB until the doctor came to the house to give me a vaccination'. Most children, however, were at the very least forewarned.

Relatives in Australia, especially if they were known from their visits to Britain, eased children's concerns as much as the parents' worries.

Phil Robinson, bred on 'glowing tales' of his mother's family in Australia, looked forward to renewing his acquaintance with Uncle Len. But, as an only child, Phil still felt 'a horrible uncertainty at being separated from my parents'.

Travel! Adventure! Many of the older children welcomed the opportunity of crossing oceans and seeing Australia with unrestrained excitement. Barbara Donald, the eleven-year-old from Tyneside, 'wanted to go to Australia because it was an adventure, and it was a new country. Most of all I think we were all enamoured with accounts of our uncles' orange and apple orchards!'

Most of the CORB boys, brought up on Empire adventure stories, were enticed by the prospect of escapades. Norman Townsend, his imagination 'sparked' by his father's accounts of soldiering in India, was convinced that 'the rest of the world sounded a fascinating place to go and look at'. John Fethney, aged thirteen, had already tasted independence in the 1939 evacuation. For him CORB meant 'the freedom to escape the parental yoke . . . The idea of escape from the war didn't really figure as much as the opportunity to get away and do something different'. Tony Houghton, fourteen, pestered his parents with a barrage of incessant persuasion. 'It had nothing to do with the possible dangers of air raids or whatever. It was the sense of adventure.'

Reg Harris, the Welsh ten-year-old, believes that his 'mother being Australian gave me an incentive to go'. But the real reasons Reg yearned to be off were a desire for adventure—and his abiding optimism:

> I loved the thought of going. I think it possessed me. I even went to a church that was on the way home from school. I remember going in there one afternoon and kneeling down and *praying* that I could go. So my prayers were answered.

Not, however, as he might have hoped.

Reg Harris was evacuated with his sister and two brothers, who also wanted to go. But Reg and Dorothy Loft were utterly at odds over CORB. Thirteen-year-old Reg Loft's immediate reaction was: '"Whooppee! I'm getting out of this." I wasn't going too well at school. Mum was very strict. Things weren't too hot in England. The food situation was crook and there was a sea voyage ahead to Australia where I was born. It was a wonderful adventure coming up.' Dorothy, though, wanted to stay, 'to fight with the rest of England'. Two years older than her brother, she was also far more interested in her life in Bromley than in what Australia might offer:

> I was still mooning over my first boyfriend, and life was just beginning to come into full bloom. I didn't want that disturbed. I just plain did not want to go, but I never would have said what I felt to my parents.

41

'2000 aluminium saucepans make one aeroplane'—and four boys and four British bulldogs in London make a striking propaganda photograph. Far from wishing to flee the war or diversions such as this, many CORB children saw the likelihood of *more* excitement overseas.

Parents were required to nominate which Dominion they would prefer their children to go to. Of those sent to Australia, over three-quarters of the parents had asked that their children be sent there. Many chose Australia because they had relatives there. The remainder did so mostly because of Australia's distance from the war or its reputation as a 'young, healthy' place with a good climate and abundant food.

Most of the older CORB children knew a little about Australia. But for many Australia was simply a far distant—*how* distant?—part of the Empire. Even children with Australian relatives generally had only stereotypes by which to picture the place: 'the outback without any cities', 'millions and millions of merino sheep', 'a land of bright sunshine and floods', 'beaches and enormous breakers', 'a place of vast distances and adventure'.

The evacuees' notions of how long they might have to remain in Australia were even vaguer. The youngest had no grasp of time at all, while most of the older children seemed unable—or unwilling—to look far into the future.

Heather Staff, just nine, thought her evacuation would last 'a short time like going to Blackpool'. For one thirteen-year-old, 'the length of time that we might be separated never came into it'; another thought 'the war would soon be over and we would be reunited'; a third recalls that 'a year might've been considered, but five years was never anticipated'. Paul Farquharson's friends were saying 'it'd all be over by the Christmas of 1940'.

Some parents, heartbroken at the prospect of a long war, told white lies to shield their children from the thought of a protracted separation. Others, little aware of military strategy and enveloped by fear, were simply unable to assess the war's likely course. Katharine Cuthbert remembers asking her parents: 'How long will it last for?'. And they replied, 'Well, we hope it may only be a few months, but it might be as much as a year.'

> I don't think that was just to comfort us, I think these were the longest terms that anyone thought of. I don't think they would ever have contemplated sending us if they'd had an idea it might be for five years.

John Hillier voices a darker thought. For some parents, perhaps many, there was the dread that—in speeding their children to safety—they might also be saying farewell:

> You don't send children to the other side of the world for six or nine months. Later I realised what it must have meant to them personally, and it was obviously a very unselfish attitude to give us the offer [of being evacuated]. Mother gave both my brother and I a Bible in which she had written words of advice, putting down her thoughts as to how she hoped we would live our lives. It was obviously in the back of her mind that she might never see us again.

The applications which flooded into CORB's headquarters created an administrative nightmare. On the day the scheme opened there was utter confusion. Amidst a melee of parents, in hastily arranged offices with their telephones not yet connected, the CORB staff worked late into the night. As Geoffrey Shakespeare later recorded proudly, 'The thin black line of the Civil Service stood its ground. Out of chaos grew, not order, but less chaos.' In ten days the staff grew from 30 to over 350.

Meanwhile, the entire scheme came close to being cancelled. The

War Cabinet considered CORB again at a lengthy meeting on 1 July. Shakespeare's broadcast a week before had done nothing to diminish parents' anxieties. Churchill remained adamant. The response to CORB, he reiterated, would 'create a defeatist spirit . . . entirely contrary to the true facts of the position, and it should be sternly discouraged'.

There were also shipping problems. The Admiralty, at last involved, voiced serious concern at the same meeting. Three factors would make it impossible, the naval experts warned, to evacuate more than a relative handful of children: few ships were capable of carrying large numbers of children; most available passenger ships were needed urgently to transfer enemy aliens to Canada; and there was the question of safety. U-boat and Luftwaffe attacks in the Atlantic were escalating and the Royal Navy was extremely short of escorts for convoys.

As Michael Fethney has argued, politicians opposed to the CORB evacuation on grounds of national morale or family bonds now had two undeniable arguments which could have been advanced to cancel the scheme: evacuating even a mere five per cent of the children already on the CORB lists would almost certainly prove impossible; and, underescorted, every evacuee ship that sailed would be exposed to extreme danger.

Before the meeting broke up Churchill once again lambasted CORB's philosophy and operation. He scornfully derided the popular view that evacuation would mean 'fewer mouths to feed'. The numbers involved were, in fact, negligible.

Churchill and the War Cabinet faced far more pressing issues than CORB. Despite their avowed opposition to overseas evacuation, they did nothing to stop—or even postpone—the evacuation proceeding. But the War Cabinet did instruct CORB to close its application lists. And, perhaps aware that it had become enmeshed in a scheme driven by crisis not rational thought, it instructed Geoffrey Shakespeare to make another statement.

Shakespeare addressed Parliament on 2 July. He raised two issues: the risks at sea could not be underestimated; and the Dominions could take only 'a very small proportion of our child population'. No mention whatsoever was made of the CORB lists having been closed. Most MPs were confused, some were angry. A passionate debate ensued. The Member for Newcastle-on-Tyne, where almost all parents were too poor to even consider private evacuation overseas and where shipyards were already being bombed, condemned the evacuation as 'trivial, valueless and disappointing'. The Secretary of the Board of Education replied that the government still hoped to make CORB evacuation 'as large as Dominion opportunities would allow'. Clement Attlee, unable to clarify CORB's evident ambiguities, closed the debate by proclaiming to rousing cheers: 'In any case, we are going to defeat the *invasion*!'.

As the CORB evacuees prepared to leave, Britain's fighter squadrons were fighting the Battle of Britain. These women, members of the Kensington W.V.S., with their load of kitchenware, were helping replace the RAF's lost fighters—made from aluminium.

For parents anxious about their children's fate the debate produced one solid fact. The next day, Shakespeare announced, 'some parents will [be] notified that their children have been provisionally accepted'.

This was welcome news. For, whatever the War Cabinet's views about panic, intelligence experts still predicted Hitler's invasion would occur. Three days after the CORB debate a Joint Intelligence Sub-Committee report concluded: 'We consider that large scale raids on the British Isles involving all the arms may take place at any moment'. The Joint Chiefs of Staff's warning concerning Operation Sea Lion, made just after France fell, still stood:

> We must regard the threat of invasion as imminent. We must not overlook the fact that a major air offensive against this country will almost certainly take place as well.

45

5   Leaving Home

Everything was hunky dory. We got on board the train,
and said cheerio. Just as the train was pulling out I
looked back—and saw my mother practically collapsed.

Few parents challenged CORB's conditions of evacuation. All were required to sign an indemnity releasing the government from responsibility for their children's safety at sea. None cavilled. The sinking of an evacuee ship could be dismissed as hypothetical; the news from the war could not. The Germans invaded the Channel Islands on 1 July 1940. The next day the Luftwaffe carried out its first massed bombing raid over Britain. A week later the Battle of Britain officially began: either the Royal Air Force would prevail over the Luftwaffe—or Britain would succumb.

The CORB forms that began arriving from 3 July at homes across Britain indicated the provisional selection of evacuees. CORB now undertook to 'do their best'

> . . . to arrange for the transport of the child to the country named [by parents], for securing the care, maintenance and education of the child after reaching that country, and for the child's return to this country as soon as practicable after the war . . .

But parents were warned: 'His Majesty's Government will not be responsible or liable for any injury including fatal injury or damage which may be suffered by children . . .'. Both parents had to sign the agreement. Children whose parents returned this form were assumed to be ready for evacuation.

'URGENT', parents read at the head of the next communication, the 'Final Notice' of evacuation. This notice alerted Local Education Authorities and schools as well as parents: the LEAs to arrange medical tests and transport to ports; schools to prepare reports to assist the integration of evacuees into Dominion homes and schools; and parents to prepare their children for departure 'at short notice'.

Evacuation was to be kept strictly secret. 'It was so difficult not to say anything about it at school', Mary Clemes recalls. 'But we were told, absolutely—no mention, not a whisper . . .' Paul Farquharson, resolved to keep scout's honour himself, 'drew five bob out of a school savings bank account' to take to Australia. Later,

> This teacher said, 'Farquharson, if you are going to go to Australia, you'll have to develop a more responsible attitude'. And I thought, 'My God, "Loose Lips Cost Lives" and ships will be sunk!'. I had to answer various questions in the playground about this Australian venture.

The 'outfit' CORB advised parents to prepare had to be packed in one small suitcase. Clothes for the tropics included '1 shady hat' for the girls, '1 panama' for the boys. One boy remembers a shop assistant 'dying to know why I needed a panama, so my mother told him some cock-and-bull story'. Mothers, being urged 'to wear flatter shoes' to save leather, stretched budgets to clothe their children for the voyage. Trying on clothes sometimes hurt as smallpox vaccination scabs were still tender. Then there were name tags, 'dozens and dozens of them' Mary Clemes recalls:

> I was told my CORB number was B2026, and that is what I wrote on the tapes. But when I got the final instructions with my name tag we discovered it had been changed to 2025. My mother wasn't going to change them. 'They can jolly well do! It can't be helped if you've got the wrong number.'

Muriel Evans' mother, on doctor's orders, had recently taken Muriel to sea aboard a Yorkshire trawler 'to help my whooping cough'. Muriel hadn't been seasick, and was 'confident I wouldn't be seasick on the voyage to Australia'. But, like half the evacuees, she could not swim. 'You'd better learn to swim in case the boat sinks', her mother told her. 'So a friend of mine took me to the swimming baths to try to learn to swim, but there was nobody there to teach us. I didn't get very far!'

Tony Smith's father, a master mariner, had spent a lifetime at sea. Tony's battered suitcase was painted with 'two cream bands across the corners so that I could pick it out easily in a stack of cases'. Then his father packed 'a torch with batteries and a blue life jacket, like a waistcoat, better than the ship's life jackets'. The final loving touch was 'a good, single-draw telescope' inscribed with Tony's name.

Reg Loft's father gave his son 'his kettledrum on its stand, the sticks and brushes and the cymbal'—all packed in a case! Though only the one case was allowed, Reg's father was unmoved: 'Take it and get it as far as you can'. For Ruth Wilson it was a 'gold watch which my father had given to my mother before they married, and a little silver horseshoe that she had been given as a child'. The watch was given back when Ruth returned after the war. The horseshoe is with her still.

Shortly before Bob Bullard left for Australia, his family had a final portrait taken. Bob, second from left, was then eight. Jean, his eleven-year-old sister, and Peter, aged six, were scheduled to go to Australia on a later CORB sailing. But, following the *City of Benares* sinking, their evacuation was cancelled.

Photographs were packed away for bedside tables in Australia. Nora Lupton, aged nine, had an album with 'photographs of all the family and the family dog, *my* dog'. Some families had formal portraits taken, as Bob Bullard remembers: 'If Hitler had carried on over the Channel the photo would have represented the last of England as it was, with us marooned on the other side of the world'.

The preparations passed some children by. Some were too young to help. Some, like Dorothy Loft, were too angry. Still somehow puzzled, she says: 'My memory seems to be of nothingness. There must have been discussions, people must have said, "Oh aren't you lucky!". But I've got no recollection . . .'

Spurred on by Geoffrey Shakespeare's example, the CORB staff worked late into the nights. They could barely cope. At the peak of their work the staff were handling over 7000 letters a day. The tasks were endless: sorting applications by age, family background, the likelihood of home areas being bombed, and Dominions of preference; assessing school reports and checking medical records; posting out notices to parents;

liaising with Dominion officials in London; administering generous donations offered for the evacuees' welfare. Preference in selecting children was given to those from less well-off families, to dampen the hostility felt by many toward private evacuation by wealthy parents.

The Advisory Committee had decided to send one shipboard escort for every fifteen children, and one doctor and two nurses for every hundred. Ministers of the leading denominations also accompanied every large group. There was no difficulty attracting men and women of calibre, despite their being offered only meagre living allowances. The advertisements seeking escorts attracted over 19 000 applications.

Meanwhile, following the CORB debate in Parliament on 2 July, there was renewed political pressure to halt the evacuation. The naval situation had deteriorated further. The destruction of the French fleet on 3 July was a massive loss to Allied strength. Three days later the War Cabinet sent a memo to Geoffrey Shakespeare warning that, with the situation 'radically changed', naval vessels must be used 'for more vital purposes than escorting ships containing children overseas'. By mid-July convoys in the Channel were coming under regular air bombardment, and U-boats were increasing their Atlantic attacks. The Admiralty advised the War Cabinet on 9 July that the Royal Navy could no longer 'provide adequate naval protection' for evacuee ships, as all available vessels were required in the Channel and North Sea to repel an invasion.

A week later, on 16 July, Attlee advised Parliament that the War Cabinet was suspending the evacuation because of the risks at sea. CORB debates dominated the House of Commons for the next two days. On 18 July Churchill himself addressed a confused and angry House of Commons about the scheme. He reaffirmed his general opposition to overseas evacuation, arguing that the scheme now had to be halted until the Navy could ensure the safety of evacuees.

Despite Churchill's statement, once again the War Cabinet did nothing to halt the scheme. Indeed, since the Cabinet did order that no evacuee ship could sail without a convoy, it almost certainly knew the evacuation was proceeding. On 18 July, the same day that the Prime Minister opposed CORB in Parliament, the first batch of 82 evacuees was assembling in Liverpool. Some time that same day Churchill fired off a memo to Sir John Anderson, the Home Secretary:

> I certainly do not propose to send a message by the senior [CORB] child to Mr McKenzie King [the Canadian Premier], or by the junior child either. If I sent a message by anyone, it would be that I entirely deprecate any stampede out of this country at the present time.

These first evacuees sailed for Canada on 21 July aboard the *Anselm*, in the 'outward bound' convoy OB189. Six days later, in clear daylight, 49 a U-boat struck. Four ships were lost, but the *Anselm* steamed through unscathed.

The CORB evacuation had begun. However, as the Admiralty had predicted, the operation was to be severely constrained by the shortage of ships—and many vessels scheduled for evacuees were sunk, damaged or rerouted before their CORB voyages began. Yet, despite appalling logistical problems, nineteen ships did sail with evacuees between late July and mid-September. Nine-tenths of the total of 3119 evacuees left on the ships which sailed during August. Only eight of the nineteen ships were large enough to take more than one hundred children.

The parents of evacuees allocated to scheduled CORB ships were immediately notified of the date and time of departure from home. Nothing was said about the children having to pass through the heavily bombed ports, but these last notices reiterated the previous warnings about the risks at sea. Parents, however, were told:

> You can rest assured that arrangements will be made for naval convoy. You can also rest assured that we shall not let your child (or children) go overseas if at the last moment we find that the situation has changed and no convoy can be provided.

For the CORB children the finality of their evacuation gradually dawned. Some, even after receiving their departure notices, remained buoyed up by thoughts of adventure. But most saw their situation in an increasingly sober light. A significant number remained shadowed by deep, mostly unspoken, misgivings.

Brothers and sisters staying behind often brought home the implications of evacuation. Katharine Cuthbert remembers walks in a much-loved garden with little Bridget:

> I can remember gradually realising what the family separation would mean, and realising that Bridget was obviously distressed at the thought of losing us. She was only four but she told us how much she minded, whereas I think our parents tried hard not to show how agonised they were until the very end.

For Michael Fethney, being photographed 'with all my choir clobber on' symbolised a final commitment—'signing on the dotted line'. One night shortly before leaving,

> My mother said to my brother and me, 'Don't forget, when you're on that ship, if anything bad happens don't worry about trying to rescue any of your possessions. You just get to that lifeboat, and make sure you're all right'. So we were aware that there was an element of danger, but it was too late to be withdrawn.

For Michael Fethney, being photographed in his choir-boy's cassock emphasised his imminent CORB evacuation—one from which there was no turning back.

On my last day at my primary school I was walking home as usual with my friend Douglas. I remember swearing him to secrecy and saying, 'Look, this is my last day at school. I'm going off to Australia and you mustn't tell anybody'. He told me recently that he went home and sobbed and sobbed, and couldn't tell his family why he was crying because it was a secret. He didn't breathe a word of it until there were public announcements about our safe arrival in Australia.

Pamela Palmer, the fourteen-year-old, was due to be evacuated with her younger sister Anne. But her mother, who some years before had had a child die, suddenly changed her mind:

It wasn't until the day before we were due to depart that mother withdrew Anne. She said Anne would be too much of a responsibility for me. Mother had photos of the three children, including the brother who had died, on the wall. She was looking at my sister's photograph when it crashed to the floor, and she saw that as an omen that she oughtn't to go. But I think it was the fact that mother had *really* lost a child. She couldn't bear the thought of parting with both of us, although it was only going to be a temporary thing.

51

The vast majority of parents had chosen to evacuate their children without any thought for themselves. For these parents, already distraught, prying neighbours sometimes made an unenviable predicament worse. A significant number of CORB mothers later recalled being harassed for evacuating their children.

Most evacuees' recollections of their final days at home are blurred. But Phil Robinson, the Birmingham boy awed by his grandfather's portrait, heard his father saying over and over again: 'Be a good fellow. Put on a good show. Take with you the Robinson tradition.' 'Goodness knows what that was!', Phil wonders. As departure approached, trivial incidents sometimes flared into dramas. The evening before Braham Glass and his sister left, Braham 'ran in between the two cases and knocked them over. This generated an enormous towering rage on my father's part, probably because he was very tense.'

Norman Townsend, whose mother had died when he was small, had never before been told, 'Your mother died on such and such a date when you were so old'. Now, on the eve of his departure,

> My father took me up to his bedroom and from a drawer took out some special things. He showed me a photograph of my mother and told me then that she had died when I was five. He gave me a copy of that photograph with her and her two sisters. I've always had the photograph.

The 577 children sent to Australia formed about a fifth of all the CORB evacuees. There were 310 boys and 267 girls. One hundred came from Scotland, thirteen from Wales and the rest from England. The children left their homes on or about 1 August, 20 August and 10 September, depending on where they lived and on which of three Australia-bound ships they were to sail.

For each, departure day finally came. Almost every family spent a bittersweet morning: the last they would share for years.

David Massey, asleep in the air raid shelter, was wakened by his mother. They had agreed on a codeword for departure. But David's mother, knowing her son's excitement, had kept his departure date secret: 'She came in and shook me and said, "Your uncle's coming to take you to the *Isle of Man*". I knew then I was on my way to Australia'.

The last-minute preparations . . . Birth certificate, identity card and ration card readily accessible. Suitcase fastened. Sandwiches and a drink in a haversack. Gas mask and overcoat ready . . . 'The next thing I know I'm labelled and given some instructions—and off we go', says Isabella Woods. Albert Young, aged seven at the time, remembers his departure in verse:

And why were only three bags packed,
What about our Mam and Dad?
The truth was slowly sinking in
To this little Yorkshire lad.

Pamela Palmer's father, an ambulance driver, said goodbye and then 'went to work like any other day'. Her grandmother, however, was grief-stricken: 'She was very, very distressed. Mother of course was trying to be brave'. Peter Edkin's mother wept by the gate as he left with his father. Their tension eased when a seaplane flew overhead, an unusual sight in London. Peter remembers, 'We had—for us—a fairly lengthy discussion, lasting a minute or two, about the plane'.

Leaving home was especially hard for children who doubted their parents' affection. Phyllis Ratcliffe says with regret: 'I don't remember ever saying goodbye to my older sister or father'. Michael Storey knew simply that he was going to 'a place on the other side of the world'. His father told him to 'keep a brave face on it'. 'Grit your teeth. It was a terrible sort of feeling . . . It hurt, it upset me. But there was the excitement and I was *told* to look forward to it—so I *would* look forward to it.'

The children faced a much more trying departure than did those in the September 1939 evacuation within Britain, who had generally left with teachers and friends. The CORB children were leaving alone or with siblings—to be sent across the world. Land escorts were waiting at main-line stations to take them on to their embarkation ports: unknown, secret destinations. Parents, not allowed to travel to the ports, farewelled their children beside coaches and trains: the evacuees now tagged with labels. For young Albert,

A lady tied a label on,
In case we three got lost,
But all I want is Mam and Dad
The rest can all get tossed.

Joan Sharp, almost seven, was enjoying 'a great adventure'. Until, hanging out of the train window, she saw her granny in tears: 'I just couldn't understand why she was crying'. Cheered then by the thought that 'everybody has an adventure once and this was ours', Braham Glass is still moved by a last image of his father. 'He was standing there as the coach pulled out, and he put his hand under his chin: "keep your chin up".' For John Hillier, bustled with his brother on to a train carriage, there came a sudden clarity—and finality.

Seeing that division—the window—between you and your
parents and others come to see their children off, and the

53

Rita Patterson kisses her brother Derek goodbye, minutes before she left from Blyth Station, near Newcastle, for Australia—and an unknown life.

singing of 'We'll Meet Again' . . . you really realised—something was happening. It became very emotional.

At Polemont Station, waiting for the down train from Edinburgh, the Cuthbert girls' father broke down. 'That,' Katharine recalls, 'was a totally novel experience.' At Blyth, Isabella Woods' earlier matter-of-factness had dissolved. She was, in fact, experiencing 'a very, very sad' farewell. The train pulled in: 'I was sick all the way from Blyth to Liverpool, sick with emotion.' Tony Houghton considered he was 'only going to Australia, not leaving home'. Everything, he remembers, was 'hunky dory': 'We got on board the train, and said cheerio. Just as the train was pulling out I looked back—and saw my mother practically collapsed. She just burst into tears and was being held up by her two sisters.'

Dressed in their best, labelled, and carrying their gas masks, seven CORB evacuees are photographed moments before leaving Blyth for Liverpool. They include Francis Woods (*left*), Isabella Woods (*centre*) and a suddenly worried Rita Jackson (*second from right*). The 'School Board' land escort stands with them.

Heather Staff, travelling with her brother on a train chugging away from South Shields and Tyneside, was bereft—but already busy building a new life: 'There were so many things to think about and people to meet and things to do, and a long train journey was something fairly new'.

Dorothy Loft was livid. Not only was she going to Australia, she was also wearing school uniform and 'the most atrocious black straw hat' her mother had insisted on. 'I hated it, and once we got on the train that went out the window. I can't remember anything else. It just went whhhht!!—straight out.' Her brother Reg, off for 'a twelve-month holiday to Australia', was swept by contradictory thoughts:

> As Mum and Dad faded away into the distance I can remember thinking, young as I was, 'I wonder if I will ever see them again.' The imminent invasion of Britain brought that to mind.

55

Awaiting embarkation, each group of Australia-bound children spent a few days in Liverpool, staying in schools, hostels and orphanages. Shipboard escorts located their children, befriended them, and organised them amidst the general confusion. Each child was issued with a metal identity tag inscribed with a CORB number. Wrenched from familiar homes, the children ate drab food and slept on straw palliasses. Every night they groped for their gas masks, then trudged down into underground shelters as the Luftwaffe pounded the city. Some were desperate to return home, some desperate to sail, some both. Many wondered why they were there at all.

Some children sent letters home. Helen Cuthbert wrote: 'We look at your photor evry day and evry body said you look very nice . . . I have not yet been sik but I have felt sik'. Young Katharine ended her spidery note: 'on the way we saw barag bloons and one coming down I give my love to you both Love from K.E.C.'. Joyce Briant wrote, 'We got a shock when we found out we had to sleep on sacks of straw and blankets'.

John Hillier managed to get off two letters. The first was relatively cheerful and ended: 'I hope you are not too sad at our leaving. Keep your pecker up, Your loving son John.' The second letter was far more distressing. After describing a midnight air raid, John continued:

> When the all clear went it turned my stumuch up side down and I felt sick. So I went to the lavatorys but was not sick. When I got up stairs dead beat I put down my gas mask and my blanket and a way went the air raid siren and down we went to the air raid shelter . . .

A few evacuees were sent home before embarkation after failing final medicals. A very few others, too utterly bereft to be reasonably taken overseas, were also sent back. These extreme cases were the tip of a much wider problem: homesickness and heartbreak in all their different degrees. Gerald and David Cox were very homesick. Their mother told them after the war that, had she *known* of the delays before embarkation, she would have 'gone to Liverpool and brought us back home'.

The escorts comforted their children: cajoling, diverting, helping them to look ahead to the voyage and to Australia. Geoffrey Shakespeare visited evacuees whenever possible. He wrote in his memoir of the homesickness he saw—'this strange disease': 'It comes suddenly like a virulent germ, and such is its physical effect on the child that it lowers all power of resistance. But the same child within an hour is laughing and joking again.'

A romantic imperialist at heart, Shakespeare was sure that 'the thrill of the strange adventure of embarking in a great ship for an unknown

Liverpool, from where all the Australian CORB children sailed, was heavily bombed while the children awaited embarkation. Here, an elderly Liverpool couple survey the damage.

destination' would overcome homesickness. People overseas, he told the children, would judge Britain by its children. He urged each group to 'be truthful, be brave, be kind, and be grateful'—unlike Hitler 'who never learnt to be truthful as a boy'. His homilies often ended with the admonition: 'When things go wrong, as they often will, remember you are British and grin and bear it'. In Australia, some children did just that.

Mary Clemes remembers Shakespeare, a tall figure, 'squatting down on his heels and talking to some of the little ones, being really very human'. His fatherly encouragement, however, sometimes failed. Joyce Briant had left her home in Kent with keen excitement. Now, about to embark, she suddenly feared that it might be years before she returned: her evacuation had 'hit home'. Shakespeare had just finished his morale-boosting chat:

He came down the centre aisle and said, 'Has anybody got any questions?'. I said, 'Yes. Can I go home?'. He looked a bit taken

57

Geoffrey Shakespeare, MP and CORB's Chairman, visited evacuees awaiting
embarkation whenever possible. A genial, fatherly figure, he tried to jolly the
children over any homesickness or anxiety.

aback, but he said, 'It's going to be wonderful, you're going to
have a marvellous time. It's going to be a lovely boat trip—and
it won't be for very long!'

Geoffrey Shakespeare had been less persuasive at home. When the
evacuation scheme was being finalised he had suggested to his own
children that they should go overseas to safety. The two youngsters
were appalled. As their father confessed in his memoir: 'They burst into
tears and emphatically refused to go'.

The Children's Overseas Reception Board was established within a
matter of weeks. The consequences of the evacuation, both good and
bad, have lasted a lifetime.

Atlantic Convoys

6

Here we were, going across to the other side of the world. Was it going to be what we hoped or thought it was going to be?

FROM the docks of Liverpool countless thousands of emigrants had left for ports of a far-flung Empire. The wide, boomerang-shaped sweep of the Mersey, the narrow neck at Birkenhead, Bootle at the river's mouth, and then the grey-green swells of the Irish Sea with Blackpool to starboard and the Welsh hills to port—all these every outward-bound migrant from Liverpool had seen in years past. But in 1940 the port had less familiar features: a curtain of barrage balloons, anti-aircraft batteries, blackened buildings, grey-painted merchant ships . . .

The Australia-bound evacuees left Liverpool aboard three ships: *Batory, Nestor* and *Diomed*. The *Batory*, with 477 children, sailed on 5 August; the *Nestor*, with 82 children, on 24 August; and the *Diomed*, with just 18 children, left on 17 September.

All three ships sailed amidst tight security as the Battle of Britain raged in the skies, and as wide-ranging U-boat attacks made the Atlantic increasingly hazardous. Allied vessels were being sunk as far as 1000 kilometres west of Britain. U-boats, many now operating from bases along the coast of southern France and so able to penetrate into the mid-Atlantic, were the greatest threat to the Atlantic convoys. Long-range bombers flying from airfields along the French and Norwegian coasts and surface raiders were lesser threats. Meanwhile, half the Royal Navy's destroyers were being withheld from escort duties as they waited in the Channel and North Sea to repel the expected invasion.

The evacuees who sailed in the *Batory* were to have left on a British liner, the *Orion*. They were reassigned to the Polish *Batory* at very short notice. The *Batory*, a 16 000 ton luxury liner of the Gdynia America Line designed for Atlantic crossings, had been launched only four years before. Since Poland's invasion she had operated under British orders, and had participated in the evacuation from Norway when her sister ship was sunk. The *Batory* arrived at Liverpool from Canada on 2 August. Two days later Geoffrey Shakespeare, concerned at reports about the *Orion*'s condition, visited the Polish ship. There and then it was agreed with her master, Captain Zygmunt Deyczakowski, that the 477 Australia-bound evacuees awaiting embarkation would sail aboard the *Batory*—the next day.

Up at dawn, the children arrived at the dock on the morning of 5 August. *Batory* officers and CORB officials hammered out last-minute arrangements for accommodating the children and 51 escorts and medical staff. The children, already homesick and weary, now confused and hungry, stood waiting on the quay. Meanwhile, to the amazement of the escorts, some 700 troops of the Gordon Highlanders, the Argyll and Sutherland Highlanders and the Manchester Regiment were seen boarding the ship. 'Far from being a children's ship, the *Batory* was a troopship. We were, in terms of war, a legitimate target', one escort later wrote.

The dock was crowded—children, soldiers, dock workers, officials, reporters and a Scots band. Heather Staff, used to Tyneside ships, was still amazed by a towering grey wall, 'this enormous ship' Norman Townsend noticed that the ship's name had been painted out under grey camouflage. However, he 'was able to read the name *Batory* as it was still in raised lettering on the side. It was a ship that none of us had ever heard of, and we wondered what sort of ship it was.'

The children felt 'uncertainty tinged with excitement'. Some felt over-whelming anxiety: one little girl, found alone and totally distraught, was sent home. Seven-year-old Albert Young, waiting with his older brother and sister, clutched a sweat-sodden sandwich:

> I've really got to tell you
> I'm a worried little bloke,
> You want me to get on the ship
> When I can't swim a stroke.

The evacuees finally boarded the *Batory* that afternoon. Dwarfed by their luggage, perplexed at having their gas masks taken away, the children clambered up the gangway—to Shakespeare, 'a thrilling if mournful sight'. Stepping into the ship the children entered an un-known world: strange smells, unintelligible orders, mysterious signs, round windows. Amidst a crush of hurrying people Peter Edkins was baffled by the maze of 'complex companionways' leading down to a cabin with no porthole. 'You lost all sense of orientation, which was front and back and side.' Lifejackets were issued immediately. Albert was petrified:

> 'This here, lad, is your lifebelt,
> Without it don't get caught!'
> My God, I thought, we're sinking
> And we haven't left the port.

60

Some of the 477 CORB children who sailed aboard the *Batory*, boarding the Polish liner at Liverpool on 5 August 1940. The escorts shepherd the girls onto their ship—to Geoffrey Shakespeare, 'a thrilling if mournful sight'.

The CORB escorts managed to find cabins for all 477 children. Then, in two sittings, they faced their first Polish meal. Later Phil Robinson found his way up to the deck. The sun, setting across the Mersey, had silhouetted a church spire. Phil thought:

> 'Well that's a good omen.' I suppose it was part of the Robinson tradition of Godfearing churchy parents. God was on our side. He was showing me that, 'There we are, there's your church. You're safe. Don't worry.'

Designed to carry 300 passengers on short trans-Atlantic voyages, the *Batory* now had a wartime complement of 1340: evacuees, escorts, troops and First Class passengers. The ship slipped her moorings at 10 p.m. David Cox was aware of getting under way: 'We were in our cabins, it was late at night and very dark . . . I heard the engines and finally knew we were off on this great trip.' One of the girls, hearing 'the pounding, the constant movement of the engines', was almost mesmerised by the throbbing of 'this fantastic, powerful moving machine'.

A dark shape in the greater darkness of blacked-out Liverpool, the *Batory* moved slowly down the Mersey. By daybreak she was in the Irish Sea amidst a gathering flotilla. When he woke, Albert,

> Looked out of the porthole,
> And as far as one could see,
> There was no sign of England,
> Just *Batory*, the sea and me.

The children, soon to be restricted to just a few decks, explored the ship. Reg Harris somehow managed to get 'right up onto the forepeak, looking over at the bow going through the water'. One small boy was discovered hanging onto a lifeboat lashed against the boat deck rails. 'Samson'

> . . . had climbed on the passenger rail, and then let himself go and grabbed the leading part of a lifeboat. He was looking down into the sea, engrossed with the waves, and that was how we found him . . . A soldier came and got hold of him.

Ruth Wilson was amazed at the sea's expanse. She wondered 'where we were going and what was happening' but, excited at the adventure, she was happy enough. Norman Townsend remembers that 'the sea was practically gun metal grey, but around the ship itself it was brilliant green with the bow wave creaming white down the side of the ship'.

WS2, the convoy that gathered around the *Batory*, was a particularly important one for it carried over 30 000 troops. It consisted of three cruisers, seven destroyers and seventeen merchant ships, every one an impressive liner. HMS *Cornwall*, the Senior Naval Escort, was leading. HMS (later HMAS) *Shropshire* covered the rear. The ships were arranged in an elongated diamond formation, with the *Batory* safest in the central position.

Zigzagging every few minutes, the grey-painted ships steamed westwards beyond Ireland into the Atlantic. The older children were encouraged by the convoy's size: 'there was this tremendous confidence in naval arrangements', one recalls. 'We felt ourselves the securest of spectators', another wrote. Boys, rather than girls, remember the details. Ted Flowers recalls: 'We were surrounded by warships and aircraft overhead. I finally realised what the Western Approaches was all about. I remember thinking, "My God, they're looking after us".' Peter Edkins' picture might have come from *The Wonder Book of Ships*:

> We had the *Stratheden*, a very big liner, dead ahead of us. We all wanted to see her from the side, but for weeks we followed her so we could never decide what she looked like. Off the starboard bow was the *Andes*, a lovely P & O liner, and astern were the *Empress of Canada* . . . the *Empress of Britain* and the *Monarch of Bermuda* . . .

On the *Batory* the escorts worked almost without respite to overcome the confusion: 'crises came thick and fast'. Meal sittings were organised, shipboard rules announced, times set for the activities that gradually channelled the children's energies and emotions.

Strict regulations agreed between CORB and the Ministry of Shipping governed safety rules and emergency routines. Evacuee ships had to put to sea with their lifeboats lowered ready, swinging from their davits and lashed against the boat deck rails. Boat drills were held daily. The escorts and crew constantly reiterated the safety rules: 'Children must not put their heads out of portholes. Children must not climb on ship's rails. Children will not be allowed on the upper deck during darkness.'

The evacuees, used to air raid discipline, responded to the situation. Beryl Speirs, an Australian escort in her twenties, thought her charges were 'wonderfully disciplined'.

> The parents who were criticised for sending their children were the same parents who had taught their children to grope for their gas masks out of dead sleep. They were the people who had disciplined their children so they were easy for us escorts to control.

One of the boys recalls: 'We always had to carry our lifejackets with us and pity help you if you were caught without it. They went to the dining room with you, they went onto your bed at night. You sat on them or lay on them on deck—you even took them to the bathroom.'

Above A camouflaged Royal Navy cruiser guards the starboard flank of an Atlantic convoy, including liners identifiable by their high superstructures. The photograph shows how spread out even part of a large convoy was. *Below* When the CORB children sailed from Britain the Royal Navy was unable to adequately protect Atlantic convoys. Many destroyers, such as these four in tight formation, were being kept in Home waters to repel an invasion—thus leaving convoys relatively unprotected.

When the boat drill siren went children had three minutes to get to their boat station. Norman Townsend remembers:

> Sometimes boat drill was notified. The alarms would go off and we would be assembled. The officers would check that everybody was in place. Then there were the boat drills without a particular time. You didn't know whether you were going to be caught in the middle of a meal or a siesta time . . . There wasn't any panic, but there was quite a horrendous sound of feet rushing up the stairs out onto the deck, pushing and jostling.

Older evacuees, like Pamela Palmer, remember the responsibility of having 'to look after the younger ones, and to make sure their lifejackets were tied on properly'. The 'Emergency Arrangements' issued to CORB escorts stated: 'Lifejackets should be tied tightly by the strings *in front*. This is particularly important with children. If the strings are not tied tightly there is grave danger of the child being throttled on getting into the water, or having its neck broken if it falls into the water from any height.'

One small boy, according to Beryl Speirs, had 'countless lifejackets'. 'Every one you picked up seemed to have his name on it. One day we found him throwing one overboard. "Look! Look! If I'd been in it I would have been safe because my lifejacket is still floating!" '

The watch-keeping officers and sailors, alert and rarely off duty, were doubly vigilant at night. The blackout precautions were unremitting; a chink of torchlight could bring a tirade of abuse. Isa Brown, a young Australian escort, wrote: 'It is strange to sit and silently watch from a darkened ship our convoy in bright moonlight forging ahead to God knows where. It is rather marvellous all the same to be a tiny atom in a system like this.'

Very few evacuees remember being extremely worried during their voyage. Phil Robinson understood the purpose of the anti-magnetic mine cable attached to the hull. However, 'it didn't conjure up visions of German U-boats springing up all round us. I just thought, "There's the anti-magnetic mine device" '. Norman Townsend expresses a view held by many of the children: 'We'd grown up with the idea that we were British, we were invincible—and the British navy was with us. We knew that ships did sink but it wasn't going to happen to us.' Pamela Palmer says: 'Being surrounded by ships gave you a sense of security, and we could see cruisers and destroyers doing their patrols.'

Others harboured private fears. Reg Loft thinks that 'If we'd been torpedoed we probably wouldn't have survived because there would have been anything up to half a dozen flights of stairs to go up from where I was to reach the boat deck.' Gerald Cox, sent for a few days to the sick bay,

... had a feeling of being trapped. The sick bay was well down in the ship ... But we were reassured that the motor launches on the boat deck were for the express use of the people in the sick bay.

Three days out from Liverpool a U-boat contact was reported, close to the convoy. In fact no U-boat was in the vicinity but the destroyers attacked, their depth charges sending up evil plumes. 'The ship trembled from bow to stern due to the proximity of the explosions', a CORB nurse wrote. Phil Robinson 'heard these explosions and looked across to where the naval ships were patrolling around the outside of the convoy ... I realised, "Well, we are at war. Perhaps something's going to happen." I was very frightened.'

Some children were simply too sick to care. There were only moderate seas in the first week, but the *Batory*'s movement, throbbing engines, strange food and shipboard smells combined to make most of the children seasick. 'Every meal I knew I was going to be seasick', Michael Fethney says. 'The advice was always: try and eat something. So I did— and then lost it.' One girl recalls nursing her cabin mate until she became so ill she was hospitalised. Reg Loft, seasick for most of the voyage, remembers:

> One morning I felt I was going to be sick so I raced up the stairs, and just managed to burst through the door onto the promenade deck and let go over the side. The wind picked it up and spread it right down this parade of troops lined up on the deck ... You can imagine the language!

The convoy steamed westwards into the mid-Atlantic, keeping well north of the area where most U-boats were sighted. Four days out the ships were beyond the greatest danger. The convoy then split into two parts, each taking troops to both the Middle East and the Far East. The *Batory* and six other liners were escorted by a single cruiser. The older children, especially some Scouts and Guides, tried to estimate the course from the sun. Paul Farquharson and his friends often leant over into the lifeboats to check the compasses mounted in their sternsheets:

> We had worked out, since we were heading due west, that we were going to go into the South Atlantic and then through the Panama Canal. But we woke up one morning and we were heading due south towards Africa, in fact to Freetown.

The *Batory* had come through the most dangerous area unscathed. But the risks for CORB ships yet to sail could not be underestimated. In late August and early September the Royal Navy, its ships still concentrated in the North Sea and the Channel, had so few escorts in the Western Approaches that outward-bound convoys were being left to

Watch-keepers on the bridge of a destroyer escort scan the ocean for signs of danger. This photograph highlights the extreme difficulty of sighting a tell-tale periscope, even in calm seas such as these.

their fate only 300 kilometres west of Liverpool. The statistics were grim: in June 1940 U-boats had sunk 58 ships; in July 38 were lost; and in August 56 were sunk by U-boats and a further 15 by Luftwaffe bombers. The Admiralty's warning that it could not fully safeguard CORB ships remained unchanged. Meanwhile, the Battle of Britain was reaching a crescendo of killing.

The second Australia-bound CORB ship, the *Nestor*, sailed from Liverpool almost three weeks after the *Batory*. A much smaller passenger–cargo vessel, the *Nestor* was better suited for the voyage. One of Alfred Holt's Blue Funnel vessels, well-known in Australasian waters, she was a tall-funnelled ship built for tropical work.

With 82 evacuees and eight escorts aboard, the *Nestor* slipped down the Mersey on the night of 24 August. She was high out of the water, loaded with a light cargo of aeroplane parts for Australia. In the Irish Sea the *Nestor* formed up with Convoy OB203 which had some 40 ships. One was another CORB liner, the *Llanstephan Castle* with 308 evacuees bound for South Africa. Mary Clemes, one of the *Nestor* children, remembers:

> We were all so terribly homesick. I think I just curled myself up in a corner of the deck with my book, just huddling into a corner trying to keep warm, reading and reading. That lasted about three days while we were sailing in convoy. I suppose, underneath, there was a fear all the time that we might get torpedoed. We had frequent boat drills when they shut all the watertight doors in the ship. Once I went back to the cabin to collect something and while I was there the watertight doors were closed. I was all by myself, in a sort of a vacuum. It was a very nasty feeling. Then one morning after four or five days we woke up and the other ships had disappeared. We were all by ourselves, just zigzagging calmly along on our own.

On 28 August two more CORB ships sailed: the *Volendam*, a Dutch liner with 320 children bound for Canada, and the *Rangitata* with 113 children going to New Zealand. Both left in Convoy OB205, together with 32 other ships. Two days later the convoy had just three escorts protecting it.

On 30 August, an hour before midnight, U-60 attacked. One torpedo ripped open the *Volendam*. Miraculously no one was killed or even seriously injured in the explosion. More miraculously still, despite a falling barometer, the eighteen lifeboats were all safely launched. As dawn broke, three rescue ships that had dropped out of the convoy picked up the last survivor. Only the purser had been lost: all the 320 CORB children were safe.

The torpedoing of the *Volendam* should have been a final warning to CORB's officials. It was not acted upon. The government and the press presented the ship's loss as a brilliant rescue—another Dunkirk, 'triumph' snatched from potential tragedy. The parents of some *Volendam* children apparently believed the propaganda; a few even applied to re-evacuate their children with CORB. For many of the children it had been a grand adventure.

The facts were different. Only the combination of moderate weather, the rescue ships' willingness to expose themselves to further attack, and the convoy's position relatively close to Britain allowed the remarkable escape. CORB officials discussed the torpedoing, but apparently concluded that the Navy still had the strength to defend convoys properly. Yet, as a convoy control officer wrote, 'Our chart always showed one convoy under attack'. Warnings which regularly appeared in the diary of the Western Approaches Command never percolated through to

The *Diomed*, a Blue Funnel ship, slips down the Mersey on a pre-war voyage. The *Diomed* left Liverpool with 18 CORB evacuees on 17 September 1940—the same day that the *City of Benares*, a CORB ship bound for Canada, was sunk with great loss of life.

CORB. One entry, made two weeks before the *Volendam* sailed, read: 'U-boats—Attacks on shipping continue on a large scale, and losses heavy. Most casualties at night. A few promising counter attacks, but generally U-boats escape without being sighted or contacted.'

As the Admiralty knew, by early September U-boats were beginning to employ a deadly tactic: hunting together in 'wolf packs' and attacking on the surface at night. London, meanwhile, was being bombed during awesome daylight raids and elsewhere in Britain there were escalating night raids. An invasion was still deemed 'imminent'.

Seven CORB ships sailed in the two weeks after the *Volendam*'s loss. The last was the *Diomed*, another Blue Funnel passenger–cargo vessel. The *Diomed* had been scheduled to leave on 13 September as the Commodore's ship in Convoy OB213. However, she was delayed for four days by a faulty boiler. Her replacement as the Commodore's ship was the *City of Benares*, which duly sailed on 13 September with 90 evacuees bound for Canada.

The *Diomed* evacuees, all boys, spent the four days of delay in an orphanage. They reboarded their ship on the evening of 16 September and sailed the next morning, the *Diomed* manoeuvring between minesweepers that were clearing the Mersey of mines dropped by the Luftwaffe. *Diomed*, 10 000 tons and eighteen years old, was loaded with aeroplane wings. She was the Commodore's ship in Convoy OB215. Donald Mitchell recalls:

> Beyond the Mersey we turned south to the assembly point off Anglesey. We were actually moored off a bay where I could see a path I'd walked around with my family perhaps two summers before: the last sight was of the mountain behind Penmaenmawr and the Great Ormes at Llandudno.
>
> The convoy was all very secure and fascinating. I can [still] see a Swedish ship on our starboard quarter, and a freighter, and I can see Norwegian tankers . . . But the convoy took form only after we picked up a Glasgow section as we were leaving the Irish Sea . . .

The night the *Diomed* left the Irish Sea, over 1000 kilometres out into the Atlantic the nineteen ships of Convoy OB213 were continuing westwards. Four days out from Liverpool they were heading towards where a U-boat had recently been sighted. The convoy's three escorts had left that morning to shepherd some incoming ships. Convoy OB213, with the *City of Benares* in the exposed leading position, was utterly unprotected. The ships were barely making seven knots. They were taking no evasive action. The weather was worsening. However, between gale force squalls, visibility was clear. U-48, commanded by Kapitanleutnant Heinrich Bleichrodt, was shadowing the convoy.

Two hours before midnight U-48 struck. A torpedo spun a ghastly trail of bubbles—then tore the *City of Benares* wide open. Two other ships were hit. The *Benares* sank in twenty minutes.

Every element combined to turn the sinking not into a 'triumphal' *Volendam* but into darkest tragedy. The weather rapidly deteriorated, none of the other ships could stand by, and almost all the *Benares* lifeboats capsized or were swamped as they were launched; the water was bitterly cold. No naval vessels were near enough to give immediate assistance. Late the next day HMS *Hurricane*, delayed by the gale force winds, began the melancholy task of gathering up the many bodies and a few survivors.

Among those rescued were two CORB girls found clinging to an upturned lifeboat: Bess Walder, aged fifteen, and Beth Cummings, fourteen. They had somehow survived a night of appalling fear and horror. Lashed by towering, spume-capped seas, surrounded by piteous, slowly fading cries, they had clung to the keel of their lifeboat. As the night wore on others clinging to the lifeboat had gradually given up the struggle—and slipped down forever. Bess remembers:

> The night was absolutely horrendous. It was the blackest of nights, and it was raining and the wind was blowing at gale

force. The lifeboat's keel was the only thing available, so our hands locked onto it. There was a row of hands alongside mine, on my side of the keel—and another row of hands on Beth's side, facing me. Bit by bit the rows of hands grew less and less as people lost their grip, or lost their will to live—and let go.

We knew that if we could hang on until daylight things would be better. We made up our minds—we were just going to go on hanging on, despite everything. Obviously in the later stages we were fantasising. We saw what we thought were enormous fish, we saw icebergs, we thought we saw ships, we thought we saw planes. We had had nothing to drink and nothing to eat, and we were suffering from severe exposure . . . I think we were very near death.

It was getting dark [on the evening after the sinking], and Beth and I had both made up our minds that this was probably going to be our last day. But there, coming towards us, at a very very creeping speed, was a black dot on a previously blank horizon seen over the crests of the waves. And unlike the other things we had seen this was definitely moving towards us. This one was real. I croaked to Beth, 'Beth, there's a ship'. When we were finally rescued they had to prise our hands off the keel.

In all, HMS *Hurricane* rescued seven CORB children, five privately evacuated children and 98 adults. Three other children were buried at sea. The *Hurricane*'s commander, Lieutenant Commander Hugh Simms, later to be killed in action, was tormented by what he had seen. Steaming to Liverpool with the *Benares* survivors he wrote,

> A cold grey sea and a cold grey mist
> Are kissing little children that their mothers kissed . . .

Eight days after the *Benares* sank the last survivors were rescued. Half-starved and thirst-crazed, their lifeboat had been sighted by a Coastal Command Sunderland piloted by Squadron Leader (later Air Commodore) W.H. Garing, an Australian. Forty-six people, including six CORB boys, were in the thirty-foot boat. Ken Sparks was thirteen: 'I don't think that any of us ever gave up hope. Then, on the eighth day, we saw this plane in the distance and our joy knew no bounds when it turned towards us.' All would have been dead but for the inspired leadership of the young Fourth Officer, a steward and two escorts, Mary Cornish and Father O'Sullivan.

The *Benares* death toll was 255, including 77 of the 90 CORB evacuees. The news was greeted with bitter condemnation in Britain and the Dominions. 'Dastardly Outrage', 'Loathsome Lawlessness of German Conduct of War', screamed two headlines. A committee enquiring into the tragedy raised serious doubts: about a ship as fast as the *Benares* travelling in a very slow convoy, about the lack of evasive

The grim aftermath of an Atlantic sinking: a lifeboat packed with survivors. Forty-six *City of Benares* survivors, including six CORB boys, endured eight days in the mid-Atlantic aboard such a boat before being rescued.

action, and about the subsequent rescue. But in the fever of war a central question was ignored: how, on a black Atlantic night, could a U-boat commander identify a ship as one carrying child evacuees—so making it *verboten*?

The fate of the *Benares* could have been that of any other CORB ship. Yet, a strong swell of public opinion urged the continuing of the CORB evacuation, if only to provoke Hitler. Indeed, Marjorie Day, the *Benares* Chief Escort, hoped—with unintended irony?—'to keep the scheme afloat'. It was, she still believed, 'a magnificently constructive piece of work for the Empire'. But Geoffrey Shakespeare, devastated at the loss of so many children, later wrote: 'It was clear that the German submarine menace had now become such that it would be unsafe to continue the evacuation scheme'. The War Cabinet, meeting at the end of September, announced that the CORB evacuation was to be temporarily suspended until after the winter. The War Cabinet had, in fact, finally resolved to end the evacuation. Its milder announcement was made to avoid offending the Dominions. The last CORB ship had sailed.

The fortunes of war, meanwhile, were turning. The decisive conflict in the Battle of Britain was fought on 15 September 1940 when Allied pilots crushingly repelled a concerted Luftwaffe attack on London, shooting down 185 German aircraft. On the same day British bombers inflicted massive damage on German invasion shipping waiting in the Channel and North Sea ports. Fears of imminent invasion were fading, though the long ordeal of the Blitz still lay ahead. On 17 September, the day the *Diomed* sailed and the *City of Benares* was sunk, Hitler indefinitely postponed Operation Sea Lion.

The escorts on the three Australia-bound ships did their best to conceal the *Benares* tragedy, but many of the evacuees heard of it. The *Diomed*, increasingly safe from attack, was west of the Azores when the news reached her. Donald Mitchell, who with the other *Diomed* boys had shared a Liverpool hostel with the *Benares* children, wrote in his diary:

> We all envied their sailing in such a luxurious ship. If our boiler had not burst we should have sailed with the convoy, and perhaps been sunk. We grumbled a lot at the time but it was an extremely lucky escape . . . It seems strange that we were talking to them and now most of them are drowned.

The *Nestor* was nearing Capetown. Mary Clemes, aware that a cousin had been due to sail on a CORB ship to Canada, 'was terrified that she might have been on the *City of Benares*, and it was a very long time before I was able to discover that she wasn't'.

The *Batory* was between Bombay and Colombo when her radio officer intercepted the news. Some of the children dismissed it philosophically 'as another piece of adverse war news'. Some, like Betty Deeley, looked inwards: 'We were past most of the dangers by then but it made me stop and think. Perhaps it was the process of growing up, where you suddenly think—"This could have been me".'

7 — Through the Tropics

We didn't know where we were going until we got somewhere.

THE imperial lifeline to Australia was the sea route through the Suez Canal. The CORB ships sailed the longer way, around Africa, so as to bypass the Mediterranean and the Italian battlefleet. Crews and escorts gradually relaxed as the ships steamed south from the Tropic of Cancer. The children, now beneath tropical skies, became absorbed in each shipboard day.

Meanwhile, parents had received letters telling them only that their children had sailed. They were warned not to expect further news until their children's ship reached Australia.

South of the Canaries the CORB ships were safe from U-boats. However, the threat from surface ships remained. During 1940 six heavily armed German merchant raiders were causing immense disruption in the South Atlantic, the Indian Ocean and the Pacific. By the year's end they had sunk 54 vessels. In London, the CORB ships' positions were plotted daily in the Convoy Operations Room, near the War Room at Whitehall. Coloured markers showed their destinations: Freetown, Takoradi, Capetown, Bombay, Colombo, Fremantle . . . Countless old pin holes, concentrated along the major convoy routes, swept across the oceans like currents.

'The sheer, glassy stillness of the sea' south of the Tropic mesmerised the British evacuees—and the colours amazed them. Pamela Palmer delighted in 'the beautiful greens with the white spray' left astern as they crossed seas that were 'green to dark blue and, in the distance, even darker blue . . .'. Norman Townsend still sees the *Batory* cleaving the ocean:

> In the tropics you had the bow wave coming down the ship's side, but you also had a second bow wave of flying fish. As the ship churned through it would disturb the schools of fish and they would fly what seemed incredible distances, zooming with their fins out from wave top to wave top.

The flying fish 'used to just plop on the deck'. If the children were quick enough, the fish could be thrown back and saved. There were

The Convoy Operations Room in the bomb-proof command centre at Westminster. The War Room, nerve centre for the British government and service chiefs, was nearby. The map indicates ships then in convoy; on the desk, beside a pigeon-hole marked 'MOST SECRET', is one labelled simply 'THE KING'.

whales 'sounding and spouting', and dolphins 'swimming alongside in schools'. And there were marvellous sunsets and violent tropical storms, 'great walls of water which just marched up on the ship, stayed there and then went on'.

To Betty Deeley—'someone who'd never been beyond Blackpool'— the buoyancy of the massive *Batory* seemed uncanny. 'The depth of the sea and how we could float on it fascinated me. I used to stand and watch the ocean for hours.' Phil Robinson, used to Birmingham's smog, was 'wonderstruck by the clearness and the brightness of the stars'. He was also drawn to the *Batory*'s wake, which at night was often luminous with phosphorescence:

> . . . this zig-zag white path across the sea, the white foam left as the ship passed through. It was never a straight line until the latter part of the voyage. From Liverpool right the way across to Singapore we zig-zagged all the way.

75

The romance of peacetime sea voyages is conjured up in this stylised pre-war postcard of the *Batory*—her bow emblazoned with the crest of her namesake king, Stefan Batory. The *Batory* was painted battleship grey in 1940.

All three ships called at West African ports for fuel and water: the *Batory* at Freetown on 15 August, the *Nestor* at Takoradi about three weeks later, and the *Diomed* at Freetown on 2 October. The children were prepared for these ports with teaspoonfuls of raw quinine. Donald Mitchell was warned—'with much finger wagging'—that they were approaching 'the white man's grave'. The *Diomed*'s aged doctor had such trembling hands that most of the quinine was spilled. Katharine Cuthbert, aboard the *Batory*, volunteered to take the first dose—'I was immediately sick'. Paul Farquharson, one of the older *Batory* boys, avoided the lunchtime ordeal:

> They put a shovelful of quinine into a glass and filled it with water which you stirred till the crystals dissolved. It was vile. Our table was close to a long window which led onto the promenade deck and, as soon as an escort's back was turned, you hulked it straight out the window.

Approaching Freetown 'the sea was still and oily'. The children, keyed up for their first landfall, saw hills rising steeply from an emerald-green coastline. Tropical smells wafted out, rollers crashed onto the shore. Native boats swarmed around each ship as it entered the palm-fringed harbour. Phil Robinson had never before 'seen such beautiful scenes'. 'The natives came out in canoes to sell us their wares, and I remember throwing coins over the side for them. They dived down in the water and you could see them going right down to the sandy bottom.'

Captain Deyczakowski noted ruefully that 'after exhausting their supply of coins, the children substituted with the *Batory*'s silver cutlery, complete with an engraved coat of arms'. 'Army issue' knives, forks and spoons appeared henceforth at meals. The children haggled for coconuts, and one boy bought a chameleon: 'this magic animal that we had never seen but which we'd read about'. He was made to return the creature because the ship 'didn't have enough flies to feed it'.

The *Diomed* entered Freetown soon after daybreak. A line of mine-sweepers was heading to sea, a convoy was about to sail, an Allied flotilla lay in the roadstead:

> Divisions were going on on the quarterdeck of one of the cruisers. The marine band were there with their helmets, all in whites, and they were playing national anthems because of the presence of various allied naval ships. It really was quite moving, somehow a visible manifestation of the British Empire.

Each CORB ship spent a day refuelling and watering at its chosen West African port. As each subsequently crossed the Equator the children were initiated into the ocean's mysteries. On the *Batory*, 'Neptune, his wife and the Captain sat on their throne, attended by slaves and courtiers. To be initiated one was lathered and shaved, then pushed through a barrel lined with soot and doused with salt water from a hose . . .'

The *Batory*, in convoy, steamed south-east past the Gulf of Guinea towards Capetown. The children had settled into regular shipboard routines. The ship, designed for 300 passengers, was carrying over 1300. The 700 troops spent much of their time below decks. The 100 First Class passengers had the spacious 'Sun' and 'Boat' decks to them-selves—and any evacuees who strayed there were met with 'pursed lips and disapproving stares'. The 477 children were mostly confined to the 'Promenade' deck, about three metres wide. Peter Edkins recalls:

> We had to rush out early after breakfast to establish a place where we could sit with our back to the saloon, otherwise you were sitting in middle of a side deck on a ship that was pitching

... We were allowed back [to our cabins] after breakfast, then we had to be out of them again before Captain's inspection.

Charles Kilby, a retired headmaster, was the *Batory*'s Chief Escort, and Bill Oats, a young Australian teacher, his deputy. With so many children they and the 36 other escorts had no choice but to organise fixed routines. Meals were when 'announcements were made, the programs for the afternoon, what was happening that night or the next morning—and also punishments. They would go crook at a few kids who'd left their lifebelts behind, or at younger ones caught hanging around the dining room.' As Derek Simpson wrote in a shipboard magazine:

'Twas dinner time on the 'Corbory'
Bill Oats came marching in,
His whistle blew, and silence reigned
To hear the dropping pin.

'You must keep to three and four decks,
But if you go on "Boat" or "Sun",
I'll wring your– – –necks,
And this is not a pun.'

The children in the *Nestor* and *Diomed* had less structured routines, for on both ships space was plentiful. Donald Mitchell and his mates

... had the run of the *Diomed* in certain ways, and we were able to contrive to have more of it than we were intended to have. There were out of bounds areas immediately around the bridge where the officers off watch were sleeping, and we were also banned from going near the galley because we cadged food.

Aboard the *Nestor* the day began with 'prayers on the for'ard hatch at seven-fifteen'. Ian Paterson, an Australian escort, continues: 'Breakfast was at about quarter to eight, and then we had callisthenics which I was in charge of. I used to do the boys and then the girls at separate times.' Later there were lessons for the younger children, with older evacuees like Mary Clemes assisting. Ronald Tubb, the young Third Mate, could see from the bridge 'six or seven hatches, and they had classes on all of them, girls aft and boys for'ard, all in their tropical clothes having a whale of a time'.

Twice a week, Mary recalls, the *Nestor* girls were taken below to the laundry to iron their own—and the boys'!—clothes. Heavily lagged pipes festooned the bulkheads, the porthole was regularly slapped by rollers:

It was terribly hot down in this place. The irons were those ones that you plug into the wall while they get hot, and then you take them out and you use them until they get cold. The boys' khaki drill shirts and shorts were horrible to deal with.

On the *Diomed* the eighteen boys spent carefree days. In the mornings they played deck games and had competitions. Sometimes they visited the engine room, 'down gallery after gallery of steel ladders'. Tony Houghton describes these days:

> About mid-morning we'd have a cup of beef tea or orange juice when we got into the tropics. After lunch the afternoons were mainly spent in the bunk, either reading or dozing. Then, after dinner, there might be a singsong in the smokeroom at night.

The smokeroom, a small deckhouse just forward of the towering funnel, had a piano, cane chairs, 'a rather jaded collection of novels', and Blue Funnel stationery that the boys longed to use.

On all the ships Sunday services were well-attended by children, escorts and crew. Ministers of the different denominations took services on the *Batory*—'a sort of mangled Matins' for the Anglicans—and on the smaller ships their captains led the prayers. All sang the haunting sailors' hymn 'Eternal Father strong to save', its lines pregnant with meaning in 1940:

> O Trinity of love and power,
> Our brethren shield in danger's hour;
> From rock and tempest, fire and foe,
> Protect them wheresoe'er they go;
> > Thus evermore shall rise to Thee
> > Glad hymns of praise from land and sea.

Mary Clemes still had her violin with her. As there was no piano in the room where the *Nestor* children had prayers, Father Ball persuaded her to play: 'Every night I had to go up and practise the hymn for the next day'.

When Bill Oats searched the *Batory*'s holds for 'the cornucopia of equipment' promised by CORB he found just 'a box of Bibles and some Laurel and Hardy films'. But 'we found much more important human resources', he later wrote. Activities proliferated: Scouts and Guides, Cubs and Brownies, informal lectures, dancing classes, gym, boxing . . .

Singing, however, became the *Batory*'s abiding pastime. Singsongs, rehearsals and concerts filled countless hours and helped soften the trauma of evacuation. Heather Staff, like many of the children, thought 'singing was the most important thing that we did on the ship'. Everyone enjoyed it: the children, the escorts, the crew, the troops, even the rather stuffy First Class passengers. The singing was inspired by Meta Maclean, one of the escorts and an Australian songwriter and pianist. To Paul Farquharson, a choir boy at home, it seemed 'the singing never stopped'. He continues:

Meta Maclean and Margaret Osborne wrote a song for the ship called 'The Call', and we used to beef it out whenever we had an assembly—

From the old lands, to the new lands,
Come Britons young and free,
With courage true, we come to you
From our homes across the sea.

Our country has taught us each to be
Steadfast and brave and true,
Now we are here, with a song of good cheer
To love and be loved by you.

The hard-pressed escorts were rarely able to relax. But, with the children asleep, escorts and officers met in the First Class lounge or danced on the afterdeck. Romance, for at least one escort, blossomed. Beryl Speirs, returning home to Australia, married Lieutenant J.D. Stevenson of the Manchester Regiment soon after leaving Freetown; 'she all in white with a bridesmaid in blue'. The ring, turned in the engine room, was made of oxidised steel. Captain Deyczakowski offered to send the newlyweds to the *Stratheden* for their honeymoon, but a senior naval officer on the *Batory* vacated the ship's bridal suite.

The heat and brilliant tropical skies brought sunburn, especially on the smaller ships with their open decks. 'Sleeves down and collars up' was the rule. The *Batory* children were occasionally hosed down to cool off. On the *Diomed* deck awnings were stretched, and a canvas swimming pool—soon punctured by 'some silly ass'—was erected beside the funnel. The boys put on their 'regulation khaki and panama hats', the girls their 'shady hats'. The shortage of suitable clothes for the children was a nagging concern for the escorts. Ian Paterson remembers:

Canada was five or six days away [from Britain] but Australia was ten weeks away, so you can imagine the problems that arose out of the CORB clothing lists being the same for each destination. Their shoes wore out when we'd been away for three or four weeks.

When the *Nestor* called at Takoradi Ian scoured its bazaars for desperately needed hats and shoes. 'Only two of us were allowed ashore because yellow fever was raging there. We drew lots, and I and a West Australian lass drew the short straws.' In Bombay, indefatigable Bill Oats made similar lightning raids to equip the *Batory* children with sandals.

Fresh water was another problem, especially on the *Batory*. The ship carried some 1600 tons of water, but 100 tons or more were consumed daily. Tony Smith, 'frequently admonished not to let taps drip or waste', realised that his father's memories of water shortages in sailing ships had not been exaggerated. Personal washing was mostly done in sea water. Reg Loft says: 'We had salt water for bathing, and it wouldn't lather. I can remember the taste of cleaning my teeth in the lousy water.' Baths gained a new dimension when the ships were sailing through seas rich in minute phosphorescent organisms. On the *Batory* the bathroom lights were controlled from switches outside . . . Pamela Palmer was bathing:

> I'm in this bath of water, when one of the boys switched the lights off. What are all these little lights in the bath?! I jumped out, opened the door, turned on the lights again—but I couldn't see the little lights I had just seen any more. We were told it was phosphorescence glowing in the dark.

At night, with cabin portholes shut to keep a total blackout, sleeping was difficult in the close heat. On the crowded *Batory* lice, measles, chicken pox, tropical rashes, boils and impetigo—spread by shared lifejackets—affected the evacuees. 'Impetigo went through the ship like a dose of salts', Braham Glass recalls. 'They set aside part of the ship for the sufferers, poor children sitting in quarantine with their eruptions painted with Gentian Violet.'

Shipboard meals provided lessons in adapting. They were more varied than at home and far more formal. Pamela Palmer felt it was 'strange to be served by stewards' and 'admired the way they carried so many plates in their arms even when the ship was rolling'. The food was far more abundant than in war-rationed Britain. On the *Nestor* 'the meals were beautiful', as a menu Ian Paterson still has suggests:

> TEA: Fried Sole; Omelettes; Minced Turkey and Tongue; Mashed Potatoes; Cold Ham; Roast Beef; Bologna Sausage; Salad; Decorated Cake; Vanilla Icecream; Orange Jelly; Preserves; Cocoa; Milk.

The old *Diomed* kept up Blue Funnel standards, but Tony Houghton remembers 'runny marmalade flowing back and forth as the ship rolled, always with a few flies in it'. The *Batory* had the strangest food, and possibly the softest cooks and stewards. One *Batory* girl put on over ten kilograms during the voyage. 'Our problem as escorts was to prevent the Poles from spoiling the children', Beryl Speirs recalls. 'You would often see a little tot coming up with a surreptitious ice cream.' Heather Staff remembers the 'slab cake' made for afternoon tea: 'We'd take it down to the cabin for a midnight feast and put it in a drawer, but the cockroaches would come and invade'.

Aboard ship, cabins replaced bedrooms, bunks replaced beds, and portholes windows. The children had also suddenly to adjust to communal living, fixed timetables and little privacy. Above all, they had mostly to cope alone. 'It was a short distance from this feeling of unfamiliarity to an intense longing for home', Meta Maclean wrote, recalling how problems often sparked—or accentuated—waves of homesickness.

Ruth Wilson, a thirteen-year-old, had experienced her first period while awaiting embarkation. On the *Batory* she was 'counting the days and expecting this to happen again, but nothing happened and nothing happened'. When Phil Robinson developed a boil on the sole of one foot the anxieties that many evacuees felt, but rarely expressed, surfaced:

> There were doctors and nurses, plenty of 'em, but I used to bandage it and attend to it myself. I had this boil for several weeks and it wouldn't clear up . . . I used to limp around the deck, but nobody spotted it. I suppose if I had been at home I would have gone straight to Mum.

For some children there were deeper disquiets: about why they had been evacuated, about how their parents were faring in the bombing, about how they themselves would fare in Australia. Today, about a third of the children remember being happy during the voyage. Rather more were 'reasonably' happy. Some were distinctly unhappy. Most children were at least occasionally homesick.

The escorts played a vital role in minimising homesickness. The nights were the most difficult. Many evacuees remember, especially in the early stages, 'a lot of crying in the beds'. Barbara Donald comforted herself with the theme song from the BBC's Children's Hour, sub-titled 'With a tender thought to all evacuated children'.

> Goodnight children, everywhere
> Your Mummy thinks of you tonight.
> Lay your head upon the pillow,
> Don't be a waif or a weeping willow.
> But close your eyes and say a prayer,
> And surely you can find a kiss to spare.
> For though you're far away
> She's with you night and day,
> Goodnight children, everywhere.
>
> Goodnight children, everywhere
> Your Daddy thinks of you tonight.
> And though you're far away,
> You'll be home one day.

'Bed wetting became a fairly common thing but we always found the Polish stewardesses were very sympathetic about it', Heather Staff remembers, and adds: 'The bed wetting, I'm sure, was related to the separation and evacuation'. Katharine Cuthbert, nevertheless, probably speaks for the majority when she says: 'I can remember the first few days being homesick all the time, but as one got into a routine life was very much happier'. And there were other sources of support, even for those most affected. Brenda Mallett, an only child, was almost constantly homesick during the voyage:

> . . . luckily, from the first day, this lovely man Stefan befriended me. He asked what my name was, then said, 'Brandy! Cherry Brandy!' He sort of adopted me. He talked to me every day, telling me about Poland and singing me songs. When we came into port he bought me a little elephant and a doll, which I still have.
> He later told me he had a wife and child in Poland, and he was at sea when Germany overran Poland—and he had been unable to get back . . . [In] his loneliness he certainly supported my loneliness. He was the most stable thing in my life.

Just under half the children were evacuated with one or more siblings. 'Children helped each other over their homesickness. The elder brother or sister consoling a little one was more effective than we escorts ever could be', Beryl Speirs recalls. Braham Glass says his older sister Essie 'took care of me and made sure that I was reasonably clean and changing my clothes fairly often. I recall being acutely embarrassed when she came into my cabin. It was like having your mum examine your ears in front of your mates . . .'

Gerald and David Cox, aged nine and seven, were very close to one another—as they are today. 'Suddenly we hadn't got a mum and dad. We were on this ship, going into the unknown', Gerald says. David continues: 'We didn't seem to show our feelings in an outward way. We kept it within ourselves. Whether that was a good thing I don't know—but we survived.' Gerald adds, 'We used to do up each other's braces, because that was always a problem for young boys, and we generally helped each other out'.

Helen and Katharine Cuthbert had often quarrelled at home, but during the voyage Helen came to 'represent' the wider family to Katharine. 'We had always been a very close family. Helen was not only my support, she was also the representative of family . . . We very much thought of ourselves as a unit in this strange environment.'

The escorts, especially the Australian ones, noted the stoicism of many of the evacuees. Some wished their charges had been less controlled. Meta Maclean later wrote of the children's 'strength of

83

character that makes them second to none'. But she thought their departure might have been less sad 'if they had been more noisily distressed . . . a little less self-controlled, a little less brave'.

On the *Nestor* Ian Paterson thought his boys were far more diffident than Australian youngsters: 'they answered better to their surnames so that's what we called them'. He was responsible for sixteen children, 'from little Arthur to Tillman who was sixteen'.

> Little Arthur was a bit of a problem. If I didn't get him up at midnight he'd wet the bed. I don't think he woke up, but I used to get him out. The mixture of ages worked out rather well, because you could have the big ones looking after the little ones.

The escorts had been appointed only weeks, and sometimes only days, before embarking. Some were British, and were to return there. Others, including Bill Oats, Ian Paterson, Beryl Speirs and Isa Brown, were Australians going home. Most had worked with children before as teachers, educators, social workers or priests.

The escorts shaped—and coloured—almost every aspect of the children's day-to-day lives. Paul Farquharson shared a cabin with Reg Loft and Tony Smith. Their escort was Eleanor Pearson. Paul says:

> I think [CORB] had done a marvellous job in London in getting the escorts they got: the Oats and the Kilbys and the Pearsons and the Speirs. These were the people that made CORB rather than the overall CORB umbrella.

Phil Robinson's escort, Miss Scott, was 'a very warm woman' in her twenties: 'She gave you comfort, she gave you confidence . . . She used to come round every night when we were in bed just to make sure we were comfortable and tucked in'. Mary Clemes remembers Father Ball as 'very human with a great sense of humour—and very humble'. Braham Glass says of the *Batory* escorts: 'They were our mentors; they were our teachers; they were the people we went to with troubles'.

Today, almost all the evacuees remember their escorts with gratitude and affection. Some of the escorts still keep in touch with their 'children'.

The halfway point in the voyages was the Cape of Good Hope. For virtually all the children Capetown was their first experience of a foreign country and of a different race. Ashore at last in the southern hemisphere, South Africa was a welcome change.

The *Batory* steamed into Capetown on 25 August, twenty days out from Liverpool. The children craned for views of Table Mountain, the

Many of the shipboard escorts were young Australians returning home from war-torn Europe. Isa Brown, pictured here with some of her girls, was one. She is still in touch with her 'bairns' today, including Rita Patterson (*extreme right*).

port's majestic backdrop. Then, as the ship came alongside, the children—boggle-eyed—leaned over the rails. Reg Loft missed none of it:

> There were negro women on the roof of the Customs sheds with large crates of Jaffa oranges, and they started throwing oranges which we hadn't seen in England for a while. They were big hefty women and a couple of oranges hit the soldiers on the promenade deck, so the soldiers started to throw them back—and an orange fight began!

'Thousands and thousands of twinkling lights' formed the breathtaking view of the port that night. The children, weary of the blackout at home and closed portholes on the ship, thought the lights glimmering across Table Bay were 'just magical'.

85

The *Nestor* and the *Diomed* called there subsequently. All three visits were marked by lavish hospitality. South Africans, from the black women at the docks to the legendary Jan Smuts, opened their hearts to these evacuees traversing the Empire. Private cars lined the dockside to take them on excursions: to parks and zoos, sports meetings and picnics, into the country, even to Government House. There were thousands of oranges, apples, ice creams, sweets. And there were families. Bobby Barton later wrote in the *Batory*'s magazine of generosity that 'surpassed all expectations', of hospitality that was 'almost embarrassing':

> This welcome was indeed from the heart. To us children it was an experience never to be forgotten, and we realised for the first time that we were part of a great and noble empire.

The welcome certainly reflected the strength of South Africans' feeling for Empire in 1940. Although the younger children generally took their reception for granted, the older ones knew it was no ordinary welcome. Some were overwhelmed at being treated 'like minor royalty'. For many of them it was the first experience of affluence and luxury. Paul Farquharson, given a little blue badge reading 'Freedom of the City of Cape Town', discovered—it worked! Shopkeepers 'dished out lollies' for the asking! Pamela Palmer was also stunned:

> I was allowed to go with a shopping list and some money to get things like hair ribbons. When I got into Woolworths they realised we were off the evacuee ship and we were told that we could have whatever we wanted at absolutely no cost.

The children made other discoveries. Heather Staff was struck by the Africans' 'very bright clothes'. Another girl saw millipedes for the first time. Reg Harris wandered along the wharf to where some 'natives' were fishing: 'One was eating a lobster with a red shell. I'd never seen a lobster before . . . I put it in my cabin for some time, but after a while it made rather a nasty smell.'

Brief as the ships' visits were, they provided the children with experiences of lives far removed from those they knew. Britain, the Empire's hub, was still fundamentally Anglo-Saxon. Hardly surprisingly, some evacuees had ingrained assumptions that blinkered them to this different, partly 'native' country. One boy says, with regret: 'We had that old imperialistic sense of superiority—you know, "The wogs start at Calais". And now we were going amongst them, so we had to show them that we were "British to the bootstraps".'

Others were more open to the different scene. Donald Mitchell was discomfited by an ugly altercation between the African helmsman of a harbour launch and an overbearing European passenger. On another occasion, he and a friend rose to give their seats on a bus to 'a heavily

Lady Smuts, wife of South African Prime Minister Jan Smuts, signs autographs for the *Batory* children during their stay in Capetown. The *Nestor* and the *Diomed*, the two other Australia-bound CORB ships, also called there.

laden elderly woman'. Their CORB escort told them to stay in their seats, 'with the explanation that one didn't give one's seat to an African'. Tony Smith, when he talked to a tall African at a sports meeting, found '. . . a very cultured sort of chap who expressed some philosophy . . . I considered him to be civilised, and it was interesting that he had a few words with us.'

Capetown also provided the evacuees with their first news of the war since leaving home. From newspapers and gossip the older children learnt something of the war's recent developments. But from their parents they heard not a word. Parents, knowing nothing about the ships' itineraries or even their names, could not write to their children. With the latest war news to hand, many evacuees felt renewed concern for their parents' safety.

Most wrote home. Joyce Briant, a week out from Liverpool, had headed a letter 'Somewhere on Earth': shipboard life was 'a bit monotonous', but she was enjoying the voyage; lifejackets were 'worse than

Three *Batory* lads at the Green Point Track, Capetown. The young 'Scottie' appears undaunted by a knee-high ball—or by the photographer who probably set up the soccer tussle. The *Batory* evacuees stayed in Capetown for a week, feted with lavish hospitality.

gas masks'; her cabin was 'quite a nice little place with two bunks, a wash basin, a writing table and a wardrobe'. Katharine Cuthbert sent an innocently charming letter home to Stirling. She said:

> we are sill having cold baths in the morning tunn a about and it is my turn to moro we do not get a bath evry night but I think I am ferly clean I am going to give yo a lot of kisses eatch and Bridget and Jillian too. Love From Katharine

She ended her message with eight lines of kisses, two each for her parents and sisters—'theses ciss are for Mummy', 'theses ciss are for Daddy' . . .

The *Nestor* and the *Diomed* each spent only a day in Capetown. The *Batory* stayed for six days, awaiting a convoy. Meanwhile, the convoy authorities had decided to transfer all 477 *Batory* evacuees to the *Stratheden* for the remainder of the voyage. The children and their escorts were stunned—and 'enraged'. Pamela Palmer recalls, 'The *Batory* had become our home by this time because we'd been at sea for three weeks or thereabouts'. The escorts cabled London: leaving the *Batory*, 'was unthinkable' and—as the *Batory*'s CORB doctor argued insistently—living conditions aboard the *Stratheden* were appalling. Norman Townsend continues:

> There was practically a mutiny. The crew didn't want to separate from the children. The children didn't want to separate from the crew, and the troops didn't want to separate. I remember our cabin steward came in practically in tears saying, 'I have to say goodbye to you'. And we said, 'Where are you going?'. Everyone's attitude was we've been uprooted once, we're here now, we're settled.

The convoy controllers, whose reasons for planning to trans-ship the children had never been obvious, wavered. Finally, impressed by the CORB escorts' and doctors' views, they relented. The *Batory* sailed on 31 August, the children still aboard their beloved ship.

8 _Voyaging On

Homeliness was what we now associated with the ship.

THE CORB evacuees were living in limbo. Their past and future homes seemed equally remote, a world apart from shipboard life. As the voyages entered their last phase the children increasingly saw their ship as 'home'. Their world-view, already vastly changed by the journey to Capetown and their time there, expanded still further in the following weeks. The shackles—or cocoons—of limited home experiences were falling away.

At Capetown, the *Batory*, *Nestor* and *Diomed* were still almost 8000 kilometres west of Fremantle. Diverted to avoid German surface raiders, all three ships steamed far further than that to reach Australia. The *Batory* left Capetown in a five-ship convoy, still with the *Stratheden*. The convoy kept close to the African coast until past Madagascar, then steamed north-east to Bombay. From there they sailed via Colombo and Singapore to Fremantle. The *Nestor* and the *Diomed*, after calling at Durban, began long—and lonely—voyages across the southern Indian Ocean.

Life for the *Nestor* and *Diomed* evacuees continued much as before, until the colder weather further south forced the children indoors. In the *Batory* the children's determination not to be transferred to another ship forged new bonds with the crew and soldiers. Games and books donated in Capetown made for more varied days. On all three ships the children turned in on their worlds: homesickness faded, shipboard friendships firmed.

Betty Deeley, who had been distressed at a cabin mate's early homesickness, was by now her firm friend. 'We started going about the ship together, always as a couple . . . We gave all boys up. We just went with each other and had a lot of fun.' Reg Loft soon forgot his girlfriend at home, and 'got mixed up with the *Batory* crowd'. Class and regional differences persisted. The tougher boys and the 'better spoken' boys generally kept apart. According to Paul Farquharson, Scottish by birth but English by residence, the Scots

> . . . tended to do more of the risky things and get into more scrapes than the English group. You'd find them hanging out of

portholes with a bit of string and a safety pin trying to catch fish when we were in port.

On the *Nestor* Ian Paterson had 'a pretty good cure' for boys who clashed: 'One of the lads had two sets of boxing gloves, so whenever we had a problem with the boys they fixed it up on the for'ard hatch'.

Donald Mitchell, one of the few boys to have been overseas, looked down rather loftily on the others who seemed 'poor and not very well informed . . . We three from the same grammar school tended to feel that we were the elite.' Peter Edkins, another grammar school boy ill-equipped to deal with tougher-talking lads, was teased and bullied because of his 'lack of strong language'. A natural loner, Peter spent countless hours making balsa wood models 'on a small flap-down table in the cabin'. Often he studied the sea:

> . . . to try and predict when a wave would break, in what way it would break—not necessarily giving a name to a type of breaking of a wave, but you had a vocabulary of wave mannerisms . . . Some others wondered how I could be so interested for so long in looking at the sea.

The children almost all gained in self-reliance, imperceptibly asserting a new independence. Exploring the ship was, for Tony Smith, a step towards his future as a seagoing engineer. 'I was fascinated by doors which led to places where we weren't intended to go: into the workings of the ship. Even then I was dipping my nose down into skylights to sniff the engine room smells.' Helen Cuthbert had always wanted her hair to have a fringe: 'My mother had said I couldn't have one. So I decided to cut a fringe myself—which was fairly irregular!' Mary Clemes faced a deeper choice: whether or not to be confirmed.

> I probably would have gone for confirmation at home because it would have been something that happened when one reached a certain age, but it certainly wouldn't have meant so much. I wasn't confirmed on the *Nestor* [just] because my parents thought I should be. It was my choice.

Growing independence, fostered by the escorts, was widened through contacts with the crews—and, on the *Batory*, the troops. The evacuees closest to their ship's officers and sailors were probably those on the *Diomed*. The eighteen boys mixed easily with the crew. Donald Mitchell lent his bathers to the pantry boy, and the bosun passed out leftover food from the petty officers' mess. There were 'educative' conversations with deck boys:

> They were not the sort of anecdotes that I think our parents would have wished us to listen to, but they took us into a world we had no access to before. The crew also volunteered to do

The eighteen *Diomed* boys, with their two escorts and the ship's Captain and Chief Engineer. Tony Houghton stands behind, and between, the two officers; Donald Mitchell is on Tony's right; and David Massey is on the extreme right, front row.

the washing for each boy, and there were almost daily diversions to the seamen's quarters on the poop to see your washerman. I had an elderly Welsh AB, Griffith Hughes, who took some care of me. He was very religious, and in fact rebuked me for listening to the deck boys.

The *Batory*'s crew had been stunned—and some of the stewards hostile—when the evacuees boarded the ship: 477 potential problems each capable of wreaking havoc in the luxuriously appointed liner. The children, unable to understand the crew, had their own misgivings. But soon the Poles, unable to return home after Germany invaded Poland, expressed their love of family to the evacuees. The children, homesick themselves, responded.

'Everybody loved the Polish crew', says Peter Edkins. Said one girl, the Poles 'just took us to their hearts'. Her own group was adopted by one of the stewards who 'used to leave tins of fruit and pieces of cake for us, all very quietly done'. Mealtimes, when stewards and children swapped mangled English and Polish, 'were always happy laughing times'. Cabin stewardesses also excelled in kindness. Ruth Wilson's stewardess brought her small cakes of soap—'different from anything that I'd had before, as I was accustomed to very plain soap. I hoarded two or three cakes of this special soap that was such a treat'.

The *Batory*'s Captain Deyczakowski with Isa Brown's girls, including Isabella Woods (*seated, extreme left*). The photograph captures the warmth that developed between the Polish Captain, his crew and the children—and the dangers at sea. The background lifeboat is ready at the boat deck rails.

Underlying the Poles' sympathy for the evacuees was their anger at the Nazi occupation of their homeland. An incident witnessed by Beryl Speirs revealed the intensity of their feelings. At a ship's 'do' she watched as British officers toasted the King. 'Then one of the Polish officers proposed "To Poland! To Poland!". Whereupon this young officer crushed the glass in his hand!'

Captain Deyczakowski often mixed with the children, who came to adore him: 'Dzien dobry! Good day!'. After Capetown they took a new interest in Poland's heritage. A portrait of King Stefan Batory hung in the lounge, and beneath it groups listened to accounts of Poland's struggles. Helped by the assistant purser Marian Slabosz, the children learnt a Polish song *Rota* and often sang it with passion to a tearful crew:

> . . . Children of Poland, freed from scorn,
> Poles to the end remaining,
> Armed by tradition, we shall fight,
> True liberty regaining.
> The Bugle of God unsheathes the sword!
> This by the help of God!
> This by the help of God!

The 700 troops added another dimension. So as to discourage liaisons between young soldiers and the older girls, the regimental commanders had initially ruled that their men were not to mix with the evacuees at all. The order was 'patently hopeless', likely to provoke outright mutiny amongst troops mostly confined below decks, and was soon largely ignored. 'Theoretically', Katharine Cuthbert says, 'we didn't have much social interaction, but in practice the troops were very kind to us. I'm sure, as with the Polish crew, we were substitute children.'

The soldiers were 'an amazing tonic' for the children, escort Isa Brown wrote. They were stationed at strategic points throughout the ship in case of an emergency, 'usually near hydrants, hoses, axes, places like that', Pamela Palmer says. 'If they found a child crying it wasn't long before there was some knee to sit on to be told a story or given a hug— or handed some chocolate.'

The *Batory*, once beyond Madagascar, was never out of the tropics until the approach to Fremantle. But the *Nestor* and *Diomed* children experienced climatic extremes. Skirting Africa they had been in tropical and subtropical zones, but sailing southwards from Durban they entered far colder latitudes as they rolled and pitched towards Fremantle with the Roaring Forties.

Albatrosses, 'those great birds with their huge wing span', constantly hovered overhead as Mary Clemes looked up past the *Nestor*'s swaying masts. At night the Southern Cross swung across the blackness. The *Nestor*, high out of the water, was by then 'right down into the Roaring Forties'—where she 'rolled steadily from side to side for a couple of weeks'. Lessons were held inside as the hatch covers were often swept by freezing spray. The escorts battled to keep their children warm. And Ian Paterson coped with 'poor Eccles':

> As soon as the ship gave the slightest movement Eccles was on his bunk, and he was there for days. Never felt so sorry for a lad in all my life . . . When we got down south the weather was very, very bad—even the crew were sick. But young Eccles, I feared for his life at one stage. He was a real cot case.

The *Diomed*, also in the Roaring Forties, at one point met a full southerly gale. The boys were both awed and exhilarated:

> We were virtually bow on to the waves. We stood up for most of the day, as long as we were allowed to, out of bounds under the bridge, watching these immense seas. *Diomed* was burying her bows and sending up great clouds of spray over the bridge and us. We went up again surreptitiously, against orders, in total darkness when lightning was also playing over this marvellous scene.

Above In the tropics aboard the *Nestor*—and a fine day to photograph the ship's evacuees. The children, almost all smiling, reflect the ship's contented life. Is 'poor Eccles' amongst the crowd, one wonders—or once again seasick in his bunk?

Below The *Nestor* escorts, all ages and styles of dress, gathered on a hatch cover after the children were photographed. The escort Ian Paterson is standing, second from left, beside the ship's commander, Captain J.J. Power. Rev. Father Ernest Ball stands on the extreme left, and Salvation Army Chief Escort Brigadier Best on the far right. The women escorts' names are not known.

Far to the north the *Batory* skirted the Arabian Sea. A fortnight out from Capetown, on 15 September 1940, the convoy steamed into Bombay. Few more impressive harbour approaches exist. To port stood the stately domed buildings of Raj Bombay. To starboard, beyond a palm-fringed shore, rose the Western Ghats. The children, a world away from drab Liverpool, hung over the rails as the anchor rattled down in India's Empire port.

'Big kites wheeling above the sea, waiting to scavenge anything thrown overboard' were Phil Robinson's first impression—and also a peculiar smell that 'pervaded Bombay and is still there today'. The *Batory* was strangely silent. 'I couldn't sleep when the engines were switched off in harbour', one girl remembers. 'We were so used to the gentle throb of it all the time at sea.' The air was motionless, the heat 'frightful'.

Ruth Wilson's English school dress, a pale blue poplin, in Bombay became 'navy blue—saturated in perspiration!'. At least one evacuee collapsed with sunstroke. But despite the enervating monsoon heat the children went ashore. Nothing they had previously experienced on the voyage had prepared them for Bombay's staggering diversity: a teeming city of Hindus, Muslims, Sikhs and Parsees, their clothes indicative of their faiths; where Gujarati, Urdu and Hindi competed amongst a babel of languages; where humans, sacred cows, vehicles, spices, dung and fires formed a cacophony of sounds and smells—an historic city of a fading Empire.

Peter Edkins, from staid suburban London, climbed Malabar Hill and visited the Parsee Towers of Silence to see 'the bodies laid out', with vultures circling overhead. Betty Deeley 'was appalled by the beggars':

> We were told that the children were purposely crippled so they could beg. I also thought everyone there had TB because there were red lumps of spit all over the pavement. You had to step over it. I found out later it was betel juice, and when they had chewed it they spat it out.

Yet Betty was fascinated. To Ted Flowers, who had seen something of hardship around Newcastle, Bombay was 'a revelation':

> There were people living under awnings, in cardboard boxes and so on. But the thing that really opened my eyes about the British Raj was this crew of twenty or thirty Indians roped together, being whipped along the street by either policemen or soldiers. I found that extremely upsetting, to think that's what the British Empire was about.

The Gateway to India, Bombay's celebrated portal, seemed to countless newcomers the entrance to exotic Asia. For Norman Townsend 'this huge arch on the waterfront that I'd heard of' was almost 'magic'.

Treading in his father's footsteps, he responded with interest and amazement to the vitality and degradation:

> Cape Town was one thing but we were meeting European people. Now we were seeing the poverty and the climate and the people and the attire that we'd been expecting to see: something much more exotic, something much more real, actually.
>
> Possibly because of the way Dad had talked, I was seeing India as India, not as ruler and ruled. He'd been up in the North-West Frontier Province as a guide and so he always worked with Indians. And I think that he always presented them to us as people, not as 'natives'. We knew that there was a caste system, but I can't recall other than seeing them as people— different to ourselves but mainly because of colour and the country they lived in.
>
> I know some of the children's attitude was they were just coolies, almost not human. There was a group who haggled with one of the trading boats that came out to the ship. The trader threw up his rope and they pulled up his basket with melons in—and then they just threw his basket down to him with no money. 'It didn't matter, he was just a coolie.' There was a lot of screaming and calling, and the aftermath was a very strong lecture in the dining room.

One of the older boys, Bill Riley, was almost killed in Bombay. Despite constant warnings he put his head out of a porthole, and was almost decapitated by a flexing wire hawser that 'ripped the side off his face'. He was rushed to hospital, the only near-fatality throughout the voyage.

The *Batory* spent only two days in Bombay itself. Then, awaiting another convoy, she anchored in the roads for four days. Unable to go ashore, now anxious to get to sea, the children endured days of steamy heat and torrential monsoonal rains. 'You could see it coming towards you. The thunder and the lightning was absolutely tremendous, it lit up the whole sea.' To Albert Young,

> Bombay it just vanished behind a grey sheet,
> Then they turned off the tap and back came the heat!

The *Batory* sailed on 21 September, in convoy with the *Stratheden* and the *Orcades*, and escorted by HMAS *Westralia*. The ships steamed southwards with the Malabar Coast hazy to port, past Goa and Calicut. They reached Colombo three days later.

The *Batory* stayed there for just one unforgettable day. Beyond a harbour crowded with every conceivable type of vessel the children were feted by colonial women again: visits to the zoo, excursions to palm-fringed beaches, armfuls of tropical fruit, and long car rides 'driving through the tropical rainforest and the palm trees'. Ruth Wilson, accustomed to 'genteel poverty' at home, rode in two cars and on one elephant—and was taken to 'this marvellous house':

> The coloured servants all wore white gloves and served at the table. We had this very nice dinner, and when we were to leave we were given big jars of sweets and a great big hand of bananas . . . No, not a hand of bananas—a *stick* of bananas with a lot of hands on it . . . The lady took all our names and wrote to our parents.

There were souvenirs and gifts. Boys bought solar topees, one a Colombo swagger cane. Heather Staff still treasures 'an absolutely beautiful shell necklace and a little shell inkstand'. Peter Edkins had been given a coconut still with its husk on, quite unlike the small hairy balls at fairground coconut shies . . . 'I had a penknife with me and I shaved away at the husk all the way from Colombo. But before we got to Singapore I got fed up with it and threw the husk and nut over the side. I never did get to the nut.' Asked by her steward to come to his cabin, Betty Deeley crept down to the crew's quarters:

> He came to the door carrying this lovely elephant. Still to this day I don't know why he bought it for me. It's about eight inches high with ivory tusks and little bits of ivory in the feet. It's got a Maharajah sitting on the front holding a sword. At the back of him is a monkey sitting with an umbrella made of a coconut shell—and he's holding it over the Maharajah's head.

The children had thought that they would 'reach Australia in about four to six weeks at the most'. They were now over seven weeks out from Liverpool, steaming to Singapore. Barbara Donald recalls: 'We knew that we were dodging around, taking the troops to drop them off at Singapore, but even so it seemed to be a very long drawn out journey'.

The voyage began to drag. One day ran into the next, time began to blur . . . Always the ships zigzagged, always the *Stratheden* was off to starboard. 'The *Stratheden* was keeping pace with us throughout the voyage. At times she'd disappear down in the trough of a wave and the next minute she'd be up high again'—as Reg Harris still sees the great P & O liner.

Petty annoyances occasionally escalated into grievances. Some evacuees, 'the novelty of mashed beetroot' having worn off and with cockroaches their excuse, petitioned the escorts about the meals. The ringleaders, Tony Smith says, were 'jumped on very quickly . . . They were told they were behaving like Nazis, and that they ought to have some consideration for the ship which was our host.'

A calm day at sea, with even George Eccles (*extreme left of group*), usually seasick, appearing cheerful! Some of the boys sport pith helmets acquired in Capetown.

The long voyage gave a new sense of distance to older children like Peter Edkins:

> For somebody who hadn't been further than the Midlands and the south coast, it put in perspective the size of the world. At places like Capetown we often went on a two hour car ride with our hosts, distances that we had never travelled in Britain.

Shipboard rumours and jokes broke the monotony. So did islands: 'There was great excitement when somebody claimed they had seen an island'. There was also 'great dispute as to whether they had seen it or not!'. If true, there was the anticipation of the hazy blob resolving into 'distinctly different colours of vegetation, towns and houses'.

Since Bombay some children, helped by the escorts Gertrude Clothier and Beryl Speirs, had been working on a magazine, *Albatross*. Dedicated to the Captain, officers and crew, it appeared en route to Singapore. The cover showed the ship between maps of Britain and Australia, in its wake the words 'Till danger's troubled night depart and the star of peace return'. Censorship demanded that the *Batory*'s name be changed—to *Corbory*—and that no ports be named.

Albatross, nostalgic and light-hearted, recalled the voyage's highlights. Fifteen-year-old Morag Donald wrote of the grey Atlantic:

> When the waves roll high,
> And the sea breeze blows,
> Then you never want to sail anymore.
> You just lie in bed
> With a basin by your head,
> Or stumble feebly down the corridor.

Paul Farquharson and Verna Lloyd recaptured the magic of Freetown, their first port-of-call:

> The hills that range the harbour round
>   Are beautiful to see.
> While here and there a stream runs down
>   Into the emerald sea . . .

Intriguingly obscure facts were reported in *Albatross*. Commander Symons, RNR, the *Batory*'s Naval Liaison Officer, had had 'the terrifying experience' of being sunk in the Baltic—aged two! Lieutenant Colonel Bowater, MC RAMC, a First War veteran, had in civilian life displayed remarkable versatility by lecturing on both 'Cod-Fish Manure Industries' and 'The Transcending Beauty of the Sunsets'. Near the two massive propeller shafts a gauge 'showed the number of engine revs made since leaving England. The last recorded figure was 3 666 510'.

'Bon Voyage', an epic written by 'Footpad', pictured shipboard life:

> Of course there are rules which must needs be obeyed,
> Such as carrying lifebelts though not on parade.
> At times though admittedly this seems a bore
> It may one day prove helpful in reaching the shore.

> A phrase often heard is 'Why aren't you on deck?'
> 'Your number? A Scottie, I thought so, by heck'.
> Our well revered Kilby, staunch leader of men,
> Has routed 'em out from their 'wee butt and ben'.

Children on an idyllic voyage . . . or wartime evacuees? News of the *City of Benares* tragedy had reached the *Batory* en route to Colombo.

The following day the children listened to a broadcast made by the King. It was both a reminder of the war and a timely morale-booster. Isa Brown noted:

> The children are magnificent, looking forward to reaching Australia but enjoying every day as it comes. The older children are noticeably concerned about their parents and the bombing that has been started in earnest. They draw caricatures of Hitler, amongst other things, and that helps their morale.

Half the world was at war; the rest would soon be engulfed. Escaping one conflagration, the CORB evacuees were unknowingly shadowed by another. In June 1940 a British intelligence report had stated: 'There is nothing to stop Japan from seizing French Indo-China, the Netherlands Indies and Hong Kong'. On 22 September, a day after the *Batory* left Bombay, the Imperial Japanese Army invaded Tonkin in French Indo-China. The *Batory*'s troops, sent to defend 'impregnable' Singapore, bastion of the British Empire in the Far East, were destined to suffer the bullets and bayonets of an Asian Blitzkreig.

Through the strategic Malacca Straits, with British Malaya to port and Dutch Sumatra to starboard, the *Batory* approached Singapore. The troops prepared to disembark, checking their equipment and farewelling the children, escorts and crew. Isa Brown retreated to her cabin. There, 'with apologies to Rudyard Kipling', she wrote:

> I am lying in my bunk
> And the screws go punk-a-punk
> Punk-a-punk and we're heading for Singapore.
> She is straining and she's striving
> Just to get that extra knot in
> We'll make port before it's dark
> The boys must get ashore . . .
> Then her bows will turn to southward
> And we'll journey down below,
> Down below the line to Sydney
> Down below the line to Home.

The ship reached Singapore at dusk that day. The following morning the troops disembarked: many would never return. Slung with packs and rifles, they filed down the gangway. The children sang through their tears 'There'll Always be an England', 'Wish Me Luck' and 'Auld Lang Syne'. Pamela Palmer remembers 'a sense of loss, we were losing a lot of our friends'. For Braham Glass it seemed 'like a family breaking up, as by then the *Batory* was our home'.

Beryl Speirs, now Mrs J.D. Speirs-Stevenson, parted from her husband of just a few weeks: 'They were already shipping women out of

101

Singapore and I was not allowed to go ashore. Heaven knew what might happen . . .' As Heather Staff sensed, the soldiers' departure marked the beginning of the voyage's end:

> I suppose it was in our minds: well, what are they going to? So the mood of the ship was rather dead but I think also it was thinking: well, we're coming to the end of our journey.

The *Batory* sailed for Fremantle on 2 October, only hours after the troops disembarked. The once-cramped ship was strangely empty. The days seemed 'longer and more tedious'. The older boys replaced the troops as sentries. There were no more concerts, there was no more whistling. 'There'd been so many other people around and suddenly there was just us.' The older children, despite the beguiling islands of the Dutch East Indies, asked for lessons. One of CORB's future representatives in Australia, W.J. Garnett, interviewed the evacuees to finalise their disembarkation ports. Meanwhile, the escorts gave talks on Australia.

Fremantle was now only days away. Western Australia's desert coast lay below the horizon. Betty Deeley got her suitcase out: 'The entire bottom was covered in sand-coloured cockroaches. There were hundreds of them and they just scuttled and vanished.'

There was an ebb and flow of excitement and anxiety. The children's thoughts focussed on families left behind, those they were soon to meet, and shipboard friends. Reg Loft could barely wait to disembark: 'All the way from England I was looking forward to this wonderful country that Digger had told us about back in England'. But George Wastell from 'Bomb Alley', now responsible for his three siblings, had misgivings:

> It wasn't only the increased space that made us so subdued. We already knew Australians were friendly and outgoing, and believed in 'having a go' . . . How would I measure up then, a boy whose instinct was to look before you leap?

The children most confident about the future were generally those going to relatives. Innate confidence, or lack of it, also affected the situation. Paul Farquharson thought that 'given the chance to have two Farquharsons anyone would swing at the chance'. Ruth Wilson, who had been happy during her 1939 evacuation within Britain, anticipated 'another happy experience'. Barbara Donald, so keen to stay at her uncle's orange orchard, now thought: '. . . this is it. I wonder what my relatives are going to be like. I wonder if they are going to like us, and I wonder if we are going to like it here. And I wonder just what is happening at home'.

Though most of the evacuees were keen to get ashore, their ship was still 'home'. Most had friendships they wished to continue. Ruth Wilson, for example, had 'some very good friends whom I would've very much liked to have lived in the same place in Australia'. In fact, very few of the children were to live near shipboard friends.

The *Nestor* and the *Diomed* reached Australia after the *Batory*. David Massey, one of the *Diomed* boys, recalls: 'I suppose to a certain extent we'd got a Flying Dutchman attitude, where we could have sailed on for ever and ever into the sunset'. Donald Mitchell, seeing in the *Diomed*'s workaday funnel and derricks the mill chimneys of the Midlands, wrote: 'Homeliness was what we now associated with the ship. The crew and the ship belonged to the world we were soon to leave.'

Evacuees, escorts and crews had been bonded. Katharine Cuthbert, thinking of 'visits to ports' and 'all the corporate activities like singing and church services', believed they had become

> . . . one big unit. As we were getting near the first Australian port, and the first group going to Western Australia were going to leave, it did seem like the beginning of another breakup—having got over the original breakup of our own families.

The *Batory*'s was the longest of all the CORB voyages, in terms of both time and distance. And the *Nestor* and the *Diomed* were at sea for a longer time than any other CORB ships, except two that went to New Zealand. Aboard the three Australia-bound vessels there had been lived, as Bill Oats later wrote, 'a lifetime of experience—of children, of human nature, of people under stress, of unexpected resources within young and old to meet anxiety and separation . . .'.

The ships' wakes, umbilical links that had seemed to disappear, stretched back to families now half a world away. The editors of *Albatross* wrote: 'This leaving of the old world is not easy, but like the Albatross we know that our sanctuary lies in southern waters. Before us is a great adventure . . .'

9 Australia at Last

Cheering and singing, a shipload of British children steamed through Sydney Heads today to make Empire history.

A<small>LL</small> three CORB ships reached Australia unscathed. They had slipped out of Liverpool under tight security and beneath grey clouds. They arrived in Australia to a blaze of publicity and cerulean skies in the southern spring of 1940. The *Batory*, with her endless zigzagging, had steamed some 37 000 kilometres by the time she reached Sydney. The *Nestor* and the *Diomed* had each sailed about 25 000 kilometres.

The *Batory* berthed at Fremantle on 9 October, then crossed the Great Australian Bight and went on to Melbourne and Sydney. The *Nestor* arrived at Fremantle in mid-October, and then sailed on to Melbourne and Sydney. The *Diomed*, after calling at Fremantle, berthed at Adelaide on 8 November. From there her eighteen boys were sent to Melbourne and Sydney by train, as concerns about mines in Bass Strait delayed the *Diomed*. Each ship was warmly greeted at the Australian ports, and at each some of the evacuees disembarked.

Empire feeling was running high. Twenty thousand homes had been offered for the CORB children, who provided a focus for Australian anger over Britain's plight. Senator Foll—Minister for the Interior in Robert Menzies' recently re-elected government—informed the press when the *Batory* arrived:

> Australia had hoped to be welcoming not a few hundred, but many thousands of British children. Unfortunately the bitter Atlantic storms of the winter months have compelled the British government to suspend the dispatch of children to the Dominions. I am sure that every Australian sincerely hopes that this suspension is purely temporary.

The Senator's 'bitter Atlantic storms' was a euphemism, an attempt to gloss over the *City of Benares* tragedy and the political impossibility of sending more British children to Australia.

The grandest of the welcomes was the *Batory*'s to Sydney. To many of her evacuees, 'Sydney Harbour and the Bridge symbolised Australia'.

There the last of the *Batory* children disembarked, together with all the escorts—and there the ship's best remembered voyage ended.

The Polish ship came in through the Heads early on 16 October. The morning was glorious: 'the sky was blue, the water scintillating'. There was no rearing Table Mountain, there were no palm trees. Instead 'tree-filled hills and gullies came down to the water's edge'. The red rooftops shone, the water was crowded with countless small craft out to greet the evacuees. Ships' sirens sounded. Then, beyond Bradley Head there rose—the Bridge! The children were lining the *Batory*'s rails. The escort Beryl Speirs-Stevenson, home at last, could see the crowds on the dock from far off. 'I was engrossed watching, when there was a hand on my shoulder. It was Captain Deyczakowski and he said, "Sydney wins!".'

The hawsers shuddered taut and the *Batory* nestled alongside the quay. High with anticipation, tight with anxiety, the children gazed at the Australian crowd. Relatives, well-wishers, dignitaries, reporters . . . The quay was packed. 'Cheering and singing, a shipload of British children steamed through Sydney Heads today to make Empire history', reported the *Sydney Morning Herald*.

Assembled on deck the children sang and listened to speeches of welcome. The friendliness of the reception was 'a wonderful introduction to Australia'. The press seized on the story of 'children escaping from a war-torn Britain'—'Britain's Crown Jewels'. For Braham Glass the voyage ended, as it had been lived, 'in a high state of excitement':

> Things were happening. Everything was different. Now here we were. I was picked to stand in front of this big wooden tripod, and the man asked me to say, 'We're a long way from Hitler now'. I added 'and he's a twerp'. For weeks afterwards I thought, 'My God, if Hitler wins he'll come and find that lad'.

The children had two concerns: the ship and crew they were leaving —and the families they were about to meet. Two months before, the *Batory* had seemed alien. Now the shore was potent with unknowns: 'the last link to our parents and home snapped when we disembarked'. The escorts, amidst the children's tearful farewells to the Poles, gathered up their groups for the last time. Then, their cases packed with mementos of the voyage, 'with Polish caps on their heads', the *Batory* children stepped off the gangway onto Australian soil.

Two boys were staring into an abyss. Before they disembarked, John and Michael Fethney had been seen by a Sydney welfare official and told that their uncle and aunt were too old to care for them properly. The boys must go to another home. Michael was 'absolutely shattered'.

> I thought to myself: what am I doing here in Sydney. I've come here chiefly to live with Uncle Harold and Aunty Elizabeth . . .

Batory evacuees step onto Australian soil at Fremantle, on 9 October 1940. On reaching Australia many of the children were torn between a desire to get ashore and meet their hosts, and a wish to stay aboard their now-familiar 'home'.

> The thought of picking up threads and living with them had kept me going a lot more than I realised. There had been an object behind this voyage—that we would eventually be living with Uncle Harold and Aunty Elizabeth, familiar faces and voices, kind people . . .

Fifty-six of the *Batory* children had disembarked in Fremantle. One hundred and eighty had left the ship in Melbourne, 142 going to Victorian families and the rest to Tasmania and South Australia. The remainder disembarked in Sydney, and of these 35 went on to Queensland. The pattern was similar for the *Nestor* and the *Diomed*, with most of their children going to New South Wales or Victoria. In all, New South Wales took 240 evacuees, Victoria 181, Western Australia 60, Queensland 40, South Australia 31 and Tasmania 25.

In Sydney, the *Batory* children going to relatives were taken to Newtown Public School. 'This was the culmination of the journey, and

The most fortunate evacuees were those who, met by relatives, felt almost immediately 'at home'. Two such children were Helen and Katharine Cuthbert, photographed here (*left and right*) with their Aunt Jeanie (Mrs Clunies Ross) the day they arrived in Sydney. Note Helen's irregular fringe!

I really wanted to get it over with', one of the boys says. Pamela Palmer, twelve kilograms heavier after the voyage, feared she looked like 'Orphan Annie': 'Mother had told me exactly what I was to wear on my arrival, but the things no longer fitted'. One boy, desperately needing to be accepted, waited alone, perched on a tall chair: 'My legs were dangling by my suitcase, there was a dirty great plaster over one ear where they'd had to lance this impetigo. I just sat there, not saying boo to a goose.' Doctors and psychologists examined the children, and escorts handed over reports on their schooling and shipboard life to relatives. There were similar procedures in the other ports, and for the *Nestor* and the *Diomed*.

Some children, on meeting their relatives, felt an immediate rapport. 'My aunt looked just like my mother', Isabella Woods remembers. 'It was wonderful! I thought "At last I'm with family again".' Helen Cuthbert assumed that 'automatically we would be happy'. Katharine and she both felt at ease when their aunt arrived. Late that afternoon the two girls reached Pymble, one of Sydney's leafy suburbs. Their three cousins were waiting by the gate:

> We got out of the car and looked at each other pretty shyly, and then Ted, the middle cousin, said, 'Would you like to come and see the house?'. He took us off and we had a tour of the house and the garden, and gradually the ice was broken.

At Newtown School Rita Patterson saw some people waving to her, but did not recognise them. 'Shortly afterwards my great aunt and great uncle came over to me. We'd been away from home for so long, and it was lovely to have someone familiar, someone that wanted and knew me.' Later, on a train to Wollongong, 'a great deal of fuss' was made of her. 'Aunty Alice and Uncle Thomas had been saying I was an evacuee, and the people were so kind. A soldier gave me some money, and someone else gave me sixpence.'

The children, already overwhelmed by the public welcome, sometimes found the Australians who came to collect them almost as strange as they had found their Polish crew back in Liverpool. Albert Young, bemused by his host's enthusiastic handshake, wondered what to say to the man who,

> Then called me 'cobber' and said 'Meet me mate',
> And asked 'Are you hungry, how long since you ate?'
> 'Let's go find a cafe and give you a feed',
> He said he was shouting, so it was agreed.

Braham Glass and his sister, met by their little-known uncle, were driven in his limousine past lavish Sydney mansions. The two East Enders arrived at 'a magnificent home in Bellevue Hill' where their uncle lived. Braham continues:

> I saw my first refrigerator, which filled me with wonder, and we had refreshments. I thought, 'This is the life. I've hit pay dirt!' There was a reporter there who took photographs of us seated at the grand piano. Then, when the reporter had been bundled out, my sister and I were driven to a less salubrious home—my aunt's, and that's where we spent the next five and a half years . . .
>
> The poor woman was a sixty-five year-old widow. She was not a child lover by nature, and she suddenly had these two Cockney kids foisted upon her, her brother's children. As time went by she learnt to resent us more and more. I don't blame her, but it was tough for us because we didn't understand.

Heather Staff noticed a couple standing by the Newtown School fence. With uncanny intuition she said to her brother, 'I hope they're not our aunt and uncle because I don't like the look of them'. The man came up to them and asked, 'Do you know Heather and Denis Staff?'

> They seemed much older than our parents. They looked strict and stern, not as we had imagined. Maybe we expected duplicates of our own parents. I don't know, but we felt very apprehensive about them.
>
> Their house had a lounge, a dining room, a breakfast room, and three bedrooms. But in it was Aunty Peggy's mother, bedridden and dying of cancer. We children were not allowed to make any noise at all, and we were always reminded that 'Aunt Jenny' was dying. A friend there to help had the third bedroom,

so I slept on a settee and my brother slept on a bed on the verandah.

Some children still had long journeys ahead of them before reaching 'home'. Paul Farquharson and his brother, who had disembarked in Fremantle, left a few days later for Kalgoorlie. The 600-kilometre train journey took sixteen hours:

> The further we got from Perth the smaller the townships became, and when we woke in the morning it was pretty arid. One place had only four houses, there wasn't even a pub. Reg and I thought we'd made a dreadful mistake, that we were going to some outback shanty town. But Kalgoorlie was marvellous, a big town as far as we were concerned because we'd lived in a village. On the station at Kalgoorlie my aunt walked straight up, saw two boys hanging out the window, and just said, 'Are you the Farquharson boys?'. We said, 'Yes'. 'Well', she said, 'I'm your Aunt Amy'.

Phil Robinson disembarked in Sydney, then travelled 1000 kilometres north to Maryborough in Queensland. Keen to meet relatives of whom he had heard 'such glowing tales', Phil went by the overnight train to Brisbane:

> The sleeper compartment was all very strange, with glasses in containers half way up the wall. I remember waking up in the middle of the night, looking out through the window and seeing mile upon mile of dead trees extending away into the distance and looking very eerie.

In Brisbane there was an 'absolutely wonderful welcome'. The 35 Queensland children, included in a civic parade to greet returning troops, were garlanded with streamers, showered with tickertape, pressed with money and sweets—and stunned by the goodwill. Phil then went on to Maryborough, where he was met by his two uncles and his grandfather, 'a real English gentleman wearing pin-striped trousers, waistcoat and a tailcoat'. They drove home through fields of sugar cane:

> No-one seemed to worry about these corrugations knocking hell out of the car. When we arrived at the house my aunt came out and welcomed me, and later that day I saw my three cousins charging up the track. There was me, all alone in this strange country, suddenly coming face to face with three unknown cousins. I found that rather overwhelming. But in no time flat we were like one family.

About a third of the evacuees who expected to stay with relatives in fact did not. Some relatives were too old, too poor, unsuitable for some other reason—or simply unwilling to take on children. The children

Children going to country hosts, or to South Australia, Tasmania or Queensland, all had long overland journeys after disembarking. Gerald and David Cox went on to Brisbane; here, David (*right*) and another evacuee arrive at Brisbane by train.

whose relatives could not take them, and those who had always been going to strangers, were billeted temporarily at hostels. In each city the evacuees were carefully assessed, in an endeavour to match home backgrounds to Australian families. In Sydney, two days after the *Batory* arrived, the Director of Child Welfare, Mr G. Martin, told reporters, 'We have made a complete study of both the children and their future homes, so that there will be no misfits'. The children had been given a written test, then interviewed by educational psychologists about their home and school background.

These assessments were clearly preferable to the almost totally random matching of evacuees and hosts in Britain's internal 1939 evacuation. However, they were inevitably relatively superficial. Chance still played a significant part in whether children went to good, adequate, poor or bad homes.

Christine Russon and her sister, confident that 'the family didn't let each other down', believed that an aunt who had failed to meet them had merely been delayed. Three days after they arrived they were told that . . .

110

Our aunt and uncle had lost their only son at sea some weeks before we had arrived, and were too upset to take us. We were going to be looked after by two ladies, Miss Daisy Malster and her sister Miss Violet Malster. We later found Violet was a victim of polio, very deformed, very sharp featured, inclined to be rather caustic. Daisy was a much easier person, but she was very strict.

When the CORB evacuation was mooted Senator Foll had promised 'to take two boys'. Soon after the *Batory*'s arrival he visited the North Head Quarantine Station, which was being used as a hostel for the children waiting in Sydney for families. John and Michael Fethney were still in limbo. The Senator, whose 'VAD' [Voluntary Aid Detachment] daughter had befriended the two boys, asked:

> 'Would we like to go and live with him and his wife because they had no sons?'. We said, 'Yes please, great!'. So off we went in his government Buick, to this house with a magnificent view looking south over the harbour.

The day after the *Batory* arrived Senator Foll had lambasted the press. 'I have been disgusted to hear little children taken to the microphone and cross-examined about their memories of air raids', the Senator pronounced, urging that the evacuees not be constantly reminded of the war. Ironically, the Foll–Fethney household lasted only a few months, in part because the boys resented their excessive exposure to interviews.

Norman Townsend puts his memorable Australian home down to quick thinking. At the Quarantine Station children were consuming huge quantities of milk each day—'two and a half pints for each child', one newspaper reported. Dr James Kemp-Bruce, the New South Wales Government Medical Officer, stopped his car next to Norman and some others at North Head one day:

> He asked me if I liked milk. I said, 'Yes, very much'. Then he said, 'How many glasses could you drink?'. I said, 'Well, that would depend on the size of the glass'. That tickled his sense of humour, and obviously made an impression on him because he then singled me out as a ward.

'Hamish', as Norman came to know the doctor, was a bachelor in his late fifties who worked with delinquent boys—'one of the finest men I've ever met, very honourable, kind, and gentle'. His ability to 'see past delinquency to goodness' presented Norman with a difficult choice concerning Sid, a Glaswegian 'who used to roam the *Batory*'s decks looking for fights'. Hamish decided to offer Sid a home also, but first asked Norman how he felt about it:

111

Senator Foll, Minister for the Interior in October 1940, introduces Norah Lupton to the delights of Ginger Meggs—and garners some welcome political 'exposure'. Two other evacuees, John and Michael Fethney, later stayed briefly with Senator Foll's family.

Sid was someone of whom I was in mortal dread. But, because this gentleman was going to provide me with a home, I didn't feel that I could say no—or explain my reasons. So I said yes. So for several months I shared a bedroom with Sid. I frequently recall waking up during the night and hearing him crying in his bed. He used to try and persuade me to wake Hamish and tell him I was dreadfully homesick, when in fact it was himself.

We came to live with Hamish, Sid and I, on a Sunday afternoon. On the Monday Hamish had to go off to his office to work and we met him in the city. We were taken to one of the top men's tailors in town and outfitted with everything, a suit, leisure wear, school wear—practically a new skin.

Reg Harris had been mildly disappointed not to be met by Melbourne relatives when the *Batory* had stopped there for a day. After some weeks waiting in Sydney, Reg—still a generous optimist—accepted that 'our relations seemed to be a little tardy in wanting to have us'. Finally, still only ten, he was sent alone to an uncle's farm in

Victoria, while his brother and two sisters went elsewhere: 'I was going off on my own, which I felt a bit lonely about, and I was a bit lost. But I still didn't feel disenchanted. Being a child, you're told to do things— you have no choice.'

Jacqueline Clout, aged twelve, and her younger brother and sister also had 'no choice'. Theirs was perhaps the least enviable situation of all the CORB arrivals. The Clout's *Batory* friends included some neighbourhood friends from Britain, all of whom were going to Western Australia. The Clout children had initially been allocated to a Tasmanian host, but on the *Batory* it had been decided that they should go to Western Australia to be near their friends. They disembarked at Fremantle but, while staying in a Perth hostel, Jacqueline was told they would have to go on to Tasmania after all:

> Our unknown Tasmanian hostess, who was very wealthy and influential, had refused to take a replacement family. She was insisting on having her 'original three'. The West Australian officials tried to reason with me, saying we were going to a beautiful home in Tasmania, much nicer than any we would have in WA; how honoured we were to be going specially to this woman. Every conceivable argument I could raise was spurned. I pleaded but to no avail. The decision was made and that was the end of the matter.

> Soon afterwards my friend Joyce Briant arrived with her new 'aunty', a very understanding woman. Until then I had managed to retain the 'stiff upper lip' expected of our race: Englishmen do not cry, neither do their children in adversity. Seeing a face from home simply opened the floodgates. I wept, and stormed, and caused a dreadful scene.

> My whole attitude towards Australia changed. I hated everything and everybody, particularly Tasmania, Tasmanians and most of all our as yet unknown hostess. We arrived about a week later. She was a spinster with a stentorian voice, and her first words were, 'I'm glad you haven't red hair or I'd have sent you straight back'. 'Please God', I thought, 'why couldn't I have had red hair?'.

The immediate problems of finalising homes for the children, and the longer term questions about their settling into new families, were barely examined in the spate of editorials published after the *Batory*'s arrival. Australia—'an environment of peace, 12 000 miles away from the devilish malice of an enemy who bombs indiscriminately'—was presumed to be a place of universal kindness and generosity. The *Sydney Sun* said:

The arrival of these little escapees from a war-torn Britain may be the presage of a greater and more permanent migration ... If we could have 1 000 000 or more British children, and keep them after the war, we would have the best possible immigrants—people who would, in a few years, be busy in building up a new and greater home for the British race away from the disturbances and problems of decadent and shattered Europe ... This country is big enough, and its people generous and warm-hearted enough, to accept British children not only as a loan but for good.

The editorial blurred the difference between wartime evacuation and peacetime migration. In doing so it overlooked a central fact: the 'little escapees' all had families in Britain. It was a confusion that some CORB officials apparently shared. Geoffrey Shakespeare, writing after the war, described the evacuation as partly an opportunity for 'the redistribution of population within the Empire'. W.J. Garnett, CORB's representative on the *Batory*, let slip on reaching Melbourne that some evacuees might well remain in Australia after the war. This would, he believed, be 'a transfer of population of a novel character'.

In October 1940, however, war was uppermost. A few Australian politicians complained about the date of the *Batory*'s arrival being kept secret until the last moment. Sir Keith Murdoch, then the Director-General of Information, caustically replied that the Admiralty had good reason to withhold the information: 'The position of German raiders is usually not revealed until a ship is sunk'.

In Britain strict security was imperative. U-boats sank 63 ships in the Atlantic in October 1940, and the Blitz was intensifying. On the day the *Batory* reached Sydney Australian newspapers reported the Luftwaffe's first massed night raid over London: 'The German flights maintained their full fury into the small hours. Bomb after bomb rained on the capital and explosions rocked a wide area.' At least 700 London children had been killed in September. Meanwhile, two million Londoners were enduring often sleepless nights in claustrophobic air raid shelters.

War continued to shadow the CORB ships and some of the escorts. The crews were feted in Sydney and the other ports, and Captain Deyczakowski went to Canberra to receive the Australian government's thanks. The *Batory*, *Nestor* and *Diomed* each in turn sailed for Europe and more Atlantic convoys. All survived the war. The hard-worked escorts were given leave in Sydney, then most of the British ones began homeward voyages. On 27 November, off New Zealand, a German merchant raider sank the *Rangitane* which was taking many of the British escorts home. Six were killed. The rest, after being held captive in severe conditions, were mostly freed and left on an island from where they were rescued by Australian vessels. Some, however, spent the war in captivity.

Above The CORB children, whatever their homesickness and uncertainties in Australia, were safe from the bombing Britain was enduring. Search lights criss-cross the sky over London in October 1940. *Below* The Blitz was entering its most ferocious phase when the evacuees arrived in Australia. Here, firefighters douse a smouldering building at Coventry, after a raid on 17 November 1940.

Across Australia, the evacuees all finally reached new homes. Michael Storey felt something of a 'highlight'—'a pommy kid who'd turned up from England'. John Hillier and his brother thought their hosts, strangers until that morning, 'very friendly and homely'. On their best behaviour, both boys knew that 'these people had kindly taken us in, and were feeling their way as much as we were feeling ours'. Rita Patterson, at her new home in Wollongong, was delighted with the dolls and prams put in her room. In bed that first night she heard her great aunt and uncle talking: 'They were saying, "Will she settle down?" and "Is she all right?"'. But despite Rita's warm welcome there had been some tension:

> They discovered within hours that I had head lice, and aunty was very upset that my mother had let me come away with lice. I assured her, which was true, that I hadn't had lice when I left home. I felt quite upset about that, the slur on my Mum.

The Cuthbert girls were delighted to get letters from Stirling when they arrived at their future home. Their aunt had already cabled their parents. That night, after giving the girls dinner in bed, she began a long letter:

> Your dear little daughters have arrived, and they are safely tucked up in bed and sleeping. They both seem well and are their same sweet selves. They don't appear to have been altered by the voyage . . . They seem to have been well looked after, and there is a very complete dossier on them. I am to be visited to see that I am looking after them properly so you need have no fear! How you will miss them . . .

The next day a *Sydney Morning Herald* reporter visited Patricia Whittaker, who was also in Sydney, staying with a woman her mother had met while serving in France during the First World War. Patricia, it was reported, was 'very happy indeed and already quite at home'. She had said, 'I only hope the other children who came out with me will be as fortunate as I am'. Her host added: 'The only trouble is that Patricia will become part of our lives and will then have to leave us'.

In the coming years virtually every evacuee faced a similar conflict: the clash of loyalties between their family in Britain and their family in Australia. And their hosts straddled a knife-edge: between nurturing their wartime charges and trespassing on parent–child bonds. The CORB evacuees had all reached their new homes safely. Most, but not all, would also come through Australia unscathed.

Settling In

10

These people were complete strangers, but they were people who were going to take the place of a mother and father.

T̲ʜ̲ᴇ evacuees had now to become Australian children 'for the duration'. Their shipboard experiences had made them more adaptable than they were when they left Britain. But the voyages had been finite: the war was not. The length of their stay in Australia was unknown. No one, least of all the children themselves, ignored the difficulties of settling into new homes—havens far from the Blitz, but in a strange country and with unknown people.

The ease of integration into Australian homes was more striking by far than the pitfalls encountered. Indeed, once over some initial hurdles, far more of the children were to find happiness and love in their new homes than otherwise. But for some the metamorphosis never succeeded, and their time in Australia was to be only bearable. Others, a small minority, were to lead wretched lives, being moved from one unhappy home to another or enduring a lack of love—and sometimes worse—with one host.

The challenges and opportunities were not only the children's. Hosts, whether relatives or strangers, had suddenly to adjust to children whose backgrounds were often very different from their own.

In each state hosts were advised how best to handle the transition. In New South Wales the Overseas Children Citizen's Committee informed hosts of the issues to be faced in fulfilling the 'honour and privilege' of helping the children of 'our kinspeople in the old land'. It was, the committee's chairman warned in a circular, 'no light task that you are undertaking on their behalf, and one which will require wisdom, patience and love to discharge worthily'. The tensions and dislocations of war, the air raids in Britain, the wrench of leaving home, and the long voyages 'cannot but have had a very considerable psychological effect on the children'. Now there were 'other people's homes and strange faces' to adjust to. Hosts, it was stressed, should make each evacuee 'just a member of the family':

> What the children need most of all is a *home*. They are not being billeted out, and a home is more than shelter and comfort.

What a child's nature asks for even more than food and comfort is love—that is, 'understanding' love.

The committee urged hosts to 'preserve the children's remembrance of their Fathers and Mothers . . . and a loving interest in their own home', through prayers, letters and photos. The circular added: 'We do not wish to encourage anything that would take the place of the Father or Mother, and so suggest that they refer to you as "Uncle" or "Aunty"'.

The evacuees' welfare and safety were the legal responsibility of the Commonwealth Government under the *National Security Act 1939–40*. Regulations detailed the very specific obligations of hosts for all aspects of the children's physical, educational, personal and moral well-being. Their actual legal guardianship was vested in the Minister of the Interior. In each state the child welfare department had day-to-day responsibility for evacuees, and liaised with CORB's representatives in Australia, Cyril Bavin and W.J. Garnett.

The CORB staff in London advised parents of their children's arrival and, throughout the war, informed them of major changes in their home or school life. In January 1941 CORB also clarified an issue that was to gain in importance as the war dragged on: Australian hosts were fully responsible for the cost of maintaining children, without any assistance from the parents in Britain or either government. The money paid by parents was to offset the cost of travel to Australia.

First impressions often created lasting patterns of happiness, uneasiness or unhappiness. Amidst their novel surroundings—spacious neighbourhoods with bungalows, gardens and gum trees—most children quickly sensed the underlying mood of their hosts.

'Settling in was really fairly easy. Everyone was very kind and I just seemed to fit in', Ruth Wilson remembers of her home with strangers in Sydney's Blue Mountains. Tony Houghton and his brother found 'a loving atmosphere' amongst relatives who 'welcomed us strongly'. But there was 'very little love or affection' for Braham Glass, whose sister Essie 'fulfilled the role of mother and took great care of me'. Donald Mitchell had left the *Diomed* in Adelaide. In Sydney, he anxiously awaited 'his' ship's arrival: 'I saw her coming up the harbour, which was fairly heart-rending because I was already in a large, very comfortable Australian house—but a rather distant one where I didn't feel very much at home'.

Conditions on the ships, especially the overcrowded *Batory*, left some children with cases of impetigo and lice. Joan Sharp, when it was discovered she had lice, found sympathetic understanding in her Sydney aunt: 'There weren't any potions then. I was put in the small tin bath in the laundry and kerosene was poured over my head. The help of the next door neighbour was enlisted, and my head was scrubbed, soaked, scrubbed, combed and combed.' Betty Deeley was less fortunate. Despite telling her host she was itching,

> No one bothered to look at my hair until the lice were dropping on my shoulders and all the family became infested with them. But the worst thing was that I was more or less sent to Coventry for two weeks. The fact that I'd got them was all that mattered and I was dirty. Raw kerosene on my head killed the lice . . . and nearly killed me.

Some evacuees, in still-strange homes and without friends or confidants, had to cope with other personal problems. Nail biting, nervous rashes and headaches were relatively common, bed wetting less so. For Mary Clemes, 'the question of reaching puberty just before I left home, and having to cope with all that, was very difficult'. Heather Staff and her brother Denis, both ill-at-ease, confronted a vicious circle: their own worries—an old, dying woman in their home—incessant domestic drudgery—and their aunt's sneering contempt. Bed wetting was the result:

> It was very embarrassing for us both. We'd never had the problem till the evacuation, but our aunt was adamant that we could control it—and that it was something we were just doing to be naughty. Consequently we were punished. We were made to wash our own sheets, and privileges were withdrawn if it occurred . . . There was never any discussion, we were just told that we were really quite disgusting to do it.
>   When you were making your bed you were expected to strip it off completely and turn the mattress every day. Just to make sure that you did this, our host would put a penny under the mattress. She checked and if the penny was still there it was obvious you hadn't turned the mattress.

Derric Webster and his sister met a very warm welcome. Their aunt and uncle had built a sleep-out, a walled-in extension on their verandah, so that Derric could have his own bedroom. It was, he remembers, 'a super place'—until some 'big spiders got in':

> I'd never seen the like of them before. I was terrified of them and gradually I got into a sort of anxiety state. I just couldn't sleep out there on my own, so they brought me in with Catherine. Then they moved me out again and put Catherine in the glassed-in part of the back porch, and from then on it sort of settled down.

Most children were expected to help with household tasks, partly to make them feel 'at home'. But some families, especially country ones,

Many children settled happily and stayed with one host family throughout the war, as Catherine and Derric Webster did. Here they stand with their Aunty Flo at the Melbourne Zoo in December 1941—two weeks after Pearl Harbor.

demanded far more of their newly arrived evacuees. Near Terrigal, north of Sydney, then an area of small holdings, Barbara Donald and her brother discovered their uncle's orchard was not all fruit for the picking:

> George had to learn how to milk a cow almost as soon as he got there. He used to go down to the orchard and empty the earth closet into the holes that he dug and cover them up. If there were any dead rats in the shed he used to have to bury those too. There were chooks to be fed and things like that. I had to learn how to clean and press my school uniform and my younger brother's.

Reg Harris was immediately set to work by his less-than-welcoming aunt and uncle: 'It was expected from when I arrived that I should do what most country boys did—chopping wood and bringing the cows in, getting the horses, helping out around the farm.' Until then cows had been 'things in picture books' for Reg.

Letters from home were particularly important during the children's first months in Australia. CORB urged parents to write as often as possible, especially as mails were sometimes lost through enemy action.

In October 1940, with the generous help of Cable and Wireless Ltd, a free monthly cable service was introduced. Parents and children could each send one of a number of standard messages: 'Miss you a lot but very happy here'; 'Always with you in thought. Writing, love'; 'Very happy in new home and settling down fine'; 'Am grateful to all those who are so kind to you, thank them. All well, love'; and the melancholy 'Have sent my cable regularly but have not had one from you for a long time. Love'.

Tony Houghton and his brother were fortunate in having a communicative and understanding father. He wrote: 'After leaving your new-found friends on the *Diomed* I suppose you may feel lonely and probably homesick, but remember you told us that you would be men and bear up, so cheer up, keep smiling, have fun, and enjoy yourselves'. The Cuthbert girls, relaxed with 'rules and outlooks that were as at home' but both rundown after the voyage, were cheered by a steady flow of letters:

> Our mother and father wrote to us very frequently, probably twice a week. We were very much aware of the day to day life in Stirling, and both our aunts encouraged us in this and also wrote frequently. So that although we felt at home in Australia we were always aware that we really belonged in Scotland. But the two families weren't in conflict in any way, they felt totally compatible. I think we very much felt part of both sides of the world.

Most of the hosts who were strangers wrote occasionally to parents, and some became firm friends through letters. Not all, however, were as perceptive as Mona Webster, Donald Mitchell's second host. Soon after he arrived she wrote to Donald's mother: 'The more you are able to tell me about him up to the time he left, the easier it will be for me to understand and help in this complicated business of growing up'.

The evacuees' ease or difficulty in adjusting to new homes rested on numerous factors: the hosts' motives in taking evacuees; the ages, size and emotional 'tone' of the family in Britain and that in Australia; their social background, 'culture', and affluence; the degree to which children's expectations and their actual situation coincided; how siblings fared; the ability—or inability—of all involved to face and resolve misunderstandings and differences; and the personalities of hosts and children.

Mary Clemes spent the war in Tasmania. She was very close to her grandmother, with whom she had assumed she was to stay. But on arrival Mary discovered she was to board in the school of which her

Australia's open-air life helped many evacuees adjust to their new surroundings and families. Gerald (*left*) and David Cox, pictured here during Christmas 1940, loved the beaches at Margate, Moreton Bay—utterly unlike Margate 'at home'!

uncle was headmaster. Feeling lost and alone, she unconsciously began to make the boarding house 'home':

> I tended to distance myself from my uncle and aunt and tried to just become absorbed into the school as a pupil, rather than as anything to do with them. I hadn't realised that I was doing that until one day my aunt said, 'You never come over in the evening to talk to us. We want you to'. Then I realised that perhaps I had rather hurt them by not doing so.

After resolving the misunderstanding Mary was much happier.

Phil Robinson 'had some ups and downs'. Unused to a large family he sometimes found his many Queensland cousins overwhelming, but he enjoyed 'a very warm relationship' with his Aunty Amy: 'I became as one of their sons . . . and felt somewhat privileged in being given a bedroom of my own, whereas my cousins had to share'. On the opposite side of the continent Paul Farquharson, confident and gregarious, 'had no problems whatsoever'. He and his brother Reg were immediately accepted 'not only by our uncle and aunt but all their friends':

> My aunt was very caring but without being cloying, and I guess my mother was much the same. I frequently got into scrapes, and I'm pretty certain I'd have copped a hiding at home. My uncle dressed me down a couple of times but he never thought it was necessary to do any more than that. He was a very masculine, outdoors type, but you always felt he was there if you needed him. Reg, though, had a bit of trouble. I remember he had a boil in a rather personal place, and he just wouldn't tell anybody. He told me and I got our uncle to sort it out, but I don't think Reg would have been any less embarrassed at home.

Joan Sharp's aunt, about the age of her mother, had recently had a miscarriage. To Joan, she and her husband gave without question 'not only material things but love and caring'. Her uncle made her 'the best dolls house that any little girl could ever wish for, complete with furniture'. Joan remembers being treated in 'absolutely the same way' as the couple's other children: 'I don't know that the word evacuee was ever mentioned except maybe when I was introduced to someone new'.

Most evacuees spent the war with families better off and more 'educated' than their own. The British government's decision that children's upkeep was to be met by host families inevitably meant that many went to relatively well-to-do homes. Most evacuees appreciated their enhanced lifestyle and the opportunities they gained. But some found more 'refined' habits difficult to accept. For John Fethney, whose second host was a doctor, meals were often an ordeal:

> You were aware that what you were doing belonged to a different social class from what you'd come from. You had butter knives, and you didn't get the butter off the butter dish with the knife you were going to use to spread it—all that kind of palaver. Spoons in the jam . . . at home you always got your jam out of the jar with your knife. Toast came in a rack, dry, whereas the normal way, as we saw it, was to get the butter on quick so it melted into the toast.

John Hillier, by contrast, was one of the relatively few evacuees who spent the war with a family less well-to-do and educated than his own 'professional' family. 'The home I came from was certainly different to the home I went to, and there were certain things which were not available to me that might have been available to me at home.' Holidays and school trips, taken for granted by his parents, were beyond the means of his host family.

Sunday School beach picnics were far removed from outings to the British seaside. Joyce Briant, who taught at Perth's St Andrew's Sunday School, picnicked with these St Andrew's children in December 1943.

Schools, churches and clubs were mostly 'very kind and accepting'. As one boy says, 'We just settled down, and started at school and the local Sunday school and church . . . We were never made to feel that we didn't belong.' However, a significant number of the evacuees recall some initial taunting at school about 'pommy' accents, or remember teachers who were less than sympathetic over evacuees adjusting to classroom subjects and levels. But far more found schools where every effort was made to welcome and integrate them. Rita Patterson's introduction to her Wollongong class was far from unusual:

> I was stood on the desk and the children were told about the war in Europe, and that Rita was an evacuee and her parents were a long way away. They all took a special interest in me, perhaps because I was the only evacuee at that school. They were all very kind, and they were always conscious of whether I was happy or unhappy.

Excessive sympathy was sometimes counterproductive. Michael Fethney, a Cub, became the focus of concern for a fifteen-year-old Scout:

He told me that he remembered me and my brother and all these evacuees in his prayers every day. It was a kind thought, but it just brought the awareness again that—yes, we were a long way from home. It was one of the rare times that I remember being reduced to tears.

Hosts' motives were probably the most critical issue in whether children settled happily or not. These varied enormously. Hosts whose primary motives had to do with caring for children tended to have happier evacuees than those more concerned with motives of patriotism, public duty, prestige, religion or the composition of their family.

Betty Deeley's hosts 'wanted to do something to help the mother country'. Betty and her brother, used to Midlands council houses, found their hosts' vineyard in the country near Perth 'a totally different life'. The family, the Makins, had ten children. The Deeleys, used to the attention that a mother of two could give, found Mrs Makin 'very strict':

At home in Birmingham, in the evening the four of us would sit down together around the fire or around the little card table and have a meal. But here there was this enormous table, there was cooking going on, and there were people everywhere coming and going.

We were very well fed and clothed and went to school, but there was little affection there for us. Things were sometimes fine, but it always wore off. Everything was very strict. I don't mind strictness, but if there had been some affection it would have been easier to bear.

Almost all the children, especially during the early stages, were in no doubt as to where their primary bonds lay. For some, especially those staying with strangers, seemingly inappropriate names sometimes created lasting tensions. 'We were often referred to as "the two little evacuees", and our aunt and uncle always introduced us as "the evacuees from England" ', recalls Heather Staff. Nora Lupton resented having to call 'these two strangers aunty and uncle'—'because I had my own aunts and uncles'. John Hillier and his brother faced an even more vexing issue, which tarnished an otherwise good situation. Their host, Mrs Ballingall, said she and her husband were 'their new mother and father':

That was very difficult to accept because I knew—I already have a mother and father. They wanted us to call them 'mum' and 'pop'. Looking back on it I'm sure that we would have had a better relationship had they asked us to call them 'aunt' and 'uncle'. We were also put on a pedestal in a way. She was anxious that we should go out with her, so that she was able to tell people that these were her two evacuees.

125

Nicknames usually indicated happy homes. Tony Houghton, for instance, was 'Swoose'—'half swan, half goose, from a song going around at the time'. His Aunty Florrie became 'Squib'—'she was smallish, and gave me the impression of a squib'.

Providing a framework of affection and discipline reasonably similar to what the children were used to was particularly difficult. Hosts often overcompensated. Some, sensing homesickness, gushed cloyingly. Others, sensing an aloof independence—the 'courage, self-possession and poise' that Geoffrey Shakespeare saw in evacuees—withdrew, so ensuring that what was often merely a facade became a deeply rooted reality that prevented any intimacy. Similarly, hosts tended to be more, rather than less, strict than the children's parents. Determined to avoid any harm to the children while in Australia, or out of deference to parents or because they misunderstood children, some hosts—especially it seems with girls—insisted on draconian rules.

Nora Lupton, staying with an unhappy, childless couple in Sydney, endured a home where people barely spoke and where she was largely confined to the house. Reading was strictly rationed; allowed to spend any amount of time on homework or sewing, Nora could only 'read for pleasure for one hour per day to conserve my eyesight'. Christine Russon, with the two kind but severe spinsters, was prevented from rejoining the Guides as one of her hosts insisted that 'she could teach me far more than I would learn from Guides'. Her friendships were also closely monitored.

Rita Patterson, staying with her previously childless great aunt and uncle, found their excessive concern and affection smothering. Being 'very conscious of her responsibility to my parents' her aunt would often comment, 'What on earth would I say if anything happened to you?'

> I wasn't allowed to have a bicycle in case there was an accident. They weren't very happy about me being out of their sight except at school. My parents were very undemonstrative, [but] very early on I found Aunty Alice would be saying, 'You can't go out without kissing people goodbye'. So I got in the habit of kissing goodbye and kissing as I came in.

For many evacuees 'fitting in' became almost a way of life. Relatively few children—the stronger, more definite ones—believe they never took on the 'chameleon' habit of 'acting to please'. Most, although they sometimes realised it was a veneer, consciously changed their attitudes and behaviour. Michael Storey's is a common memory: 'Let's face it, I felt that I should please and do my utmost to do so. The words of my father kept ringing, "Behave yourself, be a good boy and do as you're told". After all, these people were being kind to me.' One girl, then in her third home, was 'terribly anxious not to put a foot wrong . . . I probably kept quiet when I should have been more outspoken.'

Christine Russon and her sister, often very homesick, sometimes cried and said they wanted to go home. Their no doubt harassed hosts finally told them emphatically that 'unless they behaved and stopped making a fuss' they would be sent elsewhere. 'That', Christine recalls, 'frightened me into conforming, because I felt I couldn't go anywhere else'. David Massey, a working class boy, stayed first with business people living near Melbourne. There he tried hard to 'blend in' so as not to be 'too conspicuous':

> They looked after me, but I didn't feel as if I was one of the family; I was more or less a guest, an outsider living with them. I wasn't conscious of actually being good, I just tried to please. I think I just felt that I should do what I could to help because, after all, they were looking after me and I was dependent upon them . . . With me it was 'Can I go somewhere?', whereas my friends would be saying 'I am going somewhere'.

Older evacuees were sometimes able to weigh their own and their hosts' needs and duties. Some in unsatisfactory situations managed to improve matters, either alone or with the help of welfare officials. Joyce Briant was one. She was generally happy with her Perth hosts, a childless couple. However, as the months passed, Joyce 'began to feel smothered'. Used to 'a much more easygoing life' she resented having to 'tell everything and show everything' to her hosts:

> We got to a state where I really felt that I couldn't put up with it any more. In the end I said, 'Oh well, I think I'd better go'. I went into my room and started packing my case, but Auntie came in and started unpacking it. Uncle said, 'If she wants to go, let her go'. We had a bit of a barney but it cleared the air. I got what was worrying me off my chest, and they then knew that if anything was worrying me we could sort it out. We got on fine after that.
> Everything was English orientated. Auntie was English, and she didn't want me to pick up any slang or talk Australian. She wanted me to go back the same little girl that I'd come out.
> But [after Pearl Harbor] it looked as though the war was going on for ever. 'You're not going back to England just yet, not for a year or two', I thought. 'It's silly to say everything back home is best.' I then started really enjoying Australia and I got to like it very much.

Most evacuees experienced goodwill and kindness with their first hosts. However, 'Home unsuitable' was a surprisingly common comment on

CORB record cards, most often appearing in the case of relatives who felt 'obliged' and 'put upon' in some way—or in the case of volunteer hosts who were poorly matched to evacuees' backgrounds and needs. About half the children stayed with one family throughout the war. About a quarter of them had two homes, and the rest three or more. A handful lived in four or more homes. Eighty-five of the 577 children had moved to second or third hosts by July 1941. Most of these then settled happily. However, a significant number of children, although only moderately happy with their hosts, preferred not to move.

The Fethney brothers, after leaving Senator Foll's home, went to a Wollongong doctor. Many aspects of their lives there were ideal: the house backed onto untouched scrub, beaches were close by, the doctor regularly took them on trips, the community was welcoming. But for Michael something was missing:

> In all sorts of ways we were very much part of the family, but I think there was a formality that was something of a barrier. For instance no-one ever suggested more intimate forms of address than 'Doctor' and 'Missus'. Our Yorkshire taciturnity probably didn't help, but neither did the doctor's very quiet and rather nervous manner. His wife was very moody and I used to think that perhaps I'd offended her.
>
> However there was nothing that was strong enough to run away from, or to dare to say to the occasional social worker, 'No, we're not all right'. I think the thought of having to start again somewhere else was even worse than putting up with her on-going moodiness. If one could have escaped . . . If there'd been an offer, one would have had to consider very carefully. Do we start off with yet another family where it probably wouldn't be perfect? Or do we go on putting up with the known—on balance, yes we do.

The evacuees' expectations of being 'home within a year' had faded by the middle of 1941. For some, soul-searching became increasingly common: about their hosts, about their parents, about why they were in Australia at all. A larger number, happy with their hosts, immersed themselves in their new lives—and in Australia.

Town Life Down Under

11

The difference was tremendous. Australia was not just the tropical Britain many of us had expected.

Aᴜsᴛʀᴀʟɪᴀ, whatever the evacuees' preconceptions were, was not all outback, kangaroos and sheep. It was in cities and towns that most of the CORB children spent their evacuation years. They had mostly grown up in cities and towns, but the life they found 'down under' was quite unlike that they knew.

Even the two largest cities, Sydney and Melbourne, were infinitely less congested and industrial than the big British cities. The smaller state capitals seemed provincial. The towns were slow. All the cities were sea ports, ports surrounded by beaches and bushland. Spacious suburbs sprawled along wide roads. Grey-green gum trees grew everywhere. The houses were airy, outdoor life the norm.

The Australians themselves, basking in their space and sun, seemed very different from the people the evacuees had lived amongst in Britain. They were easier going, pleasure-loving, often more independent—certainly less class-conscious. There was a freshness and freedom to life: 'I saw what was the physical openness of Australia—the magnificence of the ocean and the sky—mirrored in the life people led compared to life in England'.

Almost all the CORB children came from neighbourhoods of terraced or semi-detached houses, many of them very old. In Australia almost all of them lived in relatively new houses built on quarter-acre blocks with gardens back and front. There they acquired a new vocabulary: verandah, sunroom, sleep-out, flyscreen door, garage—and dunny.

Most spent the war living with families better off than their parents. Rita Patterson's Wollongong house seemed 'like a mansion'. It stood on a hill, 'with a verandah at the front, a sunroom at the back and ground all round it'. In Port Kembla, Heather Staff and her brother spent five years in a house with 'a modern kitchen and fitted carpets right through'—a degree of domestic comfort they had never before known. Many children, for the first time, lived in houses with 'modern' stoves, refrigerators, vacuum cleaners, even agitator washing machines. In Britain very few had known telephones; in Australia most did.

Joan Sharp, whose Manchester home had no garden and who was used to fireside baths, went to live in a house that her aunt had actually designed: Number One, Woniora Road, Hurstville, Sydney.

> It was a double-fronted bungalow with a large garden at the front and back, a long driveway, and a garage. The lounge room looked onto the front garden and we had a large entrance hall. We had a bathroom with a wash basin, a bath and a shower, all beautifully tiled.

Christine Russon and her sister went to a neighbourhood on the outskirts of Melbourne. Her teacher host had a 'very comfortable home with three bedrooms, a lounge, dining room, kitchen, sleep-out, a front and back garden and a garage'. The girls' bedrooms were 'beautifully appointed'—'twin beds with matching bedspreads, a dressing table, a wardrobe, and a carpet on the floor'.

Car ownership highlighted the relative affluence of many host families. Very few evacuees' parents owned a car, but more than half their Australian host families did. Peter Edkins did not even *know* anyone with a car at home—and had 'grandiose ideas about what his host's car would be like'. But Peter was disappointed on actually seeing the vehicle, a 1926 Oakland. 'It's very old but a splendid car', his host assured him. The Fethney brothers' doctor host had two cars, one equipped with a charcoal burner to produce gas to decrease petrol consumption. John recalls,

> Dr Palmer could get petrol for his work, but he had to use charcoal when he took the Packard to the Blue Mountains on our fortnightly visits. When we had to refill the burner it was my job to take its lid off and pour in another bag of charcoal.

If most houses were comfortable and well adapted to the climate, lavatories were another matter. Although the outside 'privy' was not uncommon in Britain most of the CORB children had been used to 'going inside'. In Australia they became inured to outside 'dunnies'— and the flies they attracted! Even Joan Sharp's spacious modern bungalow had a 'pan toilet': 'It was a great ritual when the pan man came every Friday. Everyone shut the windows and the doors and stayed inside.'

Some children, visiting the dunny, sat 'immobilized, keeping an eye on the massive spiders'. Braham Glass, who sometimes slept on the back verandah, recalls his aunt 'getting up at five in the morning, drinking her Epsom salts, then walking straight down to the dunny which was not three metres away from where I slept'.

Petrol was rationed from July 1940, prompting some families to buy gas-producing charcoal contraptions such as this, mounted on the car belonging to the Cuthbert girls' relatives. Helen and Katharine are at the left and right.

There were other novel drawbacks to life in Australia's cities and towns: heatwaves, snakes, mosquitoes, flies, flies, flies . . . John Hillier, writing home after a year in Australia, was 'not bothered by the midges and gnats as much as by the mozzies'.

The CORB ships had arrived during an unusually hot spring. Most evacuees, while enjoying Australia's summers, found the heatwaves trying. Houses with corrugated iron roofs were often like ovens. Outside, barefoot, the pavements scorched. At the beach, sunburn threatened. When Wollongong's temperature soared Rita Patterson 'used to sit in a cold bath for hours trying to cool down'. Michael Fethney, also in Wollongong, remembers 'a spell of a week when the temperature never dropped below one hundred and eight degrees'. Dust blown from the parched inland filtered the sunlight eerily. When Perth became unbearable Tony Houghton used to

> lie on the kitchen floor, on the lino, which was the coolest part of the house. We didn't have a refrigerator, just an icebox, and we used to take a block and rub it on our foreheads.

In Britain, allotments had been introduced in 1939 to give people without gardens the space to grow vegetables—to 'Dig for Victory'.

Gardens were taken for granted in Australia. Gums and wattles grew everywhere; spring in Adelaide was almond and peach blossom, summer in Sydney was luxuriant hydrangeas. But the grass, often brown in summer, needed constant watering. Diving magpies demanded vigilance. In parts of Sydney there were redback and funnel-web spiders which could kill a child.

Many families had their own fruit trees. The Fethney brothers indulged in 'pears, peaches, apples, persimmons and plums' from their host's orchard. John 'took bags of apricots to school to flog them for extra pocket money'. Pamela Palmer was delighted by her Sydney garden: 'There were citrus trees and kookaburras coming down to pick bits of meat off the clothesline, and I loved the vivid colours of the subtropical flowers'. There were the subtropical and tropical fruits, so different from 'apples and plums and berries': 'The first time I tasted pawpaw and passion fruit ice-cream—that was absolute heaven! I'd grown up on just vanilla, strawberry and perhaps chocolate.'

Even before the war Australians had enjoyed more varied and abundant food than their counterparts in Britain. During the war, with Britain blockaded and severely rationed, the British simply went hungry. The amount of meat and butter Australians ate astounded the children: 'In Australia we'd get a shoulder of lamb one week and a leg of lamb the next, but at home you'd go to the butcher for a pound of this or a pound of that', one girl recalls. Some families had steak or lamb chops—with eggs!—for breakfast. Braham Glass and his sister ate 'the old traditional meals' with their aunt, 'one of the worst cooks on earth'. But they were 'adequately and much better fed than any English kid during the war'. At the CORB Christmas party held in Melbourne in 1940 'the amazing improvement in the children's physique' was obvious.

Most evacuees integrated relatively quickly into Australian city and town schools. Inevitably experiences differed widely, but most believe their Australian education was at least as good as that they would have had in Britain. Almost all found their new schools more relaxed than those in Britain.

Braham Glass was initially taunted as 'Engo, Engo the refo'—'English refugee'. He continues: 'It didn't take many weeks to adopt an Australian accent, because I realised the quicker I got to be like my classmates the quicker they would stop calling me "Engo"'. Nora Lupton, who wrote about 'me mam' in her first composition was called to the front of the class 'to explain'. 'I said that's my mother and started weeping.' However, Pamela Palmer's experience was more typical:

> I was made very welcome, and immediately made a prefect. The staff were most accommodating. The Intermediate was looming at the end of the following year, and I hadn't done some of the

Australian city and town schools were generally less formal than those in Britain. Norah Lupton, unhappy with her hosts, at least mostly enjoyed her school life. Here, Norah (*bottom row, second from left*) joins a class photo at Drummoyne, Sydney, just a month after disembarking.

subjects. They arranged for me to miss out on sports on Friday afternoons, and I had one teacher to help me catch up.

At Joan Sharp's primary school in Sydney the day began with the children lining up, the girls in their 'navy blue, three box-pleat, serge uniform and proper school shoes'—and in summer a straw hat. They saluted the flag and sang 'God Save the King', then 'the headmistress walked up and down the lines to inspect your hands and nails, and to make sure your shoes were polished'. Despite such routines Australian schools were more 'open' and informal than most schools in Britain. Rita Patterson says:

> The school I went to in England was built about 1880, 1890, with very high windows which you couldn't see out of. It was gloomy and oppressive—and so were the teachers. In Australia my school had windows you could see out of, and the whole atmosphere was entirely different. I thrived on it.

At Wollongong High, Michael Fethney's teachers were almost all 'very good and sympathetic', and encouraged 'a cheerfulness that I often felt unable to express at my host's home'. Once, during a poetry session,

133

Michael was asked to describe 'the appearance of hawthorn in spring'. Memories were slipping: what *did* hawthorn look like? But the perceptive teacher 'immediately covered the embarrassment'. Another teacher was less aware of the often subtle perplexities evacuees faced. The class was studying Rupert Brooke's *The Soldier*. Michael

> . . . resisted learning it for homework because of the words 'If I should die . . . there is some corner of a foreign field . . .'. I didn't want to die at the age of twelve. I know that wasn't what the poem was about, but the teacher insisted I learn it. We ended up with her in tears and me in tears during the lunch hour.

A few children were sent to private schools. Norman Townsend—his fees met by the ever-generous Hamish—boarded at The Scots College in Sydney. The other boarders were mostly country boys whose lives Norman 'could hardly comprehend':

> I came from the Isle of Wight, and was mixing with boys who took a couple of days to travel from their home to school. I couldn't relate to that, therefore they found me strange. And England, whilst it was known as 'Home' to Australians, was in fact mythically distant.

And yet so close . . . Ties with Britain were still very strong and often sentimental. It was the Old Country: English history and literature were heavily stressed. At the Presbyterian Ladies College in Sydney the Cuthbert sisters wore 'black-watch tartan tunics, high-necked shirts with black-watch tartan ties, long black stockings, tartan hatbands with velour hats in winter and straw hats in summer'. Australian accents were frowned on and girls with 'English' accents praised:

> Miss Knox, the headmistress, tried to inculcate what she considered a more appropriate accent, and I remember the entire school in assembly being schooled to say aloud, 'How now brown cow'—which came out as 'Heow neow breown ceow'.

Most private schools were single-sex establishments, but Mary Clemes' school in Hobart was not. 'Very shy of boys before the voyage', she remembered the *Nestor* gratefully 'because I had been thrown in with boys and learnt to make friends with them'. With many men and women away in the forces she found 'a great shortage of good teachers and nearly all ours were quite old'. Cleaners were also hard to find. The boarders managed the chores:

> There was this terrible distinction between girls and boys. We had two cows that supplied all the milk to the boarders. The boys did the milking and chopped the wood—and got paid for

Caps, ties, double-breasted suits, and Gladstone bags were de rigeur at most boys' schools during the war—and for long afterwards. Reg Loft (*centre*) sets off with his mates.

it. The girls did all the washing up and the cleaning of dormitories but never got paid.

Without the rigid bonds and barriers of life in Britain there was an easy friendliness to life in the Australian cities and towns. For Isabella Woods, Australia was 'just like another world'. The north of England, by contrast, now seemed to her a place where 'people found it hard to forgive'. In New South Wales 'the atmosphere was different altogether. Everyone was more free and easy. Once I got over my homesickness I realised I couldn't go back to England's way of life.'

Peter Edkins was struck by 'the freedom in houses that weren't closed in, the personal freedom to get around, the freedom to decide to go and swim across the river'. Some of his 'freedom' simply reflected growing up. But, as other older evacuees believe, much of it was rooted in the Australian way of life.

The evacuees' social life centred on neighbourhoods, local churches and groups such as Scouts and Guides. The older evacuees, and their boyfriends and girlfriends, met in milk bars. Pubs, and the six o'clock swill, passed most children by, though a few recall hosts who lived for 'grog'.

Neighbourhoods, if far less 'closed' than many in Britain, still had a strong sense of 'community'. Corner stores were everywhere. Life was still relatively slow, cars had not wholly displaced horses. The horses' clip-clopping was still a familiar sound, the drivers' calls of 'Rabbit-o' and 'Bottle-o' still echoed along suburban streets. On Saturdays in Wollongong, Rita Patterson's local butcher

> . . . used to take me with him in his pony and trap. He'd put all the orders in the back, and we'd go around delivering meat. The postman also used to come by trap. You'd hear him from a distance, whistling each time he put a letter in a post box. I'd be waiting on the steps and he'd lean down and give me the mail.

Church-going was a source of peace for some, but caused discomfort for others as the welfare departments did not always match evacuee's and host's denominations. John Hillier, who went to church only occasionally at home, had to go with his Methodist hosts three times each Sunday: 'There was no question of "Would you like to go?" but I fitted in happily'. His brother, however, 'only went under sufferance'. John Fethney was riled by his second host when

> . . . the first Sunday we were there he made the assumption that we'd all go off to their Methodist church together. I more or less insisted on going to the local Church of England. I think they thought it was a bit pedantic but I'd been confirmed before I left home and I was already thinking of the ministry.

Church youth groups were 'a social focus' for more than half the children. John Hillier, for example, 'enjoyed regular get-togethers after evening services, made some very good friends, and on Saturdays often went with them to dances'.

Most evacuees developed new interests. Hobbies flourished. In Perth Joyce Briant, hatted and gloved, often went visiting with her host and 'had afternoon tea in bone china tea cups and saucers with fancy cakes'. But she also kicked footballs and played cricket with a neighbour's son 'against a gum tree'. Joan Sharp, like many others, had piano lessons and often listened to Children's Hour on the wireless. Peter Edkins' model boat building, ideally suited to the climate and no longer confined to a *Batory* cabin, eventually grew beyond models to real boats: 'I was even sitting down and sewing sails with reef points, which somewhat surprised my guardians'.

Children from towns or villages in Britain found much more to do in the Australian cities. For Ken Dommerson, who lived in Sydney, 'there was far more to do in the suburbs than ever there was in our little village':

There was a picture show, two actually, and that was always a Saturday night ritual—and, if you could afford it, you went on Wednesday also. Picture shows were a big part of our life, all wartime films of course.

Heroic wartime adventures dominated cinema screens across Australia. When the CORB ships arrived in October and November 1940 the film *Convoy*—'this drama of the hour, this sensation of the war'— was 'Thrilling Thousands Daily' in all the cities.

The differences between British and Australian life were nowhere more evident than on the beaches and in the bushland fringing the cities— easily accessible, sunny playgrounds which the children loved.

Half the evacuees could not swim when they left home. Almost all learnt to in Australia, and when they left many could cover long distances. It was hardly surprising: 'the beaches were unforgettable'— 'endless miles made of golden sand not pebbles and shingle' with 'the heat of the sun and the feel of the water'. And, almost always glimmering to the horizon, was 'the blue of the sea'—'swimming just became automatic'.

Ted Flowers spent blissful summers on the beaches around Newcastle: 'The summer we arrived was as good as any Australian summer could be, very hot and marvellous for swimming'. Rearing lifesaving boats heaved out through pounding surf, and there were occasional beach carnivals. Further south, along the Illawarra coast, 'every little village had its own beach, its own small gang of lifeguards and its own flag arrangements for safe bathing'. In Sydney, Joan Sharp's favourite beach was Cronulla. Sometimes she went there by car, sometimes by train and tram—always with her surf mat:

> You would swim out beyond the breakers, and lie in the relatively calm water before the waves broke into rollers. You could hear the surf crashing on the beach. You could hear the chatter from the people on the sand. You knew that the chap watching for sharks was sitting on his look-out. And yet, you were a million miles away . . .

Bushland reached close to the edge of every city and town. There, at chop picnics and on hikes, the children found a landscape somehow primeval—and one utterly different from Britain's tamed fields and hedgerows. The plants, the animals, the birds—all were strange and new. The light was harsh, the colours muted grey-greens not emeralds. Children who wandered off could easily become lost.

Near Hobart, Mary Clemes grew to love 'the special scent in the bush'

Above The Australian city beaches, with their endless miles of golden sand, delighted the evacuees; so too did the bushland fringing the cities. Helen (*left*) and Katharine Cuthbert enjoy themselves at Newport Beach near Sydney in 1941.
Below Many of the evacuees went camping with the Scouts or Guides. Here, Donald Mitchell and his mates camp along the Yarra, near Templestowe. Note the Union Jack!

in mountains that were 'beautiful and wild, not gentle like the English countryside'. At Eaglehawk Neck on the Tasman Peninsula, she often holidayed

> . . . at this little settlement half way up the mountain called the Fern Tree where a lot of people had shacks. It was very primitive. We didn't have any electric light and many a night I would read my book with a candle under the bedclothes.

Donald Mitchell, camping with Melbourne Scouts, 'first heard kooka-burras in the tall mountain-ash gums at dawn'. Fascinated by the bush he later went on 'long hazardous hikes' through Victoria's rugged ranges. Ken Dommerson and his friends often cycled off from Sydney, 'roving through the bush for miles and miles'—'a free and easy life, sleeping in a tent, cooking over a fire, swimming in the rivers'. In Britain, near Newcastle, Ted Flowers used to be angry when game-keepers chased him off huge, walled-in estates. Near Newcastle in Australia he had 'the run of the bush'. Ted and his mates 'built tree houses well out in the scrub and went rabbit trapping at night'.

In the dry summers the bushland around the cities and towns was a tinderbox. Bushfires sometimes blackened the surrounding scrub, threatening houses on the margins. Near Sydney, Ruth Wilson's hosts were once

> . . . all packed up on the verandah, waiting with our gear in case the fire got too close. It was burning on a three mile front. Two or three houses along the end of the road were burnt out, but they got the fire under control before we had to flee.

Barely an hour's drive from where the *Batory* docked in Sydney, Helen Cuthbert watched as a bushfire swept towards a beach camp along Pittwater: 'It was very, very hot and we flopped in a small pool to try to cool off. The trees went on smouldering all night long, and my uncle and aunt took it in turns to stay awake and watch that nothing took off again.'

Some evacuees had bushland literally on their doorstep. In a house near Wollongong the Fethney brothers looked down on a sweep of idyllic beaches—their backs to the rugged Illawarra escarpment. Michael still sees it clearly:

> The back garden sloped down to a creek. There was a bridge over it into a paddock, and beyond that was another paddock—both of which Dr Palmer owned. Then you began to climb up the mountain, up the Illawarra escarpment, straight into the bush. On our hikes we'd usually penetrate a bit beyond the top of the escarpment, then have a picnic, grill some chops over an open fire—all this was part of the thrill of Australia. I sometimes

139

imagined, facing west over the escarpment with the bush stretching away, walking for hundreds and hundreds of miles. Apart from crossing a few tracks you could just walk on and on and eventually reach the Indian Ocean.

Out Bush

12

*It was a rough life but they seemed to enjoy it. The
people were very friendly, they always had a billy on the
go.*

Life in rural Australia was far removed from life in the coastal cities
and towns. For the evacuees who went to live 'out bush' the land itself
was the central fact of their existence. The realities of inland Australia
coloured every aspect of their lives: the roads they travelled on, the
houses they lived in, the water they drank.

About a fifth of all the evacuees went to country hosts. Much more
than the city- and town-dwelling children were, they were forced to
adapt. Most discovered new strengths and self-reliance: challenged by
the hardships of the bush, they delighted in its easygoing lifestyle and
novel attractions. There were 'no constraints, no fields hedgerowed in'.
Instead, the landscape had 'huge trees and enormous bull ants'. Living
there one had 'the feeling of being able to swing your arms around and
not hit anything'.

The vastness of inland Australia stunned children used to a confined
existence in Britain's cities and towns. Picked up at remote train halts,
driven homewards along dusty tracks, they were amazed by the sweep-
ing skies, the space and the distances.

Peter Edkins, a Londoner, stepped off his train from Perth at Quairading
in the West Australian wheat belt—and found himself apparently in the
middle of nowhere. He was taken home along bone-jarring, corrugated
roads. His uncle stopped by a rabbit-proof fence:

> There were plenty of rabbits on the other side of the fence, and
> Stacey got out his rifle and tried to shoot some. When we got
> back to the house a pet lamb had managed to turn on the tap
> of the two thousand gallon tank, which was our only water. He
> wasn't popular, and we had him for meals a week later.

Bullsbrook in Western Australia was to be home to Muriel Evans. The
eleven-year-old, who came from near the Yorkshire Dales, was used to
gurgling brooks: at Bullsbrook the creek sometimes barely flowed.
Familiar with solid stone cottages, Muriel found the Bullsbrook house

Muriel Evans and her young cousin Richard Pease on the wood heap at the back of Richard's home at Bullsbrook, Western Australia. The front of the house was less spartan.

ramshackle: at first sight she thought it was 'the cowshed'. Her aunt's hard-won homestead was

> . . . a weatherboard house with an iron roof, and a verandah all grown over with honeysuckle. There was a pepper tree and a mulberry tree, a hen run, and further away there was a paddock where the cows wandered. Beyond that was the real bush with blackboys and wattles.

Muriel's uncle was away in the army. Her aunt, a small tireless woman, was running the selection and rearing two children. Now there was Muriel and soon a new baby:

> The house had no taps. We got water out of the brook with buckets, and used the rainwater from the tank for drinking and bathing the baby. In the summer we used to put the water in kerosene containers, and stand them in the sun to get the water warm enough to have a tin bath. Later my aunt bought a concrete bath and we perched it in the shed. It only had a plughole, no taps or drain.

This house, a bleak monument to pioneering, was primitive even by the standards of the bush. But the people were typical: tough, resourceful and resilient, with a sardonic humour as dry as the land itself.

On another West Australian farm Paul Farquharson's hosts had 'water plumbed in from a dam so the bathroom actually had running water'. But when the dam went dry the family had to pull buckets of water from a well. There was no electricity, not even a generator. In Victoria, Reg Harris' house had the usual corrugated iron roof and wide verandahs: 'In summer you baked to death in temperatures over a hundred degrees, and in winter you froze'. Bob Bullard lived in a house that had 'grown like Topsy as the family tacked bits onto it'. Wire-meshed sleep-outs surrounded the building's only brickwork: the kitchen chimney. Peter Edkins' hosts had seen such protracted hardships and so few comforts that 'it never occurred to them that they were missing out'. Their limestone homestead had

... no water, electricity or telephone. It was a big house, but it was gaunt. There was no paint, no carpets, not even lino—just bare wood. My room had one bed, no chair, no table. Where I was to put my clothes was a puzzle the first night.

Dust-reddened sunsets turned quickly to darkness in the bush, enveloping isolated homesteads in a velvet blackness never seen in the cities and towns. Where Brenda Mallett lived, 'each evening there was the ritual of pumping up the kerosene pressure lamps. Mantles were hard to get because of wartime rationing, so it was a crime to shake the table in case the mantle broke.' Another family had 'a hurricane lamp always hanging on the back verandah at night in case you had to go down the backyard, the wick turned down low, just glimmering'.

In Queensland's cane country Phil Robinson—like most bush children—slept on the verandah enclosed with flyscreens. Beyond the wire mesh the stars blazed brilliantly. For Phil it seemed an infinite improvement on 'sleeping in a little box of a room in Birmingham'. Another boy 'never wanted to sleep inside, because there was no rain to speak of'. Betty Deeley and her brother spent the war on a small vineyard in the west with ten other children. The boys and girls had separate rooms to dress in, 'but we didn't have bedrooms as it was cooler sleeping outside'.

You could always hear the windmill whirring round and the pump working. If it stopped, you were conscious that something wasn't quite right because the sound had vanished. The crickets were always going as well, the frogs used to croak, and you often heard dingoes howling.

The summers could be fierce. Walking to school soon after arriving, Bob Bullard thought 'to hell with it!' and took off his sandals like the

143

others. 'I very quickly put them on again because I couldn't walk bare-foot on the hot sand.' Muriel Evans' aunt 'kept the Christmas jelly in a bucket down the well to keep it cool'. The Farquharson brothers suffered when their Aunt Amy decided to have a traditional Christmas dinner for her English boys: 'We finished up with roast chook, pudding and all the bits and pieces—and inside it was about one hundred and five degrees. Afterwards we were less traditional and more comfortable.'

When the rains failed the grasses turned grey-brown then finally blew away. Dust hung over parched plains. The spiralling air currents of willy willies sent up plumes of dust, and strong winds lifted stinging veils of sand. In the worst conditions sand and dust seeped remorselessly into houses, penetrating the slightest crack.

Clouds came and went, all too often bringing no rain. When finally it did rain the country was suddenly green—then came the flies. Betty Deeley never got used to seeing 'children with flies crawling in the corners of their eyes, up their nostrils, around their lips, into their mouths. They *stood still* and never brushed them off.'

Snakes, the horror of every bush mother, were a menace. Peter Edkins, soon after arriving, was startled to discover that a large snake had slithered past not three metres from where he was sitting on the ground. Barbara Donald always carried 'a razor blade and some magnesium potash to rub into a snake bite before spitting the poison out'. Muriel Evans, warned never to try to kill a snake, still remembers: 'If you saw a rat you were supposed to run away, if you saw a snake you had to stand still and shout "Snake!"—and hope somebody would come. You had to look out for another snake because they went around in pairs.'

Near country towns large birds sometimes snapped the overhead power lines. One night at Betty Deeley's, with everyone dressed ready for a rare dance, a black swan 'went into the lines and the whole district was blacked out'.

These evacuees, most of them used to large neighbourhood schools in Britain, almost all attended tiny bush schools. Remote outposts of Australian education, the schools generally had only one teacher; some had two. Many had only one small room, others two rooms divided by a folding screen. The children either baked in summer, sweaty legs sticking to wooden classroom benches, or, freezing, clustered around wood stoves in the winter.

Reg Harris walked or ran three kilometres across sheep paddocks to get to the Wahring School, near Dargalong in Victoria. One girl rode a cow to get to Wahring. Peter Edkins went to school on an old bike: 'It was five miles from where I lived. One of the miles was across deep

Muriel Evans riding to the small school she attended before beginning Correspondence lessons. She cycled some five miles to school along this sandy track—no doubt sometimes thinking of her father's cycle shop in Yorkshire.

sand that you had to push the bicycle through.' The other children arrived on horseback:

> The first day I was most taken aback at morning break when they all went and watered and fed their horses, and made sure they were in the shade—before they went and tore round the playground. It was quite a salutary lesson: you looked after your animal first.

Betty Deeley's school, built like most on low stilts to escape ants and floods, had sundry creatures living under it. On her first day there 'some of the lads went underneath, got a goanna, and chased me with it. I took off down the playground . . .' Worse still, the primitive lavatories had 'spiders, geckos and lizards running around on the seats and walls'. Barbara Donald, at school near Terrigal, found that with its tin roof 'if there was any rain the teacher just couldn't carry on with lessons. He used to write on the board "Read your books", and you'd just get on with it.'

Isolated and self-reliant, spending entire days with their cluster of children, most bush teachers or 'schoolies' knew their charges far better than city or town teachers did. The relaxed informality of bush schools allowed good teachers great scope. There were eight grades at Reg Harris' school:

145

... from first grade right through to Merit grade which, if you progressed that far, you got to at fourteen. The school varied between ten and fourteen children, with the one teacher teaching all those classes. How they did it I don't know.

Peter Edkins' schooling in London had been an ordeal. He flowered in the encouraging atmosphere of the South Caroling School, near Quairading. The sixteen other children, 'real bush kids', were fascinated by his drawings of the *Batory* and the *Stratheden*—as 'very few of the class had ever even seen the sea even though it was only a hundred and fifty miles away'. South Caroling School, though he was there for only five months, was the 'watershed' in Peter's education:

> For the first time I was a centre of interest and that did enormous good to my ego. I was somebody. Everybody tended to hang on what I said, though later one or two of the girls resented my being the celebrity. From then onwards I loved school.

Some of the older children studied by correspondence. Muriel Evans was one. 'Correspondence' relied almost entirely on reading and writing daily 'lessons', hard work for Muriel as she never liked 'the actual mechanics of writing'. There were endless pages to complete: 'It was always a push to get it done to catch the fortnightly post, but I enjoyed writing the letter to the teacher and receiving her reply a month later'.

Much was learned outside the school room, especially an appreciation of Australia's plants and animals. Near Terrigal Barbara Donald came to understand 'the tin-tinn sounds of bell-birds, the whistle and crack of whip birds, the raucous laughter of the kookaburras and the screeching of cockatoos'. New skills were acquired. In Victoria Brenda Mallett formed a 'strong friendship' with her hosts' tenant farmers:

> They were both bushmen. They grew fruit, they milked cows, and they bred cattle. Even though I was an urban child I quickly learned to milk, and in fact often had to help with milking when Ollie, the shell-shocked alcoholic, had been on a bender. They taught me to ride and so much about the bush. The children knew lots about the bush, and nature study lessons in the little school were an absolute joy. On weekends I used to go for long walks, and I became very familiar with all sorts of wildflowers, where the birds' nests were, where the possums were nesting.

And there were other opportunities:

> There was a beautiful piano in my hosts' house. I desperately wanted to learn to play, but in a remote place like that in wartime there were no music teachers. I used to pick out tunes, and I sort of learned about full and half tones. Slowly I began to

work things out . . . Then, wonder of wonders, a music teacher came to the area.

Paul Farquharson and his brother spent their first year at Kalgoorlie, Western Australia's famous gold mining town. They then went for six months to the wheat belt, where Harry Leak, a First World War digger, had a soldier settlement block near Kununoppin. His wife, a Scot, had migrated before the First War. The country was dry and the properties large. For Paul the life there was fascinating:

From memory the Leak's farm was eleven hundred to twelve hundred acres. We had a track from the house to the front gate, then it was an unsealed road lined with gum trees all the way in to Kununoppin. Petrol was rationed and the old roadster was only used if Mrs Leak was going to town alone. Mr Leak, Peg and I generally went in the sulky.

The pictures came to Kununoppin about once a month. The picture show man backed his truck up to the hall, and showed his film through a couple of slots in the back of the hall. There was an interval every time he changed the reel, and quite often there'd be a breakdown. He'd flash a slide on the screen saying 'Bombs on powerhouse, short intermission'. It was the one day in town when you could buy a pie.

The only other entertainment was dances. Peg, one of the daughters, taught me to dance on the back verandah, and perhaps every two or three months there would be a dance in Kununoppin. Everybody went, kids and all. There was a three piece band, just local people playing drums and a piano and another instrument. There weren't that many blokes around and the women danced with anybody.

An Afghan traveller, a pedlar, arrived twice while I was there—a very fine old chap and a great friend of Mrs Leak. He had a single horse with stiff legs pulling a covered wagon. He stayed at the men's quarters, a tin shed near the stable, and had all sorts of marvellous things. I bought a pocket knife from him.

Harry harvested the wheat with an eight-horse team. I helped get the horses ready in the morning, feeding them, putting on collars, bridles and reins. I'd go round sitting next to Mr Leak on the harvester. About two circuits of the paddock would fill the hopper, then we would run the wheat out into bags which were dumped at one end of the paddock we were harvesting. Then we stitched the bag and lifted it onto a dray to take down to a collecting point. Burning off the stubble was a recognised practice in those days, but the wind had to be in a certain direction. We'd get a tin of kerosene and a stick with a bit of rag round it, set a light to it, then walk along on the paddock's down-wind side setting fire to the stubble. You came in afterwards all smelling of smoke, burnt chaff all over you.

Bush children were expected—and mostly wanted—to 'work around the place'. Younger children generally only helped with small chores. Barbara Donald, for example, sometimes helped pick fruit in her uncle's orchard, but her regular task was 'every day pumping water from the big tank into a smaller one, so many pumps at a time'. More was expected of Reg Harris. With so many men at the war 'farm labour was very scarce and my uncle had quite a big sheep station'. Tough by nature, Reg still found his incessant tasks wearying. His aunt was only too happy to exploit his presence:

> Aunty did none of the outside work, but they expected me to. One of my jobs was to keep the wood bin filled with chopped wood and kindling. Sometimes when it was dark she'd expect me to go down to the swamp where the gum trees grew and pick up bark for the fire. I was terrified of the spiders that lived behind the bark.

Betty Deeley and her brother spent the war in Western Australia amongst the dry foothills of the Darling Range. Their hosts, the Makins, had migrated from Britain in the 1920s and carved a vineyard out of the scrub: 'twenty-five acres of currants, sultanas, muscatels, and raisins'. The Makins' first home there had been a tent. Everyone worked on the place, including the ten Makin children and the two Deeleys. Betty did 'exactly what the men did':

> I picked the grapes and drove the cart that we put the fruit on. I helped get the sultanas ready for dipping. We used to put the currants on racks to dry, then we used to help rub them through the racks and get them out ready to go to the cleaning plant. I used to help with the pruning, burning all the spare wood that came up. We used to pick and pack the peaches, and we'd stand for hours ironing these squares of paper ready to wrap each peach.

Droving sheep and cattle along remote stock routes epitomised the rugged independence of Australian bushmen. Michael Storey experienced a hard but memorable few weeks 'pushing stock along':

> The drovers were all on horseback but they had a Ford, a rattly old truck which carried all the camping gear. It was a long day out in the sun, your hat over your eyes to keep the sun off . . . keeping an eye on the stragglers, rounding them up, pushing them on. You got ravenously hungry and ate whatever— sausages, beans and the rest. I can still taste the billy tea!

Bob Bullard at a West Australian logging camp, with draught horses hauling felled trees to a truck. The loggers, Bob remembers, lived a rough life, but they were easygoing and friendly, with 'a billy always on the boil'.

Bob Puxted, who had grown up on a farm in Kent, was fourteen when he left home. After eighteen months in Sydney he concluded that 'the city was all rush and bustle'. Bob was then placed with a dairy farming family in the Hunter Valley, and was later employed on two other farms in the area. He found 'the type of life I liked and families who accepted me for what I was'. There Bob came to know the gruelling nature of farming in Australia:

Dairy farming is seven days a week, always early rising: getting the cows milked and the churns ready in time to catch the milk lorry. At the first place we began about four o'clock in the morning and we'd come in about six o'clock at night.

When the cows dried up we used to turn them into the bush over the mountains. Periodically we'd have to go and look for them, a day's riding rounding up the cattle to see which ones could be brought down to pasture. Mostly we'd find them down at the waterhole, so we didn't have to roam right through the mountains. But when you're mustering cattle you go all ways, you don't stick to the tracks.

Sometimes we'd take rabbit traps into the hills, set about a hundred a day, then we'd have to go round them of a night. You could bag about a hundred and thirty, night after night. We used to just take the skins off, bring them home to sell them, and burn the carcasses. Foxes were another pest. We used to set baits for them sometimes, and we used to shoot them occasionally.

We maintained all our stock yards and fences. We'd cut the trees, then split our own fence posts out of them. Two of you would cross-cut the timber, then strip the bark off, cut the

149

timber into lengths and split it. We did miles of fencing, a lot of it over the mountain, digging the stones out with a crowbar to get the posts in.

In the winter we'd go grubbing out all the undergrowth on the hills, swinging a mattock all day long, so that more grass could grow. In the very dry years we had to chop ironbark trees down for the cattle to eat the leaves. The cattle had to eat something, and the farmer couldn't afford to buy hay.

In the evenings we'd sometimes go to a neighbour's place for a few card games or dominoes, or they would come to our place. We had about eight miles to go to the occasional dance, and sometimes further. We'd tie our horses up outside the dance hall, dance, and then ride home. We'd often be asleep going home. You'd suddenly wake up and find the horse had stopped at a gate. You'd open the gate, the horse would walk through, and other than that it would take you right home.

For children with fewer responsibilities the bush provided novel diversions. Reg Harris added his small tally to the war on rabbits: 'There were plagues of them and the kids at school taught me how to skin a rabbit, hang it up and dry it'. Bob Bullard had once ridden a donkey at the seaside. Soon after he arrived in Western Australia the youngsters there got him up on horseback—'no saddle, no bridle, no nothing'. 'One of the lads slapped the horse round the backside and off it went. I ended up hanging underneath with my arms around the horse's neck, until the horse stopped very sharpish . . .' Bob, like most of these evacuees, was soon quite confident in the saddle.

Rain was so rare where he lived that 'a bivouac under a ground sheet' did for a tent when he went camping. 'An old cooking pot, masses of bread, jam and butter' together with fresh fish sufficed for meals. In Queensland Phil Robinson camped along the Isis River, named after a stretch of the Thames. However, instead of watercress, there were shrimps and prawns. These were 'never to be forgotten, heavenly days':

> Uncle Len always had a campfire going to keep the mosquitoes at bay. Round about dusk we'd go down to the river, armed with kerosene tins and a shrimp net. We'd come back with three or four tinfuls of shrimps or prawns, boil them on the fire and have a feast. For a kid from Birmingham it was unbelievable . . .

Phil's bike was made by his uncle with true bush improvisation from 'a couple of wheels and a frame he found on the dump'. Used to British handbrakes, Phil found the backpedal brakes hard to master:

> The house was on a very steep hill. Half way down it I couldn't stop because it was against my nature to pedal backwards to

The Cox brothers (*second and fourth from left*) on a 1941 visit to their great-uncle's dairy farm in southern Queensland. Their older cousin Neville (*third from left*) 'became like a brother' to Gerald and David. The old work-horse recalls C.J. Dennis' Old Grey Dobbin—with 'three upon his back'. Note the economical single 'braces'.

brake. I just couldn't do it . . . I went headlong into a barbed wire fence and ran screaming into the house to Aunt Amy covered in blood.

There was barely a rise where Muriel Evans lived. There was, however, a mulberry tree. 'I used to sit in this tree when I was feeling a bit lonely and wishing the war was over. You could just climb up to a comfortable branch and sit and think', Muriel reflects.

For such isolated children one diversion was Sunday School—by correspondence. Joyce Briant, an older evacuee living in Perth, taught children at her local church and also helped with correspondence Sunday School: 'I had about half a dozen outback pupils and I used to have to send them Sunday school lessons and questions. They would answer them and send them back to me, and I would mark them.'

While bushfires sometimes destroyed numbers of houses near the cities and towns, in the bush they laid waste vast tracts. With stock incinerated and pastures destroyed fires brought black despair to hard-pressed families. 'Snakes and rabbits and kangaroos all coming down from the bush into the school playground' warned of approaching fires near Betty Deeley's home. Only months after arriving Barbara Donald discovered how bushfires could 'come very suddenly'. Sent home from school, she led her younger brother and cousin through a sweltering, smoke-hazed afternoon. 'The ground was bone dry, the air still.'

> The main road was so hot that the tar was sticky and bursting into bubbles. The shrubs on both sides of the road were burning, snapping and crackling, sending up sparks. Snakes and toads were scuttling across the road. We could see the fire coming down through the orchards, farmers were galloping towards the flames. Some men had dug a trench nearby and were beating the fire back. When it rained afterwards I remember dancing in the garden, but the rain tasted horrible, full of smoke.

Droughts, if anything, were worse than bushfires. When the dead curse of failed rains descended whole regions suffered: rivers and creeks dried to gutters, dams became fatal quagmires, the feed vanished. Weakening, finally tottering, the stock perished or were shot. Soon after arriving in Victoria Reg Harris saw his uncles' station ravaged:

> When the drought was on there'd only be about a foot of water in the house dam. It was disgusting. The water was green, the mud was deep. It was very, very hot. Sometimes the young heifers couldn't get out, and by the time you found them they were drowned or dead from exhaustion.

Michael Storey spent the war with foster parents, Bob and Cissie Wilson. A middle-aged, childless couple, the Wilsons were operating a Melbourne milkbar when he arrived. In 1943 they moved with Michael to near Albury, where they had bought a rundown farm, 'Tara':

> There was one solitary gum by the gate, and a dirt track down to this weatherboard, corrugated iron-roofed house. The forty acres looked vast to me after Melbourne, but in Australia it was a small property. There was no running water, no electricity. There were six cows and some poultry. Bob and Cissie Wilson worked like hell, with some help from me, to make a poultry farm of it. You were involved with everything. For seven days a week you had to be up before the crack of dawn and you were working beyond darkness. It was my job each morning to milk the Jersey cow before I went off to school.
>   The drought started soon after we'd moved on to this farm. It was a part of life there, and people tried to help each other out. We had two five-hundred gallon galvanised iron tanks, and we were down to a rung and a half of water in them. We were trying to get water brought in from anywhere.

Five of the six cows died from lack of food and water shortly after we moved there. They used to wake us up bellowing in pain, desperate for food and water. One morning five came in but not the sixth. She was lying down, so weak she couldn't stand. I went back to the house and made some gruel, like a porridge, and tried hand feeding her with it. The poor thing took it, but she rolled over and died on us some hours later. When the second one couldn't stand I started to do the same thing. But Bob Wilson came up and gave me a .22 rifle. The kindest thing I could do, he said, was to shoot it. Have you ever looked in a cow's eyes close up?

13 Homes Good and Bad

They were a loving family ... I was amazed the way their only son accepted me and introduced me to his gang as his big sister.

We would be in trouble for the slightest reason, and felt very insecure and unloved ... The ultimate punishment was 'Get your bags packed and get out!'

THE children's personal lives in Australia highlighted the gamble that their evacuation involved. Their experiences varied widely. The majority spent five happy years with loving hosts. For a small minority life was bleak. A few endured years of neglect or even abuse: facing endless conflicts behind the facade of decent homes, literally or mentally on the run from damaging relationships—and endlessly seeking escape from feelings of their own worthlessness.

All host families had been given general advice on helping their evacuees 'settle' when they arrived. Their longer term obligations were detailed in the *National Security Act 1939–1940*. These requirements, had all hosts met them both in letter and spirit, would have gone far towards ensuring that every evacuee was well cared for in Australia.

The overwhelming majority of hosts did meet both the letter and the spirit of their obligations. Many examples of such cases have already been described. This chapter, however, mostly concerns the plight of the less fortunate children, those whose hosts failed to meet the spirit of the Act—or who flouted their custodial duties, and sometimes ordinary decency, entirely.

These instances of poor treatment give a hollow ring to *The Song Goes On*, a eulogistic children's book describing the CORB evacuation and published in Sydney in 1941. The introduction, written by Zara Gowrie, wife of the Governor-General, read:

> *The Song Goes On* surely typifies the valiant little ones who have left their homes so far away and come for sanctuary to this glorious land of sunshine. Here they will find peace and plenty,

Good host families often made great sacrifices for their CORB charges. One such family were Muriel Evans' hosts, Herbert and Nellie Pease, photographed here with their two children before Herbert was sent overseas. 'Auntie Nellie' then raised her own family, cared for Muriel and ran the farm—virtually alone.

loving kindness and every incentive to grow into fine, noble citizens of the Empire.

Across Australia the evacuees experienced countless instances of kindness and understanding. About three-quarters of them recall their time in Australia as memorable or at least mostly enjoyable. Secure in an atmosphere of love and understanding, these fortunate children were certain that their welfare was their host family's primary concern. Made 'part of the family', helped to make the most of Australia's opportunities rather than remain 'evacuees', they were still encouraged to keep hold of their British roots.

These hosts fully honoured the National Security Act's fourteen stipulations for 'Custodians of Overseas Children'. These included: 'To supply adequate and suitable food, wearing apparel and sleeping accommodation'; 'To afford the child reasonable opportunity for amusement, healthy exercise and recreation'; 'To ensure that any household duties performed by the child are not unreasonable for the age and physical development of the child'; and 'Generally to safeguard the moral and religious training of the child'.

Norman Townsend had Hamish and also the wider security of Hamish's brother's family: 'I was absorbed as a member of the family, not as a stranger, and I was made to feel welcome in two homes'. Anne

155

Katharine and Helen Cuthbert (*third and fifth from left*) picnicking with their much-loved relatives near Sydney. The personal photographs in this book emphasise the children fortunate enough to spend happy years in Australia; those in unhappy homes were rarely, if ever, photographed.

Ratcliffe, whose own home had been far from happy, gradually discovered the pleasures of being truly wanted: 'I loved every minute of it. It was more family orientated than I had ever been accustomed to, because our foster mother was not involved with anything else besides the home and the family.'

The happiest evacuees were usually those with outgoing hosts who encouraged their children to enjoy a wider life beyond the family. Peter Edkins was one:

> I got a lot of encouragement and met a lot of friends. I think the Gallops did an excellent job in a difficult balancing act. We were a very close family, much closer than my parents and I. But on the other hand the Gallops always emphasised that my primary relationships were in England.

A significant number of otherwise good hosts failed to meet the *spirit* of the National Security Act. A lack of understanding about children and a blindness to evacuees' subtler feelings characterised these homes. Other problems, while not stemming from the actual host–evacuee relationship, were sometimes severe enough to undermine it when not resolved. The children in these situations, often uncomfortable or mildly unhappy, were mostly not assertive or miserable enough to ask to be moved.

During the evacuees' time in Australia occasional live broadcasts were organised, linking parents and children. Here, John and Michael Fethney's parents, and their sister Barbara, listen to the two boys—and to their increasingly Australian accents.

The Fethney brothers, used to 'rabbiting on in a relaxed way' at home in Bradford, found the formality of their second hosts hard to accept. 'The adults conversed with each other and you weren't really drawn into the conversation very much at all', John remembers. The Hillier brothers, despite their hosts' many fine qualities, sensed an underlying 'strangeness' in their attitude—and their suggestion that they were a 'new mother and father' caused continuing tension. John 'liked them very much', but 'couldn't love them in the sense that you love your parents'.

Braham Glass and his sister Essie faced the opposite problem. Their aunt, far from wishing to be a 'mother', wanted as few material and emotional demands on her as possible. Her bleak outlook gave no scope for generosity or warmth, as when Braham, 'terribly excited', came home to tell her that he could join the school band. His drumsticks would cost one shilling and sixpence:

> 'You tell your teacher', she said, 'to go to buggery. If they want to make you a drummer let them buy the bloody drumsticks!' And that was that.
>
> I got a penny a day pocket money. Once I found sixpence in the gutter, and I was stupid enough to tell my aunt. She took it from me and gave it back to me at a penny a day—which saved her sixpence!

157

This philosophical thought once occurred to me: 'If my parents get killed, I'll be marooned in Australia forever'. I broached the subject with my aunt: 'If my Mum and Dad get killed can I call you mum?'—and she said 'No!' It's fifty years ago, but I still have this jumble of memories of that house in Wellington Street, Bondi—the pain and the pleasure.

Nora Lupton faced regimented silence and, because of her hosts' marital problems, continuing tension. She and her cousin, another evacuee, were not allowed to play outside the garden. Nora was stunned when she was finally allowed to join a tennis club 'and actually go somewhere on my own'. Betty Deeley and her brother spent the war with people who, while providing physical comfort, were excessively strict and seemed unable to love. 'There was no open communication, there was no privacy', Betty says. Her brother had vented his feelings in a secret diary, and Betty recalls:

> Our clothes drawers were gone through, and auntie found the diary. He'd put some comments in it about the way we were being treated, hurtful things that were said to us. She was very, very angry, but it stopped her in her tracks a bit.

A few evacuee–host relationships were so compromised by prior events that future happiness was almost impossible. The three Clout children, having gone to their elderly, slightly eccentric spinster host in Tasmania, found it almost impossible to forget or forgive the fact that their shipboard friends were all in Western Australia. The situation, Jacqueline regrets, became 'a proper little hornets' nest'. 'The decision to send us to Tasmania had a terrible impact on our lives. Our host did her best in a difficult situation.'

Ignorance about sex, and especially girls' difficulties with adolescence, sometimes complicated matters. A number of girls believe their host 'mothers' were more open and helpful than their own would have been but, especially in 'severe' homes, instances of sex being made to appear 'dirty' were common. Such attitudes were, of course, more widespread then. But, with a strange family and far from 'home', they were doubly hard to bear. One girl, already weighed down by wearying strictures at home, was panic-stricken when her first period began at school:

> The headmaster's wife explained to me what it was, gave me a sanitary towel, and said I must tell them when I got home. Auntie sat me down on the edge of the verandah and said she had been expecting it to happen. She got some very stiff calico pillow cases and I had to stitch squares of this to make into sanitary towels, which were used, washed, and used again. I found them extremely painful, especially in the heat. I was earning half a crown pocket money, so I could afford to buy

sanitary towels, but auntie wouldn't let me—'We don't talk about dirty things!'.

Children evacuated alone generally fared worst in less-than-ideal homes, as siblings were often able to reassure one another that the fault was not theirs. Outside interests and confidants helped some children forget their troubles, but many who were unhappy had no relatives, teachers, neighbours or clubs they could turn to.

The monitoring of children's situations by welfare officials appears to have varied widely. Some evacuees insist that they had no welfare contacts whatsoever, others say that they were visited regularly. Children in troubled homes were often trapped between their own reluctance to denigrate their hosts and the difficulty that welfare officials had in probing beneath the veneer of surface appearances—even in unhappy situations. Norah Lupton's is a common comment: 'The welfare people asked if we were happy, but our host was always there. It was impossible to talk with her giving us telling glances—"Yes, we were happy, everything was alright".'

Unless they lived reasonably close to one of the cities, children in the country rarely had any welfare visits. Betty Deeley, who lived near Perth, recalls a revealing incident. Cyril Bavin, one of the British government's CORB representatives, was visiting the Makin's vineyard. Bavin, the Makin family and the two Deeley children were wandering around the property:

> Everybody was dressed up in their finest. As we walked through the orchard Auntie looked around and said, 'Why's our Nell digging over there? What's she doing with the spade?' You could see this beautifully dressed girl digging behind a peach tree. The toilet had to be emptied daily, and someone had emptied one of the tubs in a hole and left it to settle before covering it with soil. Nell was frightened Mr Bavin would come over and see the mess.

About half the evacuees stayed with one family throughout the war. A small proportion of these would have preferred to move to other homes but did not. Some were fearful of going to a worse situation, some preferred to avoid the emotional upheaval of moving, some wanted to shield their parents from worry. 'I thought that I should stay and let my parents think I was happy', one says. Many, whatever their difficulties, felt a debt to their existing hosts: 'We didn't want to upset the family that had taken us. We understood the sacrifices they themselves were making'.

Moving could certainly be traumatic. However, few children appear to have had any guidance, either in being gently introduced to new

159

homes or in coping with their feelings. 'I was just told to pack' or 'All I remember is getting on a train' are relatively common memories.

Pamela Palmer, fourteen in 1940, moved twice. She went first to an uncle and aunt, a generous but overprotective retired couple. Isolated there, she was moved after a few months to a young family but the interfering wife made her life miserable. A year later she was moved again. Waiting to be seen by a welfare official, Pamela found herself sitting beside a pleasant woman:

> We had about half an hour together. She said she'd come to hear if a child was available for her, and I told her I'd come to see where I was going to be sent. A lady eventually walked out of an adjoining room and said, 'Oh, I see you two have met'. I'm quite certain it was a deliberate accident. I was so pleased when I was told 'This is the lady who's come to see if you'd like to live with her', because somehow we had gelled.
>
> They were a loving family. When I arrived I was shown which was to be my bedroom. All the furniture was in the middle of the room, and I was told they'd done that so I could put it where I wanted it. They had an only child, a son four years younger than me, and I was amazed the way he accepted me and introduced me to his gang as his big sister.

Some relatives, those who had felt 'obliged' to take evacuees in the dark months of mid-1940, saw the situation differently by mid-1942. Less well-off families, facing the higher living costs and increased taxation of the war years, saw their household budgets further depleted by long-staying evacuees. In July 1942 CORB, anxious to avoid children being moved for financial reasons, reversed its maintenance policy. Henceforth, if the Australian hosts wished to be assisted, the parents' weekly contribution of six shillings per child was to be sent to them.

Family finances had some bearing on John Speller's experiences, a story of small difficulties which became disastrously magnified because of a lack of underlying love. A shy eight-year-old on arrival, John went first to an aunt and uncle. There, 'desperately wanting somebody to love me for myself', he felt 'something of an interloper'. He knew that his relatives, already struggling financially with three children, 'were sacrificing a great deal to have me'. But, tall for his age and growing quickly, John found their meals inadequate. There were other problems as well:

> The little bit of pocket money I got was almost invariably spent on some very satisfying cake. My mother somehow got a parcel out to me with some of my toys, and at one stage I was so hungry that I started to sell off my toys. With the money I used to buy a loaf of bread and retire into the sandhills and gorge myself.

Aunt Nell invariably read my letters. Once, when I'd finished one, I sealed it up and then in the kitchen I accidentally leaned on the stove and burnt my hand. My aunt noticed the letter and accused me of saying something detrimental in the letter, because I'd sealed it up and was crying—but I was crying because I'd burnt my hand. The last thing I would have done would have been to write that I was unhappy or that anything was going wrong. I wouldn't have wanted to upset my mother and I knew that I owed my aunt and uncle a great deal.

CORB representatives came to see me at least twice, and on the second occasion they wanted to see me on my own. Even to CORB's representative I thought I was letting down my aunt or uncle if I said anything about not being very happy, so I strenuously denied that there was anything wrong. But clearly either CORB's representatives could see through what I was saying, or else my aunt and uncle made representations, because at very short notice I was told that I was going to another family (in mid-1942).

The Ruggs were middle-aged people. They had one son two years older than I was, and a small black spaniel. They turned out to be extremely kind. They were loving and really made me feel that I was being looked after and cared for. It wasn't that they were financially much better off, but they made me feel better.

I wouldn't have called myself one of the family, but I felt I was a full member of the family. The fact that they weren't real relations didn't seem to matter. I was talked to, I had things explained to me, I was treated absolutely on a par with their son John. After a while, when John was away, the spaniel came and was friendly when I called—and I felt that if the dog accepted me in some way this made me accepted by everybody.

Children who fared poorly with the relatives they were first sent to often later found happiness with foster parents, and spirits generally soared following such moves as Pamela's and John's. However, seventy or so of the 577 evacuees went on to third, fourth or even fifth homes, often with mounting unhappiness. Ruth Wilson, whose 1939 evacuation within Britain had been happy, moved home twice in Australia. Increasingly homesick, her self-concept spiralled downwards each time:

I started thinking there was something wrong with me, and that was why I was being moved all the time. It wasn't something that I ever spoke about to anyone because I was fairly reticent, but I became very anxious to return to England, to get home.

A few children remained desperately homesick during their years in Australia. For these children, often those who were poorly treated, letters from their parents were tangible evidence of solid love. But some children had both poor hosts and uncommunicative parents.

Joyce Briant (*right*) had some
initial difficulties settling in with
her Perth hosts. But as the war
continued she made a conscious
decision to enjoy her new life.
As this 1942 lunch-break stroll
through Perth suggests, she did.

The most fortunate were those whose parents' letters spoke of
continued family involvement and a future after the war. Rita Patterson's
father wrote 'long beautiful letters' and 'made great efforts to make sure
that I felt part of the family'. The Cuthbert girls' father kept up a dia-
logue over months about postwar changes to their garden, asking the
girls for their opinions and promising 'not to do anything till we can
discuss it with you'. For Barbara Donald, very unhappy with her relatives,
'letter days were just sheer delight': 'You read your letter, kept it in
your pocket, and read it over and over until you practically knew it by
heart. My father was a very descriptive writer, and you could imagine
you were back in England again.'

Some children, often the happier ones, wrote home regularly. Joyce
Briant, whose family 'were there all the time', wrote separately to her
mother, sisters and brother—'and to loads of friends'. Tony Houghton
kept his promise to write weekly, and to report his younger brother's

activities. The 'marvellous flow' of letters between Tony and his father never faltered:

> I kept copious notes in notebooks made from strips of paper and a bit of cardboard and string. Every day I'd write a note about what we'd done, or what we were going to do the next day so I'd know what to write in the next letter. Although some letters did go astray we never felt far from home.

Others, though keen to hear from home, wrote back rather less often. Some, busy enjoying their new lives, did not find the time to write. For some life was too bleak to encourage letters at all. These children, already unhappy, often had their mail strictly censored by uneasy hosts. Many, even if they had been allowed to write home candidly, were unwilling to reveal their unhappiness to their parents. Braham Glass, forced by his overbearing aunt to write home each week 'by way of punishment', began his letters 'the same way every time'—'Dear Mum and Dad, I am well and happy as I hope you are'.

Long delays in the mail heightened some children's sense of remoteness from their families. 'You lost all sense of being able to write and get a reply, letters were divorced and isolated', Peter Edkins says. The situation improved vastly in June 1943 when 'airgraphs' were introduced, photographed letters which were airmailed to and from Australia as negatives and printed at their destination. The free Cable and Wireless telegrams were valued by most of the children. However, for those in unhappy homes, their set messages—mostly variations of 'chins up' cheerfulness—made a mockery of thoughts and feelings.

The number of cases of severe mental, physical or sexual abuse amongst the CORB evacuees was very small. The precise number is not evident from CORB record cards, but a recent questionnaire survey suggests that less than five per cent were abused. However, for each child who endured abuse, often for years, the effects were devastating. Feelings of fear, guilt, worthlessness and self-degradation shadowed the victims for years afterwards. Some have only been able to talk openly about their suffering in recent years, mostly only to their intimate circle of spouse and children.

Barbara Helliwell, nine in 1940, was destined to spend vagabond, loveless years in Australia without any sustained relationships. She stayed in five homes, and in most suffered a degree of mental and physical abuse. The marital problems of her first hosts, a great aunt and uncle, soon propelled Barbara to another relative, a hot-tempered woman 'furious' at her intrusion. She was told emphatically that 'no one in the world liked me or loved me, which was why my parents had sent me

163

away'. Feeling 'scarred and worthless' she went to a third home. She stayed there for over two years, at last happy in a loving home. Barbara's stay there ended abruptly when her 'aunt' died of cancer. Shunted on to some other strangers, she was 'welcomed' dismissively: 'Don't think I've taken you out of the goodness of my heart, I can't get a maid of your age', her new host warned her. The family was excessively religious—and warped:

> Playing was 'evil', I wasn't allowed to read anything but the Bible, and I started getting a few hidings. I began to wet the bed, and the more I did it the more hidings I got. The mattress would be taken outside, and the neighbours and the children would be called round to have a look, and then my bottom was bared. I dreaded going to sleep.

Barbara then moved in briefly with a war widow before finally returning to her great aunt. Still haunted by these experiences, 'a wall built round me' remains her defence against the world: 'The things that were said have stayed with me all through my life and play over and over in my brain . . .'

Brenda Mallett, an only child, went to live with strangers in the Victorian countryside. Her hosts, an unmarried man and his spinster sister, were reclusive, somewhat eccentric Baptists—hardly ideal hosts for a sensitive ten-year-old Catholic. They were very strict. Brenda's disquiet increased when, on receiving letters from Stefan, who had befriended her on the *Batory*, she was forbidden to continue this 'undesirable friendship':

> They didn't trust a Polish man corresponding with a young girl, and no more letters ever arrived. I was very upset, and in secret—using some of my Christmas money—I sent off a letter telling him to write to me at my English address after the war.

On Sundays little activity was allowed and Brenda was never taken to Mass. 'I was very lost', she says. 'The Church didn't know I was there, and I didn't know where the Church was.' Initially sent to a small bush school Brenda was later, against her wishes, sent to board at a Presbyterian school in Melbourne:

> Once again I felt I was the outsider, the loner. They kept calling me a refugee and asking me if my parents were dead. There were sermons about the wickedness and evil that existed in the Church of Rome. I felt very uncomfortable, and wanted to stand up and say, 'I'm a Catholic, it's not like that'.
>
> I stuck it out for a term and a half, but after a tremendous row about Catholics I knew that I didn't belong. I couldn't take any more of it. I had a little pocket money, and I decided I

would try to stow away on a ship and get back to England.

I got on a train for Port Melbourne, but there were so many drunks on board I went back to the city. I didn't know where to go, but I thought the tenant farmers on my hosts' farm might hide me. So I got on a train for Ferntree Gully. It was late at night, and I tried to make myself as unobtrusive as possible. When I got to Ferntree Gully there was no bus, so I hid in the Ladies Rest Room.

I was very cold and tired, and I must have been half asleep when I heard a voice. Soon afterwards a policeman arrived, and I was taken back to my hosts' house. I was in disgrace. I can see now that they were terribly hurt, but I think I might have been a bit more hurt and upset than they were. I lay awake most of the night wondering what was going to happen.

Despite her troubles Brenda, like many others, felt torn between her own needs and 'disloyalty' to people who—whatever their faults—had taken her in and provided for her generously. Back at school she was branded by the girls as 'a sort of scarlet woman' and condemned by the headmistress as an 'ungrateful, rebellious child'. Finally, after again running away, Brenda was sent to a high school near her hosts' home where she gradually began to enjoy herself. Later, American marines flooded into the area to train nearby:

The American officers were really wonderful, very kind and good, and everything seemed a lot more human when they were around. They actually introduced a new facet of life to my maiden aunt which made my own life a little bit easier.

The most painful recollections are those involving sexual abuse. One girl, an eleven-year-old who went to stay at her uncle's farm, suffered prolonged abuse there. Soon after she arrived her uncle began to interfere with her:

Every night when I went to bed I used to pray that something would turn up so that I could get away from the whole situation. I didn't know what I would do if something didn't turn up. When the Japanese came into the war my aunt said that it would be much safer for us all to be sent inland. So my sister, two brothers and I were sent to two families in Wagga, for which I was eternally grateful.

It was terrible to live through. It made you feel, especially as you were told that you mustn't tell anybody, that it was partly your fault. There was no one to confide in. I often wished that there had been some contact with somebody from the CORB, but I never saw anybody. It stayed with me for years after I came home. I told my mother after the war, but I loved my father very dearly and I just didn't want him to know that his brother could have done such things.

At Wagga she went to live with a doctor who welcomed her as 'part of the family'. However his adult daughter was overbearing and prone to administering severe thrashings without her father's knowledge. The young girl was then sent to board at a country school. Teased unmercifully, she was almost totally shunned by other boarders:

> 'Where should I run to if I ran away?', I thought. If I went back to Wagga I would probably only have to go to a new home and it might be even worse than the boarding school. So I decided I'd just put up with it, and that's what I did until I went into hospital to have my appendix out. There I got a letter from everybody in the class saying that as I'd been a good sport I was now one of them.

The emotions generated by prolonged abuse were overwhelming. While desperate to unburden themselves to a confidant, most of the abused children had such severely damaged self-esteem and self-respect that seeking one out was virtually impossible. A conspiracy of silence between abuser and abused resulted, with the children usually shielding siblings, parents and even welfare officials from their horrors. Feeling bereft, abandoned, and almost totally alone, most put up barriers and 'withdrew'. Some, those who escaped into fantasy worlds, lived double lives: one oppressive and all too real, the other imagined and comforting.

One sister and brother, aged nine and eleven in 1940, spent almost their entire time in Australia with an aunt and uncle south of Sydney. There, domestic drudgery, niggardly allowances, draconian rules, harsh punishments and a total lack of love all combined to make their lives a misery. The sister remembers:

> We would be in trouble for the slightest reason, and felt very insecure and unloved. If [my brother] transgressed at all, or was idle and didn't do as much gardening as was expected, he would be beaten by my uncle with his belt. He was even beaten with the buckle end, which really made a mess of his back. The usual punishment was isolation in our bedrooms with no food, no drinks, not even a book.
>
> The ultimate punishment was 'Get your bags packed and get out!' I can remember quite consciously thinking, 'I'm damned if I'll take anything that she bought me'. I used to just put in my bag what was left of the things I had brought from England. I remember standing by the door with [my brother], tears streaming down, wondering where on earth we were going to go. Then she would say, 'Alright, you can stay this time'.
>
> No one else suspected what was going on. My aunt was very

charming to outsiders, and she was frequently commended for the way she had taken in two evacuees. We certainly never intimated to anyone outside that things were not as they should be. We were too frightened to do so. We assured welfare visitors that we were quite happy. I think we both felt that we could not open up as no one would have believed what was happening and we had always been told to respect adults who knew best.

These two children's letters home were always vetted, and altered to their aunt's satisfaction. The girl had little that was happy or innocent to write about. She was old—and torn by loathing and shame—before she reached her teens:

> My uncle started to touch me before the onset of puberty. I think I would have been about ten years old when he began, and it went on continually until I left—'so I would understand about men when I grew up'. There was never actual intercourse, but there was everything else. He would wait until my aunt was out, then come quietly to my bedroom and say, 'Come into my bed'. I would have to go.
>   I had an absolute dread of it happening, hating every moment of it, and hating him because of it. Also, because I allowed him to do it, I was not punished as much as my brother. Only in the last year or two have I found out that he also tried this with his other Australian nieces. They reported straight to their mother. If they knew he was like this, why did they not protect me? I was only a child.

Unable to prevent the abuse, unable to escape from her tormentor, she sometimes turned on a friend she was particularly fond of:

> We would just have a childish difference and I'd lift my hand and slap Mary hard across the face, leaving clear finger marks. I was always very upset when I'd done it, but for some unknown reason I just had to slap Mary . . . I can only think I was jealous because she was so loved.

Reg Harris, so keen to go to Australia that he had actually prayed to be sent, paid heavily for his evacuation. Only ten in 1940, he was first maltreated and exploited as cheap labour on his uncle's sheep station in Victoria. Finally he ran away. Young, alone and vulnerable, he managed to get to Melbourne where some other relatives took him in. Reg, barely tolerated there, was then sent to some strangers. 'From the first day there was criticism':

> The woman was the bottom of the pit. There were many, many difficulties, mostly associated with her being a fanatical gambler.

167

She'd play cards about five days a week at other women's homes and they would come to her house. I had to cook the tea before she got home from the cards. When I'd got that on I had to go out and garden until it was dark, and then come inside and set the table. She'd come home and put the tea out, then I'd have to wash up. I would often have to play cards with her. She was quite impossible, she had to win.

I just had to tolerate her violent behaviour and her attitude towards me because I'd been in so many places, and the Children's Welfare were probably sick of trying to find places for me. It wasn't until she was violent outside the house, in front of neighbours who complained, that the Welfare decided to do something about it.

While I was there, when I had no one else to turn to, I was attending a gymnastics class at a Methodist church. The older chap taking the class could see that I was unhappy, and he asked me to stay back afterwards so we could talk. I confided in him, but he not only talked to me—he also sexually abused me. But he did set the ball rolling, and with the people next door complaining to the Children's Welfare Department all of a sudden they took me away.

Many things that happened to me I kept to myself. People just didn't believe what some people could do to others, particularly when you're in their care.

[Later] a chap and his wife offered to keep me on a temporary basis until something permanent came along, and I went to Mr and Mrs Thomas on that understanding. They were wonderful people. I felt wanted, I was treated as one of the family. They were absolutely marvellous because they were doing these things for *me*—not for any ulterior motive.

The evacuees who spent the war in loving homes mostly recall their Australian years with nostalgia and often with delight. Many of those whose lives were only bearable remain anaesthetised in some way. And the few who were abused recall their suffering with bitter regret. Some, those who have transcended their experiences, look back on their tormentors with pity—or at least a degree of understanding: 'Although we were so vulnerable it seemed to be human nature to take from you', one says. Others, still dominated by their abuse, cannot forgive or forget.

Of all the previously unknown situations the evacuees faced in Australia none were as daunting as these instances of maltreatment or prolonged abuse. Remarkably, despite appalling experiences, these children all held on to some straw of hope. One of those worst abused, today a devoted parent, says:

I had no one to turn to with my troubles. You felt yourself just on your own, and you built a shell around yourself to try to protect your inner-self from all the things going on around you. But somehow I always looked ahead, and believed that things would be better some time.

14 _The War Drags On

If the Japanese came I wasn't running any further.

Some military genius decided that the Japanese would find the Bondi 'piers' a great advantage, so they blew them up.

THE Blitz was headline news when the CORB ships reached Australia late in 1940. Newspaper photographs of bombing raids on Britain's cities showed children crouched in trenches or bedded-down in air raid shelters. In September alone some seven thousand civilians had been killed in Luftwaffe attacks, almost one thousand of them children.

Events in Australia seemed something of a sideshow. The day the *Batory* reached Sydney, for instance, the *Sydney Morning Herald*'s report titled 'Heat Wave Chased by Breeze' was as long as one on the city's proposed air raid shelters. A 'Cigarette Drive', the paper announced, was being run 'to send smokes to the troops'. Another article warned that 'Pen-friends May Be Nazi Spies'. The United Kingdom High Commissioner urged Australians to 'spend less on things which have no relation to the war'.

About a year after the evacuees arrived the shadow of conflict with Japan became a reality. Australia was menaced as war spread into the Pacific. In the event, the Japanese attacks on the Australian continent itself proved as nothing, mere pinpricks, compared with the horrors suffered by Britain.

The evacuees, meanwhile, were marooned in Australia. Most of them took a close interest in both the European and the Pacific campaigns. Pangs of guilt troubled some. Far from home, comfortable if not always happy, they were not sharing their families' hardships and dangers.

The war, especially for the older boys, remained 'a predominant part of life' throughout their years in Australia. Wireless broadcasts were listened to nightly, often in silence, sometimes 'slavishly'. Reg Loft had 'the usual map with flags marking the European fronts and later the Japanese job'. At some schools the war was 'almost a subject'. Reg Harris' teacher had him 'draw a black-board map with the front lines to mark the way the war was going'. John Fethney, 'somewhat peeved' at the

The horrors of modern warfare: a child being rescued after a pilotless plane crashed onto a house in southern England, June 1944. The CORB evacuees, safe and spared the day-to-day hardships endured in Britain, often felt guilty at their own comfortable lives.

slight news coverage of the British Army compared with that given to the much smaller Second AIF (the Australian Imperial Forces), felt 'cut off from what the British Army was up to'. Saturday night Movietone newsreels kept Pamela Palmer 'aware not only of what was going on in New Guinea but also the war in Europe. I used to feel very saddened, say seeing Regent Street on fire and thinking "I've walked down there".'

For the evacuees perhaps the most telling accounts of the European conflict were their parents' descriptions of German bombing. Some parents, hoping to avoid needless worry, rarely mentioned the war in letters. Others, hoping to allay their children's fears, were almost totally explicit.

In Ruth Wilson's letters from home 'the war wasn't mentioned at all'. Peter Edkins' parents 'played it down so much that it was actually difficult to detect there was a war going on'. But the Cuthbert girls' father always commented on developments, and in March 1941 sent them a typed report graphically describing a near miss at their grandfather's

171

house—'a terrific bomb blast' that shattered the windows in all but one of his rooms. The Cox brothers were very distressed when a cousin 'blurted out that our house had been bombed', but later found from a letter that their parents were safe: 'The whole roof of our house had collapsed but the family were in the Anderson shelter'.

Until the Blitz ended in May 1941 the evacuees were very conscious of the dangers their parents faced. Mail delays and censorship often heightened concerns. Norman Townsend, whose brother was at sea in the Royal Navy and whose father was a poor correspondent, remembers often wondering how they were faring

> . . . until I received a copy of the local paper which described rather graphically one raid that flattened most of the houses in our street. Some of the neighbours that I'd known had been killed, which brought things home very much. From then on I was always wondering, 'Who is surviving and are they telling me the truth?'

Letters from Britain tended to be more heavily censored than those from Australia. Mary Clemes remembers hearing very little about 'the secret comings and goings of the war'. Paul Farquharson's letters to his mother

> . . . seldom, if ever, had anything chopped out, but we frequently got letters from her with whole chunks cut out, especially her news about relatives in the forces. There was this real cloak and dagger secrecy in Britain that we only saw on films in Australia.

Australia's position changed overnight when Japan attacked Pearl Harbor on 7 December 1941. A grim resolve to defeat the Japanese was born: 'Whatever our British kinsmen have endured, with unwavering fortitude, we may now be called upon to suffer too though on a lesser scale', the *Sydney Morning Herald* said two days afterwards.

The fall of Singapore on Sunday 15 February 1942 brought home the dangers to Australia. The two months since Pearl Harbor had seen a ferocious Japanese advance of bewildering speed. Singapore, the British Empire's 'impregnable fortress' in East Asia, had long been seen as the front line of Australia's defence: a tropical Maginot Line. Suddenly, ignominiously, it was gone. Some 85 000 troops were lost, some killed but most captured. Among them were many Australians. Already lost beneath the South China Sea were the British battleships *Prince of Wales* and *Repulse*. Singapore's collapse was, the *Sydney Morning Herald* said, 'the culmination of a series of disasters [which] leaves Java as the last bastion between this country and the Japanese'.

'It was a black day.' Ted Flowers, thinking of the troops he had known on the *Batory*, 'had a naive belief that good would triumph, that this was just a temporary set-back'. Tony Houghton, then working in a Fremantle office, remembers that immediately after the news of Singapore's fall was broadcast:

> People became very despondent, very quiet. They went mute, practically, until we went home. We felt that a terrible thing had happened. Most people felt apprehensive about the possibility of an invasion.

Rita Patterson was 'personally never terribly frightened' by the Japanese onslaught. But her great aunt was 'devastated' because 'she knew how many friends I had made with the soldiers on the *Batory*, and she felt that I had gone from one war and now here was another one starting'.

On 19 February, just four days after the fall of Singapore, Australia itself was under attack. The 89 Japanese bombers and fighters that raided Darwin that day killed over two hundred people. Fearing that the attacks might be 'the opening shots in the Battle of Australia' the *Sydney Morning Herald* wrote the next day: 'The news that blood has been shed and damage wrought in Darwin means to Australians everywhere that their country is at last exposed to the ordeals of merciless war'.

Fears that the entire Australian seaboard—and especially the southern cities—might now be attacked and possibly invaded galvanised the nation. For the evacuees, especially those living near Perth, the city closest to the Japanese advance, 'the war had actually reached our doorstep'. Bob Bullard recalls 'the vivid stories' of a rubber planter who had 'scrambled out of Malaya just before the Japs got there'. For John Fethney the immense difficulties of defending Australia 'were beginning to filter through, this small population in a vast country, and the sense of isolation'.

Many of the evacuees, however, aware of the horrors of the Blitz, thought the Japanese threat to Australia overrated. For one boy in the west, 'the odd Japanese submarine off the coast of Australia seemed small fry by comparison with what was going on back at home or across the Atlantic'. The bombing Peter Edkins had experienced in Liverpool was still vivid, and he was 'rather contemptuous of the Australians who panicked in certain areas after the bombing of Darwin'.

The situation of the CORB children was indeed ironic. By early 1942 Britain itself was no longer seriously threatened, while Australia was. The American forces flooding across the Atlantic virtually assured ultimate victory in Europe, but even America's power might conceivably fail to halt the Japanese in the vast Pacific. The evacuees, unable to

Japan's blistering land, sea and air advance towards Australia during early 1942 directly threatened the country. Defences around the nation's vast coastline were rapidly strengthened, as here near Darwin.

return home until victory was won, seemed to be caught in the wrong hemisphere.

On 20 March 1942, a week after General Douglas MacArthur abandoned the Philippines and moved his headquarters to Australia, CORB wrote to the children's parents to assure them that:

> . . . arrangements have been made by the Australian authorities to evacuate children from danger points if this should be considered necessary . . . Should it be decided to evacuate children from any district the parents will be informed as soon as possible.

Australia was put on full alert. City defences were strengthened: major buildings sandbagged against bomb blasts, trenches dug, gun emplacements established, air raid sirens installed, blackouts practised. Straggling barbed wire barricades were hastily erected along sections of the vast—

174

and mostly uninhabited—coastline. At Bondi, where Braham Glass lived, two concrete 'piers' jutted into the ocean:

> Some military genius decided that the Japanese would find the piers a great advantage, so early one morning they blew them up. For the rest of the war it was very easy to stub your toe on the lumps of concrete in the sand. Then they erected barbed wire halfway up the beach to stop the Japanese.

John Speller, living near Newcastle's strategic shipyards, had a host who kept a .303 rifle in the house. Every evening John, though still only at primary school, 'used to get the rifle and practise loading, aiming and firing some dummy rounds. If the Japanese came I wasn't running any further . . .' Far away in Western Australia, in a little-known vineyard community, Betty Deeley and her school friends began digging a large L-shaped trench. 'If a plane comes down and machine-guns one way, you nip into one side of the trench—and vice versa', their teacher told them. The playground, just cleared bushland, was baked: 'Digging the trench was hard work!'.

The Japanese midget submarines that slipped through the defences into Sydney Harbour on the night of 31 May 1942 brought the war to south-eastern Australia. Compared with the concurrent British raids on Cologne—on one night alone over 1000 bombers devastated the city—the damage done by the three midget submarines was forgettable. But as the *Sydney Morning Herald* said on 2 June, the attack, although 'enterprising and recklessly courageous' rather than effective, nevertheless dispelled

> . . . any lingering popular belief in southern Australia that 'it cannot happen here' . . . The risks under which Australians live belong no more to the realm of theory, nor can official warnings be regarded merely as exhortations.

In the ensuing mild panic some Australians living along the coast moved inland to be safer. Even near Albury, two hundred kilometres from the sea, Michael Storey remembers how—on the 'bush telegraph'—'the sense of jitters got passed around and there was a lot of talk about going bush'. For Heather Staff, evacuated from an industrial port in England, 'Port Kembla became almost like South Shields and people thought there was imminent danger of the Japanese landing'. A friend was taking her own children inland, and

> . . . my brother and I were invited to join them. The five of us lived in Mittagong for about six months. It was just a little fibro hut, with one bedroom, a kitchen and a living room, but we took it in our stride and had a very happy few months.

One girl's Sydney house had 'large picture windows' facing the ocean. Her hosts, rather than blacking them out, decided to move elsewhere— a few suburbs inland! The Cuthbert girls were on holiday at Pittwater, near Sydney, when the midget submarines attacked. A bushfire then burning near the coast was a more likely threat than further Japanese attacks, but their aunt and uncle led them away from the coast into some scrubby hills for the night. To avoid getting lost Helen left a trail of bread crumbs:

> We felt like Hansel and Gretel as we walked up through the smouldering trees after the bushfire. The holiday came to an abrupt end the next day and soon afterwards we were sent off to a cattle station near Yass with our cousins. We stayed there for eight months.

John Fethney, a Wollongong Scout, was sent with two hundred others to Moruya on the southern New South Wales coast. The Scouts were employed there 'putting bits of hessian into camouflage netting for aircraft'. It was piecemeal, tedious war work:

> We were down there for nearly six weeks, and it involved letting us off school for three weeks which registered how important it was . . . One afternoon a Lockheed with about a dozen Air Force officers came down, obviously for a riotous afternoon and to get some Moruya oysters.

John described his Moruya interlude in a letter to his Bradford Scoutmaster, always known as 'White Arrow'. Soon afterwards the Wollongong police called John in for questioning. They were 'dead serious':

> My letter was in the sergeant's hand, with great chunks of it to do with the visit of this Lockheed plane scored out. 'Aren't you happy out here under the British flag?', the sergeant asked. They honestly believed I was writing a letter to a spy, because of this difference between the name on the envelope, Bill Smith, and the name inside, 'White Arrow'.

The fear of further attacks—and the instances of paranoia—soon faded. The Battle of the Coral Sea, fought in early May 1942, prevented the Japanese from capturing Port Moresby and greatly boosted Australian morale. A month later the Battle of Midway, the first clear sea victory over the Japanese, proved the decisive turning point in the Pacific War. In August 1942 the Americans recaptured Guadalcanal, and a month later Australian troops began forcing the Japanese back over the Kokoda Trail in south-eastern New Guinea. Victory still lay far into the future, but Australia itself was no longer directly threatened. In the next three

Parades of departing and returning troops, often intended to boost recruitment levels or to raise war loans, became a feature of city and town life during the war years. This Melbourne march-past was for the latter purpose.

years, as the Americans and Australians slowly advanced through the islands, new names became familiar to the British evacuees: Bougainville, Manus, Guam, Halmahera, Morotai, Mindanao, Leyte . . .

Australia, meanwhile, had become a vast staging post for MacArthur's island-hopping forces. At the peak there were a quarter of a million Americans stationed in Australia, vastly outnumbering the Australian forces. In Melbourne Donald Mitchell was 'immensely impressed by the Americans' splendid new military equipment'. Peter Edkins, living near the Fremantle naval base, remembers the rivalry—and sometimes resentment—between Australian and American sailors. Joyce Briant found going to night school in Perth 'quite hazardous': the Americans 'nearly all stopped you and asked if you wanted a nice evening out'. Mary Clemes, 'somewhat galled' to think that Australia's defence depended on American not British might, found 'solace to hurt pride' when the American Liberty ships' crews 'became a laughing stock in Hobart because they couldn't find the mouth of the Derwent, and landed their vessels up in all sorts of odd places'.

As the war dragged on some evacuees grew old enough to help with war work. Ken Dommerson belonged to the Red Cross Junior Set and with his girlfriend helped at a 'Repat' hospital: 'My now wife and her sister used to go there and entertain the wounded soldiers. They played the guitar, rather badly, and sang, rather well!' Pamela Palmer managed to 'do her bit' at lunchtime:

> You could make camouflage nets for half an hour, and at Manly they had a canteen on the foreshore for hospital patients. Some of them had their arms in plaster, and we'd write letters home for them, or perhaps darn some socks.

Not everyone supported the war effort. During the severe drought on his uncle's sheep station, Reg Harris was stunned when his aunt exclaimed: 'Why don't we give it all to the Japs? There's nothing much here anyway.' To Reg the thought seemed a terrible slur on all those struggling for victory. And his later hosts' 'entire attitude was to get out of war service if possible'.

Newspapers, with their daily lists of those killed, injured or taken prisoner, brought home the sacrifices. About half the CORB children had relatives serving in the British and Australian forces. A few, how many is not known, lost fathers or brothers. There was a special poignancy in these instances where evacuees' relatives were killed. Isolated in Australia they sometimes heard the news long after the event, unable to share in their family's grief.

The shortage of shipping and the need to limit consumption forced the Australian government to introduce rationing: petrol from July 1940; tea, clothes and some other goods from mid-1942. Donald Mitchell wrote to his mother in June 1942: 'Clothes rationing starts next week but you can still get any amount of oranges, apples, bananas, grapes etc'. Clothes were later hard to come by, but rationing in Australia made people 'careful rather than threadbare'.

Sweets were another matter. Before the war 60 different kinds of halfpenny sweets filled the glass jars in corner shops. But by late 1942, with sugar rationed, the *Sydney Morning Herald* reported that only three kinds could be had—'chocolate frogs, cricket balls and clinkers'.

Rationing in Britain was far more severe, and many of the evacuees and their hosts sent food parcels 'home'. In June 1942 Donald Mitchell's host, Mona Webster, wrote to his mother: 'We've tried to get things that would be a treat, but Nestle's tinned cream is off the market for the duration'. Joyce Briant faithfully, once every month, made up a food parcel for her family in Kent. Custard powder, chocolate and jellies were often included:

> My mother liked the Oxo cubes and the chicken cubes especially, because she could make a meat meal with them. At Christmas Auntie would make a Christmas cake, Uncle would buy a special tin, we'd solder the lid on and send it off. We sent

one to my brother in Malta, but it took about three months to get there and it had gone mouldy.

Very occasionally food parcels came the other way. Christine Russon's mother, on hearing that tea was to be rationed in Australia, sent some from Britain: 'It didn't suit the Australian water at all but it was a nice gesture' Christine recalls.

Very few evacuees recall being taunted in Australia for 'running away'. However, as the war continued, a significant number themselves questioned their comfortable lives there. John Fethney, like many others, would not have experienced any bombing even if he had stayed in Britain. But, as others were, he was 'certainly aware of eating in a fairly luxurious manner compared to the way people in Britain were having to survive'. Peter Edkins, after seeing a graphic newsreel about conditions in London towards the end of the war, wrote home saying that he

felt like a rat deserting a sinking ship. My father replied very robustly. He said there was no question of that, and to make the most of the opportunities that I had in Australia.

By 1943 the oldest CORB boys were eighteen. Between then and 1945 almost seventy of them joined the services, the majority of those eligible to do so. They enlisted, John Fethney believes, partly 'to show that we hadn't run away. I've no doubt that in 1940 parents thought they were sending us to safety, but I don't think getting to safety was one of the motives in most of the evacuees' minds.'

Virtually all the evacuees who enlisted joined the Australian forces or the British Army in India. John Fethney, who in early 1945 joined up in India, chose the British Army rather than the Australian forces because of the better postwar educational opportunities for British servicemen. Tony Houghton and Phil Robinson were others who enlisted before the war ended: Tony with the Royal Australian Navy, Phil with the Royal Australian Air Force.

Not all the evacuees could enlist. Near the war's end half were still young enough to be at school, and some were pursuing further training. Some of the older boys, then serving apprenticeships, were directed to 'protected industries' by manpower regulations. Reg Loft, for instance, was working in a Melbourne foundry making 'short howitzers and seventeen-pound anti-tank guns'. 'We got fed up with not being able to get into the services because engineering was an essential industry, and they had a manpower organisation sorting out the men who were left in Australia.'

The older girls were mostly either beginning post-secondary studies or working in 'civvy street'. Some joined the women's auxiliary services, some were nursing. Mary Clemes was a student teacher, Joyce

179

Left By 1943 some CORB boys were old enough to enlist, and many later did so. Phil Robinson joined the RAAF, and trained as a pilot at Temora, NSW, in the Empire Air Training Scheme. This 1944 portrait was a Silver Wedding present for his parents. *Right* Tony Houghton in July 1944, as a RAN Officers' Steward. He trained at the Flinders naval depot, and spent the last months of the war on a corvette in the South China Sea. Tony later pursued a career in the Merchant Navy. Sadly, Tony died in July 1993 while this book was being completed.

Briant was a trained secretary, Ruth Wilson worked at the Ministry of Transport, Pamela Palmer in a Sydney bank. When Pamela was given the job

> . . . men were being called up rather quickly, and although we were a staff of seven when I started there was soon a period of ten months when we were reduced to just the manager and myself until they'd got more women trained up.

By mid-1944 it was almost certain that the Allies would finally triumph. Italy was out of the war, the Americans were 'island-hopping' northwards through the Pacific. On D-Day, 6 June 1944, the Allied armies landed in Normandy. Ten days later the Americans made their first bombing raids on a Japanese home island. Meanwhile, Hitler launched his last desperate attacks on Britain with V-1 and V-2 rockets. In a final flurry children were briefly evacuated from British cities. In September 1944 Britain's blackout was finally relaxed. A month later the Americans landed in the Philippines.

Germany surrendered unconditionally on 7 May 1945. For every CORB evacuee the victory in Europe was an enormous relief: 'a great weight rolling off you because you didn't have to worry any more'. Above all, 'Mum and Dad were safe no matter what happened now'. But for those anxious to return home, peace in Europe seemed 'something of a false finish'. Only slowly did Rita Patterson realise that 'we had to wait for another victory. It was a blow to find that I wasn't going to be on the next boat home.'

Three months later, on 14 August 1945, the Allies accepted Japan's capitulation. Tony Houghton, at sea off the Philippines in an Australian corvette, was sleeping in the shade of a lifeboat when 'the news came through'. Michael Fethney was playing a wintry game of football at Wollongong High:

> 'Dreamy' Hastings strolled off the pitch—he never did more than stroll. He came back actually in haste and announced, 'The war's over, lads. You might as well go home'. By jove, that was quite a day . . . But there was a note of gloom too, that it had required the atom bombs.

In Hobart the student-teacher Mary Clemes rushed out of her school with the others ringing the handbell. 'We rang it all the way down Elizabeth Street to the Post Office. Everybody else was congregating there . . . We just went mad. Then we all went into the Cathedral for an impromptu service of thanksgiving.' Barbara Donald heard the long-awaited news in her boarding school dormitory. An English woman teacher, her eyes wet, raced in to tell Barbara the war was over:

> The other girls couldn't understand why we were crying when we were so happy. I said, 'You go home at the end of each term and during half-terms, but I haven't seen my parents for nearly five years'. I think they began to understand.

181

15 Thoughts of Home

*My world was Australia and I was really an Australian.
But I had come away because of the war, and now I
was to go back.*

*I was an English girl waiting to come home, even though,
deep down, a little part of me was Australian.*

F OR most of the CORB evacuees, in Australia 'for the duration', peace spelt a return voyage and long-awaited family reunions. But some felt tense and uncertain. For them the war's end brought confusion and internal conflict as a troubling question came into focus: 'To which family, and in which country, do I belong?'

When the evacuees had left home most had expected to return within a year or two. Five years passed between their departure and the Allies' final triumph. By 1945 a gulf of years and experiences separated them from their parents: the youngest children had spent almost half their lives in Australia, the oldest had grown into young adults.

Many left Australia happily, though some of these planned to return. Others departed with misgivings and deep regret. For some, leaving Australia seemed a more real 'evacuation' than leaving their families in 1940: a journey taking them back to their 'roots'—but away from 'home' . . .

Meanwhile, as the war had worn on, some parents continued to agonise over whether they should have sent their children away. CORB maintained regular communication with the parents throughout. Elspeth Davies, CORB's calm and diplomatic Welfare Director in London, spent much of her time easing parents' concerns:

> I encouraged them to come and talk about anything that was worrying them. Among their friends and relations in Britain there was sometimes little understanding of why the parents had sent their children, and it was important to give them an opportunity of talking about it. They did have worries, sometimes about plans that the foster-parents were making for their children, but on the whole there was remarkable understanding between most of the foster-parents and most of the parents. Most foster-parents

By the war's end, many evacuees felt very close to their hosts, and these children often felt torn about returning home to Britain. Here, earlier in the war, Derric and Catherine Webster nestle up to their Uncle Dick and Aunty Flo (Webster).

were very good in communicating direct to the parents, and many of them really kept the children's memories of their parents alive.

CORB's correspondence with parents involved all aspects of their children's welfare and—increasingly often as the war continued—their return home. By 1943 it was clear that some children hoped to stay in Australia permanently. In November that year CORB raised the possibility of parents migrating to Australia after the war, and advised them how to apply. Four months later, in February 1944, CORB circularised parents again. While 'deeply sympathising' with the feelings of parents separated from their children for so long, the organisation advised that—despite 'the tide of war turning in our favour'—the dangers at sea and the shortage of ships meant the children could not be repatriated until victory was final.

By late 1944, no doubt aware that many of the CORB evacuees sent to Canada were returning, some parents again approached CORB about their children's repatriation. The seas around Europe were relatively safe, but the Japanese war and the distance from Australia made the return of children from there very difficult. A very few did return to Britain between late 1944 and mid-1945, but the rest remained in Australia until the Pacific war ended.

As victory approached almost all the evacuees began thinking more of 'home', though not always of returning there. As the years had passed some children's recollections of 'home' and family had remained sharp and clear. Others had faded. And—especially amongst the youngest children—some had almost entirely disappeared.

Katharine Cuthbert, although happily settled in Australia, still knew that 'we were just there for the duration, as it was put. After the duration—I don't think I quite knew what the word meant—then we would go home. We were aware that our parents were very much missing us.'

Others felt more neutral. Pamela Palmer's family in Britain had 'never faded'. But she lived in the present: 'I had a contentment here. I thought about the future, I suppose, but there was always that uncertainty about it.' Those whose time in Australia had been particularly happy, especially if they were older, often felt increasingly drawn to life there. Phil Robinson, for instance, had discovered an independence that he cherished. He did not think 'any less or any more' about his parents, but

> I was capable of looking after myself, capable of finding my way around. I was twenty in 1945. I'd become a man, more mature I think than anybody who'd remained in England would have been.

Almost all the children who had experienced unhappiness or abuse longed to be home with their parents. Barbara Donald, whose time in Australia had proved a misery, 'felt the same way about the family' in 1945 as she had five years before: 'I knew they were just waiting for us to all get back, just as much as we were waiting to go home, the sooner the better'.

The least fortunate were those who, unhappy in their family life before 1940, had also been unhappy in Australia. For them the options seemed about equally bleak. Braham Glass was one:

> My memories of England before coming to Australia were always dark grey. The colours were muted, there was no sunshine. My thoughts about Australia were like looking at sunshine through a Polaroid lens—dark, but not as dark as England. I wasn't terribly happy here in Australia, but I was happier here than I was in England.
> I can honestly say that I never entertained the thought of going home. England was the place where my parents lived. I didn't miss them, I never felt homesick, just a bit sad when I was in trouble with my aged aunt.

By late in the war many of the evacuees had firmly bonded with their relatives or foster parents. These children, however close to their own parents, valued their wartime homes and relationships—and wished to maintain them. David Massey, unaware of the possible hurt, wrote home in 1945 saying: 'I've got to stop and think sometimes . . . Mrs Edwards is not my mother but I look upon her as mother'. Michael Storey, whose father was domineering, had spent five years with a couple who had given both confidence and interest to his life. He felt torn between 'duty' and 'warmth':

> I had little arguments with myself. I used to say, perhaps I should think of Mummy and Daddy more often and in a better light—as they *are* my mother and father. But they were so distant. Cissie and Bob Wilson had been my aunt and uncle, they'd looked after me and I was part of their life. They were part of my life in Australia and I wanted to make my life there.

Many of the older evacuees had also formed independent relationships. Earlier in the war boyfriends and girlfriends were mostly passing teenage passions, but by 1945 a number of the 'children' were engaged—often further complicating their thoughts about returning to Britain.

Some evacuees found it increasingly hard to visualise their parents and siblings. Film was difficult to obtain in Britain, and photographs sent to Australia rare. Heather Staff could clearly remember only her father. Moreover, with a baby grown to a young child and another one born during the war, she thought 'It was a completely new family that I was going home to'. For Michael Fethney, 'conjuring up a mental picture of my mother, father, and sister became more and more difficult, and eventually impossible'. Joan Sharp was barely seven when she left home:

> My memories faded as the years went by and later I thought of my parents very little. About two or three years after I'd arrived here I began to doubt whether the letters I was getting were actually from my Mum. I remember thinking that perhaps my parents were dead and that that had been caused through the war. I don't really know why . . .

In a very few instances one or other parent had died or been killed, and a handful of evacuees heard in Australia that their parents were separating or divorcing.

CORB get-togethers in Australia might have helped resolve some of these conflicts, by allowing evacuees to share their thoughts and feelings about 'home' with others who could understand. However, very few CORB gatherings were held during the war.

The evacuees' thoughts about their future sharpened after Germany's surrender. They came into still sharper focus after the victory over

Relatively few CORB get-togethers were arranged during the war years. This one, organised for the Tasmanian children to mark their first year in Australia, was held in Government House, Hobart. The formality was softened with Mickey Mouse and Goofy coasters!

Japan. On 16 August 1945, the day after the Japanese surrender was accepted, the *Sydney Morning Herald* reported that Sydney's 'immense crowds' were gripped by 'delirious joy' and 'unprecedented emotion and gaiety'. The King's broadcast of thanksgiving, published the same day, read in part: 'Let us pray that one of the results of beating Japan may be many happy reunions of those who have long been separated from each other . . .'

For the CORB evacuees the King's message held both a promise and a caution. The war was over: all who wished to could now return to their parents. But was 'home' now to be found in Britain—or in Australia?

Evacuees, parents and hosts often had mutually antagonistic desires. About half the evacuees felt that they belonged with their family in Britain, and about a quarter felt that they belonged in Australia with their host family. The remainder were uncertain. Of the parents, three-quarters wished their children to return. However, almost all the parents of those children who wished to stay in Australia wanted them to come home. Of the hosts, about half hoped—at least vaguely— that 'their' children might stay on. The 'transfer of population of a novel character', predicted by a CORB official when the children reached Australia in 1940, was for many to prove distressing.

For some, whatever their own inclinations, the choice was clear-cut. Ken Dommerson saw 'no question whatsoever'—'I looked upon going back to England as a duty and would have done so no matter what'. The Cuthbert girls' relatives, much as they would have liked them to stay, 'made it very clear' that they felt it was right that the children should go back to their parents. 'We had become part of their lives and would leave a gap, but in the selfish way of young children I was much more aware of what I was going to gain by returning.' For those whose lives had been miserable there was a powerful need to 'escape' as much as to 'return'. Australia, for Heather Staff,

> . . . could have been a very happy experience if it hadn't been for our home life. All the people that I knew had always been very kind to us, but the separation combined with this feeling at home made it a very bad experience.

Some others, although they experienced deep conflict about whether or not to return, were still determined to do so. Rita Patterson 'sounded Australian, and had studied Australian history and geography'. In fact, 'My world was Australia and I was really an Australian'. But she was nevertheless intent on going home:

> My great aunt and uncle had made me theirs. But I had come away because of the war, and now I was to go back. I was quite single minded about it. There had never been any thought that I would stay, it had never crossed my mind. My home was home—and like a lot of other evacuees, to me I was always going home . . .

Some evacuees, like John Hillier, consoled themselves with the thought that returning to Britain need not be final. He left 'with the feeling that I would go back to England, see what had happened, and then probably return'.

The love some children had found with their hosts in Australia could not easily be let go—and vice versa. Some childless hosts, numb with sadness, planned to adopt other children to fill the coming gap. Joan Sharp, almost twelve, was initially delighted to know she was returning. Her thoughts about departing palled as the realisation of leaving her Australian relatives penetrated: 'I didn't want to go, and it had a very unsettling effect on me. Home was England, as it always is for a Pom, but my real home was here in Australia.' John Speller, the boy who initially went hungry, had 'never liked change'. With the Ruggs, his second hosts, he had found security and love. Now—'I was going to have to leave all that and start back again at home with surroundings that were unknown':

> By 1945 I was 14, and I was beginning to think for myself. I had made very definite and strong bonds with the family that I was staying with. So it was much harder to leave them than it had been to leave my mother and brother in 1940.

Joyce Briant's hosts were 'devastated' when she told them she was going back to England. Then engaged to an Australian who was beginning two years' theological training, Joyce planned to return to Australia and marry when his course was finished: 'I'd got to like Australia very much, and I always wanted to come back'. Pamela Palmer wanted to stay, but felt an 'obligation' to see her parents. Engaged to an Australian serviceman then in Germany, she decided to return to England 'for a period', marry there, and then come back to Australia with her husband.

> I'd mapped out in my mind that I was going to do the right thing by both my parents and my hosts, that was to go home and stay for a while and then come back to be with my Aussie parents. I thought I had reached a compromise that would hopefully satisfy both sets of parents.

Joyce and Pamela both returned to Britain. But in the end both stayed there, their engagements ended.

Some evacuees hoped their parents would migrate, so resolving their parent–host dilemma. Reg Harris, despite his having been abused, loved Australia and its life. His parents were amongst the small number who did migrate soon after 1945. Had they not, Reg 'would have gone back to see them' but not to stay. However, most parents were unwilling to leave Britain. Tony Houghton raised the issue, but his parents felt too settled. 'I'm sure they would have made a go of it, but they didn't want to come. I preferred to come home to my parents than stay in Australia without them.'

Educational options complicated the choices facing many older evacuees. Peter Edkins knew his life in Australia was far better than what he would find in Britain, and returned mainly to pursue his engineering in London. Despite their heartbreak his hosts told him: 'You must go back to your parents, that's where your education is'. Mary Clemes, part-way through her teacher-training in Hobart, 'wasn't in any great hurry' to return—and when she left for Britain felt 'a lot of heartache, wondering whether I'd ever come back'. Paul Farquharson 'always intended to return home'. But in 1945, with his parents' and hosts' support, he stayed in Perth to complete an apprenticeship—and

188

The poignance of many evacuees' Australian leave-takings is captured here. Francis Woods (*centre*) did not sail for Britain until well after the war. His Aunt Nelly (*right*), with whom he had stayed, returned with him to visit 'home'. But Francis' girlfriend, Vanda Jones (*left*), remained in Sydney. Francis and Vanda still correspond.

only finally returned to Britain, after flying as an aircraft engineer in India, in June 1948.

The evacuees who did not return home were, almost without exception, the older ones. Those aged eighteen or over were legally able to decide their future. David Massey, very settled in Werribee, Victoria, had almost no desire to return home. But he was only seventeen:

> If my parents had said I could stay, I would have. But a welfare official told me, 'If your parents say you've got to return then you've got to return'. If I could have got the clock to stand still, I would have. I did not want to go back.

A few of the older evacuees never went back to Britain. Bob Puxted stayed farming and working around Newcastle. Ted Flowers, studying at Sydney University, was determined to stay on. For him Australia was 'a land of opportunity'—and he felt an Australian. 'I had cut myself loose from any close family ties, and over the next few years I constantly made excuses not to go back.' His mother visited him once, but did not stay.

Some evacuees returned only after the lapse of decades. Norman Townsend was one. Despite loving his father, he had found a richer life in Sydney with Hamish. The doctor, very fond of Norman, had talked of adopting him but also kept alive Norman's memory of his father. By the war's end Norman 'wanted to go back but didn't know how to go back'. He was then eighteen:

> Hamish and my father were two distinct men in my mind. My father was still my father, but I was also extremely fond of Hamish. If it had come to the point of Hamish adopting me there would have been a deal of soul-searching on my part. But, knowing Hamish, he would not have adopted me unless I had gone back to talk with my father. To have been brought up as Hamish's son would have been a privilege but there would still be that old blood and water tie to my father—which [is rather belied by] the fact that I never ever saw him again.

Anxious to repatriate the evacuees quickly, CORB was ready to begin embarking them following the Japanese surrender. But, as in 1940, ships were scarce. The war had decimated the merchant fleets, and in August 1945 there were more urgent voyages. Many ships were sailing mercy missions to Asia and the Pacific, taking food and medicines for prisoners-of-war and internees released by the Japanese—and, afterwards, repatriating the victims.

It was only as berths became available on ships bound for Europe, often with only a few weeks' warning, that the evacuees could leave. Most sailed in small groups on ships departing from mid-October 1945 onwards. By February 1946, when CORB officially closed, 446 of the original 577 had returned home or were about to. The last CORB evacuees left Australia in early March 1946.

The farewells, even of those happy to leave, were often harder than when the evacuees had left Britain. In 1940 the sense of crisis and wartime secrecy had lent necessity and speed to partings. In 1945, in far happier times and with departures talked about, more people were involved in the partings: schools, work places, churches, families, boyfriends, girlfriends. The evacuees had matured, their feelings ran deeper. For John Hillier, the boy for whom a window had symbolised the finality of his evacuation in 1940,

> The leavings were two different things entirely, different ages and different emotions. Leaving Melbourne was probably less emotional than leaving home. But we were leaving people who we were very attached to, a whole circle of friends—whereas in 1940 we were leaving mainly our mother, father and sister.

Once again came bittersweet moments. In Western Australia Bob Bullard packed a large wooden box with his treasured possessions, saying: 'I'll just have a look at everything in England then come straight back'. In Brisbane Gerald and David Cox went searching for 'Bobby', the family's blue heeler cattle dog, 'a law unto himself'. Sensing that the boys were leaving, the dog had hidden under the house. 'We found him and said goodbye . . . It was very difficult. Saying goodbye to an animal is saying goodbye forever.' Phil Robinson, surrounded by tall seas of sugar cane, stood on a Queensland country rail platform with his uncles. CORB had not advised him that, aged twenty, he could have chosen to stay:

> I was saying goodbye, and wanting desperately, so desperately hard, to just say, 'I don't want to go. Please can I stay behind?' I felt it was my duty to go back, but there was one enormous internal turmoil in those few minutes. I can't remember going down to Brisbane, I can't remember getting on the boat . . .

Braham and Essie Glass had occasionally seen their rich uncle during the war. Now, 'in yet another American car', he gruffly collected them from their Bondi bungalow and drove them to Wolloomooloo. They stopped at the children's great-uncle's home. It was early morning:

> The window flew up and my great-uncle looked out in his pyjamas. My uncle said, 'The kids are going back to England, governor'. My great-uncle looked at us and said, 'Goodbye'—and closed the window. We were taken down to the *Stirling Castle*, where a photograph was duly taken of my sister and I with our aunt. Then my aunt said 'Goodbye', turned around and walked away . . . and that was that.

For Heather Staff, leaving an unhappy home, 'the excitement of packing to go home was unbelievable'. The long-awaited day finally came. Heather, her brother Denis, their aunt and uncle and some other relatives went together to the Sydney docks. Some of the relatives 'were very distraught'. Heather 'just could not raise a tear'—indeed felt 'quite guilty because in no way could I feel any sadness'. Neither could her brother.

Escorted by her great aunt and uncle Rita Patterson boarded the *Andes*, then went to find her cabin. 'Uncle Tom inspected it, and I was exclaiming about how wonderful it was.' When Rita turned around her aunt and uncle had gone. 'I ran after them and saw them disappearing down the gangway but they didn't look back.' Her uncle wrote later to say that he had had to take Rita's aunt away—'there was no way that she could stay to say goodbye'. The couple were again childless.

Joan Sharp had been seven when she left Britain in 1940, carefree and unknowing, baffled by her grandmother's tears. Now, on 26 October

The CORB evacuees mostly left Australia between mid-October 1945 and February 1946. The *Stratheden*, which had accompanied the *Batory* to Australia in 1940, sailed from Sydney on 26 October 1945 with twenty-seven evacuees—when this photograph was taken by one of the foster parents.

1945, a spring morning five years to the month since she arrived in Sydney, Joan was taken to Pyrmont to embark:

> I remember being quite excited when I saw the *Stratheden*, but not wanting to say goodbye—hanging round my aunty's neck, crying, not wanting to get on board that blasted ship. My cousins, Peter and Pat, didn't realise what was going on. I learned later that Peter (born during the war) was desperately asking, 'But why does Joan have to go?'.

The *Stratheden* steamed out through the Heads later that day carrying 27 evacuees. A week afterwards the ship left Fremantle, having collected more CORB children there and in Melbourne. In Fremantle Peter Edkins' parting from the Gallops had been 'emotional'. But, once beyond Rottnest Island, the first Australian land sighted five years before, his thoughts of the voyage ahead eased the pangs of parting:

> There was this new ship. I'd enjoyed the *Batory* and here was the *Stratheden*, the ship I'd looked at off our starboard beam for weeks and weeks in 1940. Four weeks, with a stop at Bombay again, and then back up through the Suez Canal—back home on 3 December. Miss Pearson, my escort coming out, had married an Australian clergyman, and she was our guide going back.

The evacuees' voyages home were far more carefree than their wartime voyages to Australia. Here, in March 1946 aboard the *Rangitiki*, Tony Houghton (*background*) and some other CORB evacuees gather on deck around their two Salvation Army escorts.

On the morning of the day he was to leave Australia another of the *Batory* evacuees crossed the creek into the house paddock for the last time—to gaze in awe at the primeval beauty of the Illawarra escarpment. Later that day, by coincidence aboard the *Nestor* this time, he sailed southwards from Sydney leaving Wollongong and the Illawarra to starboard:

> I could see every detail of the coast, from Bald Hill right down to Bulli Pass and Sublime Point, Mount Kembla and Mount Kerra. Gradually the sunset lit up the escarpment. You could see every bump that I knew so well—this wonderful part of the country I'd been living in these last five years.

Another evacuee had been in tears at home on the last morning. Later, aboard a train bound for Port Melbourne, this seventeen-year-old stared fondly at Werribee and its cattle pens until they were lost to sight.

We sailed about seven. As the last streamer snapped I kept shouting 'I'll be back! I'll be back!' As we sailed down Port Phillip Bay I could see the lights from the shore, and I like to think I could see the lights from South Werribee. Standing there I was wishing that the umbilical cord could not be broken—but it was broken—and I entered a new phase of my life.

Australia had left an indelible impression on the CORB children. And, whatever their experiences there had been and whatever their feelings as they sailed back across the oceans, all had been spared the direct impact of war. Countless other children elsewhere had been less fortunate. One CORB evacuee remembers another girl travelling home to Britain on her ship. She was a survivor of the Japanese camps: '. . . a young girl of about fifteen who just hadn't developed at all. She was a little thin child with no bosoms, no shape, with arms and legs like sticks.'

Back in Britain

16

I went back to England with a great deal of anxiety.
I didn't know what I was going to find.

It was just heavenly to be home again, all of us under
the same roof.

THE ships that brought the CORB evacuees back reached Britain in late 1945 and early 1946. Their voyages had been uneventful. But, as the evacuees steamed 'homewards', undercurrents of regret and uncertainty at leaving Australia mingled with thoughts of coming reunions.

Newspapers and newsreels seen in Australia had shown the bombing and hardship suffered by Britain. But the scale of the destruction, the dismal heartbreak, the real hunger—these waited to greet the returning 'children'. As they left Australia, newspapers there were publishing 'grim warnings' of epidemics and mass starvation amongst Europe's countless displaced people.

Most evacuees knew they themselves had changed. Many realised or guessed their parents had also. But few could grasp the depth of the differences. Even those whose parents had maintained close contact felt apprehensive about meeting their families.

Many homecomings were joyful, others more tentative. Some were bleak and distant. Often, though not always, these initial encounters set patterns for the months and years to come . . .

But, as the returning evacuees passed the Bay of Biscay, Britain still loomed ahead. One boy thought, 'Good grief, I'm almost home again'. Then, 'But this isn't home—my home should be Australia'. A girl, one from a particularly close family, sat on a darkened deck lost in thought: '"Will I recognise them?" Photos had gone to-and-fro and of course I knew exactly what they looked like. But I still had this awful sinking feeling, "What will it actually be like?".'

The British ports at which the evacuees disembarked were a world away from the Indian or Pacific Ocean ports they had visited. 'It was intriguing to see England again, everything was so muted, so sombre, compared with the brilliance of Bombay and Fremantle', one evacuee recalls. For another, 'there was this heavy overcast, the rain was horizontal and it was sleeting'. But Britain, war-damaged and in mid-winter,

195

A group of Australian CORB evacuees photographed aboard the *RMS Andes*
on their arrival at Southampton. This arranged photograph, and the children's
expressions, camouflage the uncertainties that some were no doubt feeling about
returning home.

could still move Rita Patterson. As her ship steamed up Southampton
Water, she

> couldn't believe the beautiful green—it was all green and it was
> mine. There was a band on the dock, and I cried and cried. The
> next morning there was ice crackling on the ground. It was
> lovely!

On arrival, virtually all the others found Britain dispiriting: 'We disembarked onto a small island that was approaching winter' . . . 'Everything seemed grey, everything seemed small' . . . 'There was no colour'
. . . 'It was dingy, dismal, austere, awful' . . . 'Everything was cold, dark
and drab' . . . The people looked 'tired and worn', the cities 'dirty, war-
damaged and very different from attractive Australia'. Michael Fethney,
who disembarked in Liverpool, was stunned. This was not the Illawarra:

> The train journey from Liverpool to Bradford was increasingly
> depressing. It wasn't so much the bomb damage but the fact that

it was getting misty and murky—just four o'clockish and it was getting dark.

Heather Staff, travelling home on a train to Carlisle, chewed through every finger of her gloves—'literally'. But at Carlisle she 'fell out of the train into her family's arms'. Heather, Denis and their parents 'knew each other immediately'. Christine Russon's father—'a really burly Yorkshireman'—was in tears. So was her mother. 'I remember putting my arms around them and saying, "It's all right, we're home now"'. The Russons' street was 'decked with bunting and flags'. Nora Lupton's family had saved a tin of salmon for years to celebrate her homecoming; the sandwiches were a rare treat. Another girl, not aware of how precious they were, was given some chocolates.

In 1940, when the *Batory* reached Sydney Rita Patterson had been thrilled to see the Harbour Bridge, so like one she knew well. Rita realised she was home when, from a train, she glimpsed the Tyne Bridge again:

> As we pulled into the platform I saw Mum, her two sisters and my gran. They all ran along the platform, I leapt out—I'll never forget it—to see them all again. My Dad was standing quietly at the back, waiting for all the women to get their tears over. Dad had hired a taxi, which was a big thing then, and we cried and cried the whole way home. It was so cold, but it was lovely to be home. Mum and I shared the same bed that night. I kept getting up to get things out of my case to show her, and we talked until the day broke.

Not all family reunions were so joyful. Peter Edkins and his father met in London, at Waterloo. They only half-recognised one another, once again joking to cover their unease: 'I remember distinctly saying to him, "Your name *is* Edkins, isn't it?" '. Some instances of 'lack of re- cognition' covered a deeper gulf. John Speller, waiting alone on a station, was finally met by a mother who 'stood some distance away and didn't recognise me'. She was the same mother who, a few years before, had coldly told John in a letter that his father had 'gone'. The Clout children returned from Tasmania to discover that their parents had separated.

David Massey, standing in a Customs shed still thinking of Werribee, heard a woman say 'Which one is David Massey?' It was his mother. David turned away, began to walk away—'But somebody stopped me and said, "Is that your mother there?".' Barbara Helliwell, still numbed by her vagabond years, stood on Leeds Station:

> There was a heavy mist swirling and everyone had gone. I'd passed this couple about three times. They didn't know it was their daughter, and I didn't know it was my parents. I felt so lonely, as if I was the only person left in the world . . .

197

Barbara Helliwell (*left*) aged fourteen, reunited with her parents and sister Andrea in 1945. A family photograph taken five years before, with Andrea still a baby, had been inscribed 'Parting Casts its Shadows'. For Barbara, Australia had held other 'shadows'.

Braham Glass had found Southampton's weather and bomb damage 'one hell of a shock'. Now, back in London, 'two little old people' came down the platform:

> I just stood there, just being embraced, not embracing back—and they were my parents. They were terribly happy to see us, but I wasn't the least bit happy to see them. My sister had exactly the same feeling.
>
> I think we had forgotten the past unhappiness in the family. But I wasn't used to being embraced—after five years of unembraceable existence—and I felt awkward. We were taken home to this block of flats that had suffered some bomb damage. I can still remember the depression, *looking* at this building after the sunshine of Australia. I said to my sister, 'I'm getting out of here'.

For Joan Sharp, returning was 'a great relief' . . . an immediate let-down . . . and a continuing disappointment. The girl who had fantasised that her parents were dead, the girl who had lived in comfort at Number One, Woniora Road, Hurstville, stepped out of a taxi into the darkness of Manchester:

> My mum said, 'Look up, Joan!' What she wanted me to see was a Union Jack and a huge sign, 'Welcome Home, Joan'. But what

I saw was this row of very dark, miserable-looking terrace houses.

Inside I was asked to sit down at the table. There was no bathroom, I had to go into the scullery and wash my hands in the sink. When I sat down I had a small plate with a slice of boiled ham. I looked to the left and there was no bread and butter plate or knife. I had no napkin, and in the middle of the table was a bowl of tomatoes and a huge plate of bread, already buttered and cut in halves. I'd never seen that before. And that was the meal.

The following morning I pulled the curtains open. All I could see was the backs of these terraces, no gardens, and in the next street was a big woollen mill. I wondered what on earth I was doing there.

For five years letters had been the only real communication between the evacuees and their parents. Their regularity or infrequency, their intimacy or distance, reflected family attitudes—and affected the ease or otherwise of homecomings. Those children and parents who had written about the changes they were living through bonded again more easily. But some experiences were very hard for others to comprehend; some went so deep they could barely be mentioned.

Children who had grown up and matured often found parents whose wartime hardships had aged them prematurely. Betty Deeley and her brother, both adolescents, found a father who 'seemed to have shrunk. It was hard to recognise him at first because he looked so ill.' A foundry worker, he was suffering from emphysema. Paul Farquharson did not recognise his mother when he returned in 1948:

> She had dark hair when I left, and she was almost white when I got back. She'd lost a son at sea, she had two sons in Australia, and she'd had to cope with my younger brother growing up when my father was frequently away for long periods.

Some parents had suffered still more severely. For these the horrors of the war—the Blitz, the fears of screaming bombs and crashing masonry—often only surfaced afterwards as nightmares and phobias which shadowed the future.

Sunderland's shipyards had been heavily bombed and many nearby houses destroyed. Ruth Wilson returned there to an emotional home-coming, when she gave back the gold watch her mother had entrusted to her in 1940:

> My mother had been very badly affected by the war, psychologically more than anything else. She'd taken the other children to a very isolated spot in the country. My father had to

199

stay in Sunderland because of his job, and the house two doors from ours was totally demolished by a bomb. My mother was worried about what was happening to me, the family was split up, and then she lost a baby.

There was a lot of heartache. It was a real struggle for me, for quite a while, to come to terms with meeting up with the family again, having been totally estranged from them. I had this feeling of separation, of being cut off—I was outside the window, looking in.

The older 'children', especially the girls, often found their new-found maturity reflected in their family relationships. Mary Clemes and her mother could now 'talk as equals'. Mary was surprised and pleased: 'I found I could be much more frank and open with her'.

The children most profoundly changed by their evacuation were those who had been abused. Some revealed all their horrors, others could tell only part of what had happened. Reg Harris' parents, by then in Australia, were appalled by his frank revelations. His mother was adamant that she could never again face 'the trauma of knowing or imagining that things were going wrong'. One of the girls who had been sexually abused was never able to tell her mother or father about it. Some years after marrying she finally told her husband. But Heather and Denis Staff were 'fairly open' about most of their experiences:

Our parents were very indignant, and my mother was very regretful that she had ever sent us. I think that had been so ever since the day we'd gone, but more so when she found out what had actually happened.

It took us a while to get trusting again. My mother was very possessive, and tried to show her affection by cuddling a lot. I had been so unused to that for so long that I couldn't handle it. She didn't seem to understand, and we had a little difficulty over that. Also the first month I was home I didn't have a period, and she was very concerned in case I'd become pregnant. The trauma of returning had stopped it.

Some CORB families, after the anguish of their lost years, were determined to push their five-year separation into the past. For others, however, the reunion marked the beginning of ever-deepening divisions. Many of the children settled into home easily and enjoyed renewing their family life. But about half the returned evacuees felt tense and distant. And some parents and children looked at one another across an unbridgeable gulf. The parents of these children and young adults could barely comprehend the changes in their offspring—who, often, felt equally perplexed.

The family reunions concentrated into days changes that families ordinarily experience over years. The degree of parental understanding and patience concerning this 'telescoping' of change drastically affected each evacuee's reintegration into the family. A 'here and now' attitude, tempered by parental interest in the Australian years, helped. So too did the natural closeness of families, the warmth and regularity of wartime letters, and similarities between the Australian and 'home' families. Lack of acceptance that the children were older and more independent tended to force parents and children apart, as did major changes in family structure since 1940. Resentments at the evacuees' 'easy' war, at their more affluent lives in Australia, or at bonds forged with their Australian hosts were always counterproductive.

Tony Houghton thought his parents 'looked rather drab'. But the pleasure of being reunited pushed aside superficial appearances: 'We'd never been out of touch. It was as if we'd never been away, we all just fell back into routine and everything went swingingly'. For Barbara Donald 'it was just heavenly' to be home again, 'all under the same roof . . . There was the same family feeling that had always been there.'

Helen and Katharine Cuthbert 'slotted back amazingly quickly' into the family's life. The girls, immediately and totally accepted, were not made to feel restricted at all. For Katharine,

> The house was just as I had remembered it. Bridget was thrilled to see us and seemed very grown up. She was nine, having been four when we left. But Jill, who was just five and whom we'd never known, was extremely shy and wouldn't really talk to us. Bridget had related to us throughout our time in Australia, but Jill couldn't at all.
>
> We continued to write to our aunts in Australia, but it was with nothing like the same regularity that we'd written home when out there. We didn't forget them, but I ceased to feel part of their lives in the way that, while out there, I'd still felt part of Scotland.

Joyce Briant's mother seemed 'a bit of a stranger'. Their terrace house had been bombed, and Joyce returned to another one nearby. But she still 'slipped back in where I'd come out of':

> On the boat going out we made our bunks every day, and in Australia I used to make my bed every morning. When I came home, the first morning I left the bed for my mother to make— and she made it! Later Mum asked me to walk up and get some groceries at the local Co-op. When I got to the till the girl said, 'What's your number?' 'Two one three six . . .' I hadn't said the number for nearly six years but I knew it.

For some returned evacuees the process of mixing into family life was more gradual and uncertain. Christine Russon and her sister had been slightly spoiled in Australia. On returning they had 'all the glory and all the fuss', they were sometimes too demanding—and so they upset a younger sister used to being the eldest. John Speller had never been as close to his mother as to his father. Now his father was gone. His mother tended to treat him as an eight-year-old—yet there was friction with a younger brother who 'bitterly resented' John 'acting the father'. Michael Fethney's evident enthusiasm for his life in Australia sometimes created unease. His mother 'felt that life in Bradford was being unfavourably compared to life in Wollongong'.

> That wasn't my intention although I'm sure I wasn't totally blameless, because I was sometimes so upset at my mother's resentment that total strangers had shared those five lost years that I said things to irk her.

A virtual chasm lay between some parents and their children. A significant number of CORB families never effectively revived—or built—meaningful bonds. Brenda Mallett and her mother were 'like two strangers'. Brenda, unable to confide in her mother, could not shed the hurt she had felt in Australia. Soon after returning came the letter Brenda had asked for from Stefan, her *Batory* 'uncle'. He had lost his wife and son, victims of the Nazi occupation of Poland. Unsympathetic, overbearing, Brenda's mother

> . . . also decided that the friendship should not continue. She told me that she had approved of my guardians' action in preventing Stefan corresponding. My mother took the letter and the envelope with his address and burned it—the end of a beautiful friendship.

Isabella Woods had been happy in Australia. Tyneside's severe bomb damage was dispiriting, her family's nightmare memories of the war another burden. When she arrived home,

> The foghorn was blowing and the shipyard buzzer was blowing. I thought, 'Oh dear, what have I come back here for?' It was exciting for the first month because I had so many people to see, people who wanted to know everything about my life in Australia. I was a VIP—but then it all collapsed.
> We were four strangers living in a house. The bond had gone, absolutely completely gone. My father gave a party and he stood up and said, 'My daughter's home now for good. She'll never leave us again'. I hadn't the heart to tell him but I thought, 'I'm definitely not going to stay here'. My mother wouldn't talk about anything. We remained friends, but the mother–daughter relationship had gone completely.

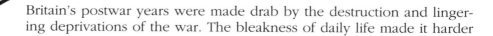

Britain's postwar years were made drab by the destruction and lingering deprivations of the war. The bleakness of daily life made it harder still for children to readjust, especially where family troubles also existed.

'England seemed claustrophobic' say many of the evacuees. Houses seemed suddenly to have shrunk, there was scarcely space to turn. Ken Dommerson, 'more or less obliged to stay inside' to escape the cold, remembers 'heavy curtains at the windows and the doors'. Life for children used to being out-of-doors seemed 'condensed'. Donald Mitchell was 'full of nostalgia for the Pacific seas and the bush'. He wrote 'increasingly gloomy' poems: 'For four long weeks I haven't seen the sun . . .' one began.

The severity of postwar rationing surprised many of the evacuees. The Cox brothers found people's clothing 'very drab'. Their parents were 'hard put to it to clothe us all properly'. Food rationing was even more keenly felt: 'food was still very scarce', and some people as a consequence were disgruntled and dissatisfied. Ken Dommerson returned with a few bags of rice and sugar, and the resulting rice pudding was 'a big occasion'. Fish was not rationed, and 'eating herrings till you were fed up' was common.

Ruth Wilson remembers 'snow in the streets and ice everywhere' that first winter of 1945–46. Local people 'with sacks and sledges were flocking down to the beach' to fossick amongst outcrops for coal. Joan Sharp's father warmed her hands with hot water from the kettle on the stove. Allowed only a small amount of coal each week,

> At night we would let the fire die down and then back it up with tiny pieces of coal and shovelfuls of slag. My grandmother and I used to take an old stroller and some bags to where the trucks from the coal mine tipped the slag, and we'd pick out pieces of coal from the rucks.
>
> We'd always had bananas in Australia, but in England they were almost non-existent. If the fruit shop had any the word got around like wildfire. You could only get a banana if you had a green ration book, if you were under eighteen or pregnant.

If such rationing was alien to children used to antipodean affluence and plenty, so too were the barriers of British class-consciousness to young people impressed by Australia's more egalitarian life. Some of the evacuees felt a guilty disdain for their parents' seemingly narrow and unambitious lives. Many felt 'cut off' from their peers.

'Britain was very tight, very structured and socially conscious', Betty Deeley decided—'people seemed to exist in cliques' more than in Australia. At work her broad Australian accent baffled the others: 'They used to sit me down every afternoon and give me lessons on how to speak English'. On arriving in Australia in 1940 Braham Glass had found 'nothing in common' with his new school friends:

The first full winter in Britain for the returned children was that of 1947, photographed here near Joyce Briant's home in Kent. Some evacuees were overjoyed at seeing snow again, others yearned for Australia's sunshine.

Five years later it was the same. I had been brought up on chocolate milk shakes, McNivens ice cream, Marchant's lemonade, and *Search for the Golden Boomerang*. When I got back to England I found I had no shared memories with my contemporaries, and I couldn't discuss these things.

Worse still, the evacuees had few memories of the war in Britain and none of the worst periods of the Blitz. The mild guilt some had experienced in Australia often intensified when they returned. For Mary Clemes

. . . looking down on all the bomb damaged buildings, the squalor and the dirt, and talking to people about the experiences they'd had—that was what started me feeling guilty about having been to Australia. It seemed awful to have missed all that.

Instead, the CORB evacuees had voyaged across the world and spent five years in Australia—experiences that were to affect and often shape their future lives. When they left Australia each was presented with a government booklet. The lavishly photographed, thirty-page publication recorded their lives there and the country itself, and was clearly intended to entice the evacuees and their families back as postwar

Many CORB evacuees felt at least a degree of disquiet at not having shared the war's hardships, such as those experienced by these customers queuing at a wartime fruit barrow amidst bomb-scarred buildings.

migrants. Arthur Calwell, the Minister for Immigration and Information in October 1945, wrote in the introduction:

> Australia has tried to be a true friend to you, and we feel sincerely, now that you are going home, that you will be true friends to Australia for the remainder of your lives ... At some future time, we hope to see you back in this sunny land, if not to make your homes here, at least to visit us and renew the friendships that you have made during your stay with us ... To those remaining in Australia, I am happy to convey the nation's sincerest wishes for your happiness and success as Australian citizens.

Despite Calwell's hint most CORB evacuees finally made their homes in Britain. Many of these, however, stayed only because of family ties and some still yearn for Australia. Others, unhappy in Britain and missing Australia, emigrated in the late 1940s and early 1950s. In subsequent decades still others finally decided to follow their hearts and migrate. About a third of the CORB evacuees live in Australia today.

Some evacuees had always known that Britain was 'home'—and would be forever. And even of those who had planned to return to Australia many soon settled firmly back into life in Britain. Generally their future was sealed within a year or two of their returning, often with only mild regret. Joyce Briant, by 1946 engaged to a childhood friend, 'loved living in Kent so I made up my mind to enjoy life there'. Barbara Donald, happy to be near her family, decided to work for Barnardos helping children. John Hillier, like many others, decided he could not justify 'just upping and leaving' his parents again:

> You were torn a little. I think we did say to our parents, 'Would you like to go to Australia?' But they weren't interested in cutting their roots, and so we decided we would stay. If we got the opportunity of going back to Australia later—then so be it.

Others who settled in Britain were, at least for some years, much more 'torn'. Rita Patterson, despite her joyful homecoming, soon began to feel swamped by her four siblings. She missed her great aunt and uncle. She missed Wollongong. Indeed, although her parents were 'totally against it', Rita 'growingly got the feeling' that she should have stayed in Australia:

> Eventually, after much upset, my mother said that if that was the way I felt I could go. I wrote and said I would come back, but then realised that it was the wrong decision. My family was here on Tyneside and this was where I belonged.

David Massey, too young to opt to stay in Australia, was too old to escape from Britain . . . Two days after getting home to Liverpool, he

> . . . went down to the shipping pool to try to enlist in the Merchant Service. A chap there asked how old I was. 'I've just turned seventeen', I said. 'Oh', he said, 'that's a pity. If you'd have been sixteen we could have taken you on as a boy.' I was on the point of doing one of two things: I was either going into the Navy or I was going to emigrate. But then I met my wife and I suppose I thought that we'd see if anything developed. It did . . .

Whatever the appeal of their families and of Britain, some who returned there were determined to make their future in Australia. A number, like Paul Farquharson, Mary Clemes and Ken Dommerson, left again within only a year or so. For Paul 'home' was no longer London or even Scotland. It was Perth: 'I'd grown up there, my friends were there, my ties were there'. The open-air life and opportunities were other magnets. Mary felt very drawn to Tasmania and her friends in Hobart. She went to live there for some years, but finally returned to Britain to be near her elderly parents. Ken's heart was also in Australia and, like Paul's and Mary's, his mother eased his decision: '"It's up to you", she said. I was now eighteen, my own person, and she let me have my head. I was very anxious to return, but that break was probably harder than the break when I was thirteen.'

Others, much as they longed to return to Australia, stayed reluctantly in Britain. They were held by ever-changing webs of family obligations, work, marriages, children . . . and inertia. Much later, in some cases after decades, they finally left to settle in Australia—to 'come home'.

Joan Sharp married in 1950. For many years she endured living in Manchester but it was not Australia. Periodically she would get 'this terrible urge' to return. Disconsolate, Joan would wander down to Australia House in Manchester and browse through the Australian newspapers looking for jobs. 'If only we could migrate . . .'

> I was always very close to my gran. Before I married we did everything together, but later her health faded and finally she barely knew us. We had arranged an interview in Australia House—at last—and it turned out to be on the very day of my grandma's funeral. As we came back from Australia House to go to the funeral I realised that I could now leave England happily because I didn't have to say goodbye to gran.

When Braham Glass returned to Britain he 'clung to an Australian identity'. At school he was 'the colonial'. When he was photographed in his first suit—bought with clothing coupons—he had an AIF hat badge in his lapel:

> Australia was my home. I felt alienated in Britain, and Australia was always at the back of my mind. But for various reasons— mainly my parents threatening they would drop dead if I left again—I never took the opportunity to go back. In 1963, my wife finally turned round and said, 'Let's go to Australia'. It was a terrible winter, and she hit me at the right moment. My mother was widowed and getting on for seventy. We decided that we'd all come or all stay. My mother, who had never left England before, came.

Isabella Woods married in 1951. 'Australia never left' her. But her husband's work was in Britain, and leaving again would have devastated her parents. In 1963 her father was killed in a shipyard accident; her mother died a few years later.

> My husband came home one day and said he didn't like the way things were going in Britain, so would I like to emigrate to Australia? I went running upstairs—'I'm getting the cases!' I had to bide my time for another twelve months, and when I landed at Sydney Airport I felt as if I'd never been away. All those years had just blotted out. I was home.

They built a house in a leafy Sydney suburb. Today, widowed but surrounded by her native-born grandchildren, Isabella helps care for her very elderly Australian 'mother'.

Pamela Palmer had returned to Britain in mid-1945, one of the few evacuees to leave Australia before the war ended. As her train approached Waterloo Station from Southampton she glimpsed Big Ben still dominating the Thames. But London seemed 'grey and dirty'; bomb sites scarred the suburbs and city.

As the train pulled to a stop I saw my mother, father, a ten-year-old and a baby in arms. I thought, 'They are definitely my parents'. But again this feeling of greyness. They seemed so much older than I remembered. We'd been away five years, but they looked about fifteen years older. Mother had gone completely white, my father looked much leaner and balder and older.

I got out of the train to run towards them but then I couldn't. My feet had gone to lead. I got back into the train and said, 'I can't face them'. The four girls with me said, 'Of course you can', and physically pushed me out of the train. In the end I went up to them, Mother burst into tears and Dad hugged me. It was one of those ironies. They seemed more pleased to see me then than I did to see them. I don't know whether it was easier for them getting one person back than for me having to see four people. I was bewildered, overcome by it all.

My friend had made this sign over the front door, 'Welcome Home Pamela'. She had drawn a map of the world with me making my way by a devious route to Australia, and she'd drawn the route back to England starting as a dot in Sydney which became a question mark that got bigger and bigger as it approached England. It was so true. My parents weren't too sure who or what was coming back. Coming back *was* a question mark.

Although it was still summertime when I got home I missed those clear blue skies. Everything appeared grey. The houses were unkempt. People hadn't been able to paint them during the war, they hadn't been able to replace curtains, garden railings had been taken away . . . It had been mend and make do. I immediately thought how lucky I had been to be sent to Australia. I'd had a marvellous war compared with the things they'd had to endure. I didn't play down my experiences in Australia, because they made mother feel that she had done the right thing, that I had had these advantages by being away during the war.

Mother was aware how relaxed I was with Australians, and

she felt she wanted to repay Australia. I was working in Australia House, and had lots of contacts with Australian forces personnel. Mum used to say, 'If anybody wants a bed for the night they're always welcome', so quite often we had three or four Australian personnel sleeping on the floor. Somebody painted out the name of our road and put *Anzac Club*, with an arrow pointing down to our house.

Pamela maintained close contact with her wartime hosts and always had a deep desire to return to Australia. In 1974 an opportunity to migrate arose, and Pamela and her husband left Britain for Australia. They settled at Harbord, close to where Pamela remembered spending her happy wartime years at Manly.

Also destined to return much later to Australia, Phil Robinson, a handsome twenty-year-old in an Air Force greatcoat, strode down a Birmingham platform early in 1946. He recognised his mother, then saw his father—and immediately compared him with his uncles in the sugar country. Phil's father 'didn't measure up'.

When I left home my mother had assured me that everything in my bedroom would be left exactly as it was, and I was looking forward to getting my hands on my childhood possessions again. I was longing to play with my train set and ride my bicycle, which I worshipped . . . Stupid! But I discovered my father had given my things away, probably to some poor youngster who'd been bombed out. But it was a really traumatic experience to suddenly find that the things that I'd treasured in earlier life just weren't there any more.

From then on the relationship between my father and I just folded up. They were never close again, right up until the day he died. When I got back I felt he was always treating me as a child, and I also felt that he resented me coming back to take up some of Mother's time and affection. Mother and I always were close, although as the relationship between me and my father collapsed she had to support him.

My father was an out and out city man, and he could never understand that people could be happy in the wide open spaces of Queensland. Later I said to Dad, 'I might be going back to Australia or somewhere else'. And he said to me, 'How could you break your mother's heart a second time?' That shattered me. I was getting the blame for their own decision, and also being blamed for wanting to branch out and be myself.

In Australia I had learnt Banjo Paterson's poem 'Clancy of the Overflow' parrot fashion. When I got back to England it seemed to me that the poem outlined my life exactly, from the time I came to love Australia and Queensland—until the time when I was having these rows with my father. I saw myself as Banjo

209

Paterson, suddenly back in Birmingham and expected to work there—'the foetid air and gritty of the dusty, dirty city . . .' It described Birmingham and my feelings to a T.

I began working with my father in his business in 1946. It took me two years to pluck up courage to tell him that I just couldn't stand the environment, and that I was going to go. I landed up in Somerset where I lived from 1948 to 1989.

Ever since I got back I had split loyalties. I felt that I belonged to both countries and yet belonged to neither. There are different appeals. I've got deep connections now in Somerset, my daughter, son-in-law, grandson and ninety per cent of my friends are there—whereas in Queensland I've got seventy-three relations.

I tried for years to persuade my wife to emigrate to Australia, but she was an English girl with very deep roots. But in 1977 I had the opportunity to go to Australia for a holiday. I came over on my own, and met the family again—the welcome I got you just wouldn't believe! I came over again in 1984. My wife was ill and I had been advised to disappear for a few weeks, but she died a few months after I returned.

My mother was still living in England. She was nearly ninety and I felt I had to stay there to look after her. Ironically all her relatives lived in Australia. She died in 1987. I was suddenly relieved of all my obligations. The dilemma arose, 'Should I come to live in Australia or shouldn't I?' I couldn't make up my mind so I went into the local village church to plead for guidance. The feeling came over me that if I could find anything in that church which was connected with Australia, then I should come. I was drawn to the visitor's book. The last person to have signed that visitor's book came from Melbourne, from the suburb next to where my cousin lives. So I bought a ticket and came.

In Queensland Phil later met an Australian woman. They married in 1990 and live today in the Blue Mountains. From there they make regular excursions to the sugar cane country near Maryborough to visit Phil's Australian relatives.

Postscript

17

Some 3100 evacuees sailed from Britain aboard CORB ships. However, due to the sinkings of the *Volendam* and *City of Benares*, only some 2700 reached their destinations in the Dominions—577 of them in Australia. Although the Children's Overseas Reception Board provided havens in the Dominions for these 2700 children, in doing so, the scheme separated these children from their homes and parents for some five years. The CORB scheme also led to the deaths of 77 children at sea, proportionately some three hundred times more than were killed or injured during the Blitz—but perhaps less than might have been lost had Britain been invaded in 1940. The evacuation's long-term effects on the 'children', both good and bad, continue today.

Child migration within the British Empire has had a long, and often harrowing, history. The CORB evacuation reflected, and was driven by, Empire loyalties. Ironically, by 1940 the Empire was already in fatal decay—and the Second World War marked its passing.

In 1940 Jean Lorrimer wrote in *The Pilgrim Children*, her eulogistic book about the CORB scheme, of the evacuation's 'rich Imperial harvest that was ripe for the gathering'. Indeed, she hoped CORB's benefits in future might be 'woven into the permanent woof of Empire':

> Why should not streams of British children each year flow to the great Dominions under a scheme similar to that found to be so acceptable in wartime. British stock is sorely needed. Children are ideal settlers. Will parents in peace-time part with their children? This is the crux of the problem . . .

Four years after the war ended, Geoffrey Shakespeare wrote in similar vein: 'I had always taken a special interest in the problems of migration and the redistribution of population within the Empire. [In 1940] it would have been foolish to let this [CORB] opportunity slip.'

Did Shakespeare seriously believe that one aspect of the evacuation was to 'redistribute' children to the Dominions? Or, in saying so, was he in fact clouding CORB's wartime objectives with subsequent rationalisation? The latter was almost certainly the case. For CORB, despite its fine ideals, had proved—and continues to prove—a very mixed blessing.

Jean Lorrimer also predicted in 1940—surely with a degree of blind optimism—that the CORB experience 'cannot fail to benefit each one

Some *Batory* evacuees aboard their well-loved ship once again, at the event held to mark the liner's last trans-Atlantic voyage in 1969. For one 'CORB' who attended, the occasion seemed like 'coming home'.

of [the children] mentally, physically and socially'. For most, though not all, this indeed proved true. But fifty years on many evacuees, even many who enjoyed their years in Australia, look back on the saga with dismay.

There were undoubtedly gains and losses: personal and educational, social and psychological. For no two evacuees were the benefits and drawbacks, or the balance between them, exactly the same. Even siblings often have very different thoughts about their evacuation. And, it must be admitted, innate personal traits, family backgrounds and prior experiences coloured both the evacuees' years in Australia and their perceptions today.

The majority of 'CORBs' believe that their education benefited from their evacuation. For most evacuees the wider experiences of travelling to and from Australia, and living there, fostered an awareness of diversity—and so of tolerance for people and lifestyles different to those they previously knew. These mostly positive recollections are confirmed by Patricia Lin's research, which indicates that overseas evacuation generally brought significantly greater educational opportunities.

Allied to, and no doubt reinforcing this, many—perhaps most—of the evacuees believe that their CORB experiences created a strong sense of independence, self-reliance and confidence.

Geoffrey Shakespeare was thus largely right when he wrote of the 'breadth and independence of outlook and a wider vision' that the evacuees would return with. And undoubtedly, many evacuees' war-time education and general experiences enhanced their later study and employment opportunities—though other postwar factors clearly also contributed. (Conversely, a number of evacuees believe that their later choices to pursue careers in 'caring' professions—teaching, nursing, and childcare in particular—were at least partly due to their own un-happiness while in Australia.)

Many evacuees, however, including some who have 'prospered', be-lieve that the purely personal aspects of their evacuation caused much greater drawbacks than benefits. 'Confidence' was often double-edged. It sometimes camouflaged individuals better able to 'cope' with life—and to change, chameleon-like, to suit others—than to choose how to live themselves. Others believe that their mild phobias, and especially their difficulties in forming close ties, are rooted in the sundering of family bonds by evacuation.

Misgivings about the protracted break with their natural families are the single common denominator of the CORB experience—and its most potent legacy. For most this involves no more than mild regret at the 'lost years', tempered by the knowledge that the war changed other lives far more drastically. For others it is a deeper loss, a grief for bonds broken too soon—and, often, never again solidly joined. In a few cases these feelings are far stronger and more damaging, often reflecting instances where children doubted their parental love and experienced a clear sense of rejection on their departure from Britain in 1940. Con-tinued insecurity and depression, at least partly rooted in the war years, have shadowed a very small minority of the evacuees.

Other feelings concern the evacuees' wartime hosts. Those evacuees who were shown kindness and love in Australia, and whose hosts ac-cepted they were merely 'wartime parents', almost all have great fond-ness for their hosts. Some evacuees living in Australia today now care for their elderly 'Aussie parents'. Others, either because they received too little or too much understanding and 'love', regard their hosts with mixed, often unresolved feelings. Those who were maltreated or abused have mostly, though not all, transcended and forgiven their experiences.

The overwhelming majority of evacuees later married and had families. For these, their children highlighted the poignancy of their own evacuation—and, in almost all cases, emphasised their own parents' selflessness and anguish in 1940. Many evacuees believe that the closeness of their own subsequent marriages and family life reflect

Many of the evacuees who settled in Britain have made nostalgic returns to Australia, and some have visited there a number of times. Here, in 1978, Christine Russon (*left*) and her sister Doreen enjoy recapturing the past with their wartime host, Daisy Malster.

deep-seated thoughts and feelings about the parting from their parents in 1940.

Virtually without exception, all these CORB parents state categorically that they would never have parted with their own children in similar circumstances. 'Even if Britain (or Australia) were facing possible invasion . . . ?' Recalling the dark months of mid-1940, a few mildly qualify their original statement. The majority do not. Whatever gains CORB gave them, the losses they—and their parents—experienced today loom greater in importance. For these evacuees, potential dangers, even actual conflict, could never justify the break-up of their families. (Could the children now suffering in today's war zones, they wonder, conceivably be happier elsewhere—without their families?)

Elspeth Davies, CORB's Welfare Director throughout the war, said in 1983: 'The scheme was a mistake from the start. There was a desperate atmosphere at the time. This, alone, can explain what now appears so absurd.' Indeed, in part CORB *was* absurd. As Geoffrey Shakespeare wrote in his memoirs:

CORB children they were called, and CORB children they remained. Every child who left our shores carried a bootlace round its neck with a magic disc bearing its CORB number, framed in a substance claimed to be proof against salt water, and so strongly made as to be indestructible . . . It was the outward and visible symbol of a great adventure, on which each child was embarked.

The evacuees' lives have moved on. Superficially, very few remain locked in their wartime experiences. But the thoughts and feelings described above linger on—and, with them, the sense of divided loyalties that their evacuation very often created. Noone interviewed for this book produced a CORB name tag. But, in every 'CORB' home, Australian souvenirs hang in British living rooms, British mementos on Australian sunroom walls: Britain or Australia, parents or hosts . . .

Periodic CORB reunions have revived the CORB evacuees' shared experiences and bonds. The first and perhaps most nostalgic reunion was held in February 1969 aboard the *Batory*. Moored at Tilbury on the Thames, the veteran ship was dressed in bunting to signal her final trans-Atlantic voyage. Four of the ship's wartime crew, some fifty evacuees and some escorts were there. One of the 'children' wrote in thanks: 'It is impossible for any words to express my very deep affection for the *Batory*. Yesterday, to me, was like "coming home".' It was a moment of goodwill in the bleakness of the Cold War.

Twenty-one years later, the most moving of all the CORB reunions were held to mark the fiftieth anniversary of the children's departure from Britain in 1940. The largest reunion was held in August 1990 at York in Britain; smaller gatherings were also organised that year at Sydney, Melbourne and Brisbane—and in the other 'Dominions'.

The York reunion included some 200 evacuees, mostly those who had been evacuated to Canada or Australia. Elspeth Davies, in 1990 the sole remaining representative of the CORB organisation, attended, together with some of the elderly escorts. In Sydney, where the largest Australian reunion occurred, 27 evacuees and one escort gathered at the North Head Quarantine Station. The weather was 'scintillating'— just as when the *Batory* had steamed through the Heads half a century before. There were smaller reunions in Melbourne and Brisbane.

For some evacuees, the 1990 reunions were simply nostalgic. But for many others they had a deeper, often lasting, significance. In the intervening years most evacuees have had few contacts with other 'CORBs'. Some have had none at all. At the reunions experiences—and troubling or painful memories—were shared. One of the York organisers recalls:

A lot of people wrote afterwards. I was amazed how many people used the word catharsis—and how many others were

John (*left*) and Michael Fethney, with three of the CORB 'girls' at the 1990 reunion held at York University. Rita Patterson, photographed fifty years before kissing her brother a fond farewell on Blyth Station, is on the right.

talking about catharsis without actually using the word. People who'd had unfortunate experiences, who'd buried painful feelings for many years, discovered that others had had very similar experiences. There was a release and a lot of healing began.

Notes on the oral history

The recollections of some 50 evacuees were my key resource. During 1990 I interviewed eighteen evacuees living in Australia for the Australian War Memorial's Keith Murdoch Sound Archive (coordinated by Australian Heritage Projects Ltd). In 1992, with the assistance of an Australia Council Fellowship, I interviewed 25 evacuees in Britain. Four evacuees were also interviewed by Harry Martin for the Australian War Memorial. Some others whom I was unable to visit sent me recollections. Three of the shipboard escorts also contributed interviews.

CORB reunions held before and during 1990 had resulted in a widespread network of ex-evacuees, some living in Britain and some in Australia. Three reunion organisers, Norman Townsend, John Hare and Michael Fethney, kindly gave me full access to their invaluable lists of names.

Selecting interviewees from the CORB reunion lists posed a danger of slight bias, as those who responded over the years to reunion newspaper publicity might have had unusually—and perhaps disproportionately—strong memories, whether good or bad. However, as I hoped to produce a vivid account, not a strictly historical or sociological work, this possible imbalance was accepted. (Further publicity seeking other interviewees would probably have unearthed mostly the same individuals.)

Almost all the 'CORBs' I approached, including some with deeply troubling memories, agreed to record their experiences. To make sure of interviewing a balanced group, I sought out a representative cross-section of evacuees by gender, age and evacuation experiences. Interviews were based on a sequence of roughly standardised questions which, depending on each person's power of recall, were opened out more or less. Taped interviews mostly lasted for about an hour and a half, although some were significantly longer.

To underpin the evacuees' recollections a questionnaire was sent to everyone on the CORB network (in all, about 150 people in Britain and Australia). One hundred questionnaires were returned completed, representing 17 per cent of the original total of 577 evacuees. The seven-page questionnaire covered most aspects of the evacuees' previous

A once-in-a-lifetime gathering: some 200 CORB 'children' congregate for a group photograph during the 1990 York reunion. For many of the wartime evacuees, meeting other 'CORBs' at reunions has helped to resolve personal conflicts—the legacy of their CORB evacuation.

lives in Britain, their journey to Australia, their lives there and the long-term effects of their evacuation.

The completed questionnaires had two specific uses. First, they gave hard data on many personal, social and historical matters, providing an objective framework for the recollections. Second, they gave reasonably reliable figures from which to construct a cross-section of evacuees.

To provide continuity through the story the recollections of some of the evacuees have been emphasised. These main 'speakers' were chosen for the strength and breadth of their memories, with roughly equal numbers of them now living in Britain and in Australia. The final selection of speakers also reflected the following cross-section of evacuees, as indicated by the questionnaire:

- A little over half the children were evacuated alone and the rest with one or more siblings.
- In Australia, about half the evacuees stayed with relatives and the remainder with previously unknown foster parents.
- About half the children stayed with one family throughout the war, about a quarter with two families, and the rest with three or more families.

- In Australia almost two-thirds of the evacuees lived in cities, with the remainder about evenly divided between towns and country areas.
- Finally, and perhaps most important, of the 100 evacuees who answered the questionnaire: 38 describe their evacuation as 'memorable', 35 as 'mostly enjoyable', 17 as 'bearable', 5 as 'unhappy', and 5 as 'traumatic'.

Editing the oral history to meet constraints of length forced many hard decisions—and the deletion, with great regret, of much fine material. Minor rearrangement of verbatim transcripts was sometimes made to improve their flow. However, the thrust of speakers' memories and views was kept intact.

The book's interview tapes and transcripts, and the completed questionnaires, are now held by the Australian War Memorial. The War Memorial's generous assistance with many aspects of the work is acknowledged elsewhere.

The contributors

The 48 CORB evacuees whose recollections appear in the book are listed below. Names used in the book are wartime names; married names appear below in brackets. I apologise to any contributor who, through oversight, has not been mentioned.

Boys
Bob Bullard, David Cox, Gerald Cox, Ken Dommerson, Peter Edkins, Paul Farquharson, John Fethney, Michael Fethney, Ted Flowers, Braham Glass, Reg Harris, John Hillier, Tony Houghton, Reg Loft, David Massey, Donald Mitchell, Bob Puxted, Phil Robinson, Tony Smith, John Speller, Michael Storey, Norman Townsend, George Wastell, Derric Webster, Albert Young.

Girls
Joyce Briant (Hazeldon), Mary Clemes, Jacqueline Clout (Dorman), Jean Cole (Singleton), Helen Cuthbert (Mann), Katharine Cuthbert (Blake), Betty Deeley (Jeffreys), Barbara Donald (Saum), Muriel Evans, Essie Glass (Gordon), Barbara Helliwell (Hanna), Dorothy Loft (Laing), Nora Lupton (Fernie), Brenda Mallett (Murray), Pamela Palmer (Squirrel), Rita Patterson (Jackson), Anne Ratcliffe (Groth), Phyllis Ratcliffe (Holdsworth), Christine Russon (Chitty), Joan Sharp (Jones), Heather Staff (Weedon), Ruth Wilson (Hay), Isabella Woods (Summerbell).

CORB's Welfare Director in London, Elspeth Davies, was also interviewed, as were two of the escorts: Ian Paterson and Beryl Speirs (Daley). Another escort, Isa Brown (Lupton) sent written recollections; the escort Bill Oats' comments are from his book *Headmaster by Chance*. The Third Mate of the *Nestor* during her CORB voyage, Ronald Tubb, was also interviewed.

Others who provided recollections include survivors of the *City of Benares* and the *Volendam*: Bess Walder (Cummings), Beth Cummings (Williams), Ken Sparks, Colin Scott and Robin Scott.

The following people kindly assisted with various documents, letters or cuttings: Isa Brown, Helen Cuthbert, Katharine Cuthbert, John Hillier, Tony Houghton, Donald Mitchell, Phil Robinson, Beryl Speirs, Michael Storey and George Wastell. Tadek Dobrostanski of Melbourne provided a most valuable translation of the log of the *Batory*'s CORB voyage.

CORB evacuees sent to Australia

The total number of CORB children evacuated to Australia was 577. The Australian contingent included slightly more boys than girls, 307 compared with 270. The children's ages in October 1940 ranged from five to fifteen. About 14 per cent were aged from five to seven, 29 per cent were aged eight to nine, 45 per cent were aged eleven to thirteen, and 12 per cent were aged fourteen to fifteen.

The names of all the Australian CORB children appear below, set out in order of their CORB embarkation numbers. These identifying numbers were based on 'ship batches' and home localities. Asterisks indicate siblings. Identical surnames from the same locations, not asterisked, are often cousins.

I am indebted to Michael Fethney for this list, compiled by him from original CORB records and first published in *The Absurd and the Brave*.

* *Indicates brother or sister follows in list*

87 HARRIS, Eleanor, 15, Barry *
88 HARRIS, Melvin, 13, Barry *
89 HARRIS, Reginald, 10, Barry *
90 HARRIS, Ruby, 7, Barry
91 MATTHEWS, Margaret, 15, Barry
92 DAVIDSON, Frederick, ?, Bridlington
93 SCHULTZ, Phillip, 6, Hull *
94 SCHULTZ, Hester, 5, Hull
95 BROWN, Joan, 11, Birmingham
97 DEELEY, Betty, 12, Birmingham *
98 DEELEY, Philip, 14, Birmingham
99 JONES, Sheila, 7, Swinton

100 HAWLEY, Anthony, 10, Barnoldswick
101 SALT, Albert, 12, Birmingham
102 SPINKS, Iris, 9, Birmingham *
103 SPINKS, George, 7, Birmingham *
104 SPINKS, Joan, 5, Birmingham
106 BRENNAND, Anthony, 13, Blyth
107 BROWN, Evelyn, 11, Blyth
110 PATTERSON, Elsie, 9, Blyth *
111 PATTERSON, Jean, 13, Blyth
112 PATTERSON, Rita, 8, Blyth
113 WOODS, Francis, 12, Blyth
114 WOODS, Isabella, 11, Blyth

115 BULLEN, Donald, 9, Liverpool
118 DUFFY, Francis, 13, Bradford
119 FAREY, Doreen, 12, Bradford
120 FETHNEY, John, 13, Bradford *
121 FETHNEY, Michael, 9, Bradford
122 FIELD, May, 14, Bradford
123 HARDISTY, Helen, 13, Bradford *
124 HARDISTY, Ian, 10, Bradford
125 LANGDALE, Keith, 15, Bradford
126 LEE, Allan, 12, Bradford
127 METCALFE, Kenneth, 15, Bradford
128 RUSSELL, Jack, 13, Bradford

129 STANWAY, Robert, 14, Bradford
130 WEBSTER, Derric, 9, Bradford *
131 WEBSTER, Catherine, 7, Bradford
134 LITTLE, Phyllis, 14, Cardiff *
135 LITTLE, Isobel, 11, Cardiff
136 JONES, Lewis, 12, Cardiff *
137 JONES, Lillian, 7, Cardiff
138 RICHARDS, Ruth, 12, Cardiff *
139 RICHARDS, Barbara, 11, Cardiff
140 THOMAS, Denis, 12, Cardiff
141 WILLIAMS, Dorothy, 11, Cardiff
142 COLE, Jean, 15, Grays
143 CORNISH, Patricia, 10, Loughton
144 COX, Gerald, 9, Chelmsford *
145 COX, David, 8, Chelmsford
146 DIXON, Joan, 11, Chelmsford
147 LAMBLEY, Winifred, 10, South Benfleet *
148 LAMBLEY, James, 5, South Benfleet
149 SOLE, Kathleen, 12, South Benfleet
150 BOWCOCK, Arnold, 13, Colchester
151 BURRELL, Dennis, 14, Colchester *
152 BURRELL, Trevor, 10, Colchester
153 CAPPS, Victor, 13, Colchester
154 GRAY, Michael, 9, Colchester
155 HADDOCK, Vernon, 7, Colchester
156 WARD, Michael, 15, Colchester
157 WIGHT, Richard, 12, Colchester *

158 WIGHT, Rex, 10, Colchester
159 WHITTEN, David, 13, Southall
160 WILKINSON, Sidney, 12, Colchester *
161 WILKINSON, Philip, 12, Colchester
166 BAKER, Dulcie, 14, Darlington *
167 BAKER, Arthur, 10, Darlington
168 BELL, Margaret, 8, Darlington
169 COOPER, Launa, 9, Darlington
173 WILLIAMS, Doreen, 10, Manchester
174 KERSHAW, Evelyn, 11, Darlington
175 LUPTON, Nora, 9, Darlington
176 McLEISH, Margaret, 14, Darlington
177 SIMPSON, Jean, 12, Darlington
178 SNAITH, Sheila, 13, Darlington *
179 SNAITH, Noreen, 12, Darlington
180 THOMPSON, Sylvia, 8, Darlington
181 ANSELL, John, 11, Doncaster *
182 ANSELL, Julie, 9, Doncaster
183 HIGGINBOTTOM, Geoffrey, 8, Doncaster
184 HOGARTH, Stanley, 10, Doncaster *
185 HOGARTH, Betty, 9, Doncaster
186 HOWARTH, Brenda, 13, Doncaster
187 LOXTON, Joan, 7, Doncaster
188 SMITH, Geoffrey, 9, Doncaster
189 WARD, Eric, 11, Liverpool *
193 WARD, Phyllis, 13, Liverpool

190 FLOWERS, Edward, 13, Chester-le-Street
191 HOLMES, Violet, 12, Newcastle-on-Tyne
192 ROBINSON, Rosemary, 13, Middlesborough *
194 ROBINSON, Lilian, 8, Middlesborough
195 TEMPLETON, John, 11, Hartlepool
196 WILLIAMS, Marie, 13, Newcastle-on-Tyne
197 ASCOTT, Kenneth, 12, Greenford
198 BERNARD, Robert, 10, Hanwell, W7
199 BYFORD, Iris, 12, Hanwell *
200 BYFORD, Lawrence, 7, Hanwell *
201 BYFORD, Maureen, 7, Hanwell
202 COLES, Richard, 13, Greenford
203 GIBSON, Janet, 9, Wycombe Marsh *
204 GIBSON, Robert, 9, Wycombe Marsh
205 GRANT, Olive, 13, Northolt *
206 GRANT, Roy, 10, Northolt
207 GREENING, Patricia, 13, Northolt *
208 GREENING, Terence, 14, Northolt *
209 GREENING, Shaun, 9, Northolt *
210 GREENING, Maureen, 7, Northolt *
211 GREENING, Dominic, 6, Northolt
213 HILL, Patricia, 8, W. Ealing
214 HILLIER, Frank, 13, Hanwell *
215 HILLIER, John, 12, Hanwell
216 JOHNSON, Robert, 12, Greenford
219 OWEN, Roderick, 8, Greenford

220 ROSS, Gordon, 13, Hanwell
221 SAUNDERS, Stella, 8, Ealing
222 WOOLLEY, John, 11, Hanwell
225 BARKER, Derek, 9, Enfield
226 HARKNESS, Deirdre, 12, Enfield
227 HENRY, John, 7, Enfield *
228 HENRY, Pamela, 6, Enfield
235 BERTRAM, Doreen, 13, Durham *
236 BERTRAM, Robert, 10, Durham
237 CLOUGH, Greta, 10, Gateshead
239 LAIDLER, Margaret, 13, Felling
240 SIMPSON, Derek, 13, Gateshead
241 STONE, Lillian, 13, Felling
242 TIMMINS, Alan, 11, Gateshead
243 WAUGH, Wilfred, 13, Gateshead
244 WEATHERBURN, Peter, 7, Gateshead
247 BRYDGES, Mary, 12, Grimsby
248 BUDDERY, Leonard, 10, Grimsby
249 CORMACK, Kenneth, 11, Grimsby
250 CUCKSON, Peggy, 13, Grimsby
252 SMITH, Iris, 13, Grimsby
253 SMITH, Nan, 14, Grimsby *
254 SMITH, Sheila, 14, Grimsby
261 BARRETT, Edward, 13, Hull
262 BORRILL, Herbert, 10, Hull
263 CRAWFORD, Brenda, 10, Doncaster
264 FARROW, John, 12, Hull

265 GOODFELLOW, Rita, 12, Hull *
266 GOODFELLOW, Barbara, 10, Hull
267 SCARBOROUGH, Jean, 9, Hull
268 TAYLOR, Maurice, 13, Hull
271 WHYTE, Cynthia, 10 Ilford
272 BARTON, Patricia, 11, Carisbrooke, IOW
273 EEDLE, Donald, 12, Sandown, IOW
274 KENCHINGTON, Agnes, 12, Newport, IOW
275 PENNY, Michael, 14, Undercliffe, IOW *
276 PENNY, David, 12, Undercliffe, IOW *
277 PENNY, Margaret, 9, Undercliffe, IOW
278 PIGGOTT, Bernard, 8, Freshwater, IOW
279 TOWNSEND, Norman, 13, Newport, IOW
280 WHILLIER, Jean, 14, Gatcombe, IOW *
281 WHILLIER, Joan, 12, Gatcombe, IOW
282 ALEXANDER, Joseph, 11, Canterbury
283 ANDREWS, Elizabeth, 12, Leeds *
284 ANDREWS, Audrey, 13, Leeds
285 BELMAR, Leon, 15, Eltham, SE9
286 BOWMAN, Terence, 8, Welling
287 BRIANT, Joyce, 14, Ashford
288 CLOUT, Jacqueline, 12, Ashford *
289 CLOUT, Yvonne, 10, Ashford *
290 CLOUT, Alan, 9, Ashford
291 COLEMAN, John, 12, Bexley *
292 COLEMAN, Frederice, 10, Bexley *

293 COLEMAN, Anthony, 8, Bexley
294 PERREN, Doreen, 12, SE9
295 DEACON, Joan, 7, SE9
296 EDNEY, Frank, 14, Tonbridge
297 GALE, Audrey, 9, Edenbridge *
298 GALE, Shirley, 9, Edenbridge
299 GOLLOP, Joyce, 11, Bexley
300 HADAWAY, Bernard, 13, Sittingbourne
301 HANSON, Frederick, 12, SE9 *
302 HANSON, Richard, 10, SE9 (* 304)
303 WALSHAM, Doris, 11, Liverpool
304 HANSON, Derek, 5, SE9
305 HARRIS, Geoffrey, 5, Bexley Heath *
306 HARRIS, David, 11, Bexley Heath
307 LLOYD, Verna, 13, Bromley *
308 LLOYD, Clarice, 11, Bromley
309 LOFT, Dorothy, 15, Bromley *
310 LOFT, Reginald, 13, Bromley
311 PACKMAN, Betty, 13, Ashford
312 PARRETT, Joan, 15, Sevenoaks
313 PEMBERTON, Leo, 11, Bromley
314 PUXTED, Robert, 14, Tenterden
315 ROACH, Yvonne, 9, Welling
316 ROSE, Arthur, 12, Dartford *
317 ROSE, Jean, 6, Dartford
318 SMITH, Anthony, 13, Glasgow
319 WASTELL, George, 14, Mottingham *

223

320 WASTELL, Alan, 13, Mottingham *
321 WASTELL, Edna, 11, Mottingham *
322 WASTELL, Colin, 7, Mottingham
323 SHARP, Joan, 6, Pendlebury
324 WHITTAKER, Patricia, 13, Orpington
335 COATES, Alan, 11, Leeds *
336 COATES, Dorothy, 13, Leeds
337 JONES, Margaret, 13, Manchester
338 CLARKE, Patricia, 14, Liverpool *
339 CLARKE, Billie Diana, 11, Liverpool
340 HARDCASTLE, Shirley, 7, Leeds
341 HARDCASTLE, Harry, 11, Leeds
342 HELLIWELL, Barbara, 9, Leeds
343 MACDONALD, Jessie, 15, Leeds
344 MORRIS, Irene, 8, Leeds
345 RATCLIFFE, Annie, 9, Leeds *
346 RATCLIFFE, Phyllis, 14, Leeds
347 CARTHEW, Roland, 13, Peckham
348 COHEN, Sidney, 14, Hackney *
349 COHEN, Ralph, 12, Hackney
350 DICKENSON, Audrey, 12, Charlton
351 GLASS, Essie, 13, E1 *
352 GLASS, Braham, 7, E1
353 GOLDRING, Pamela, 6, E5
354 HOUGHTON, May, 13, E3
355 McGINTY, Patricia, 8, Liverpool
356 JEFFREY, Alan, 10, SE9 *

357 JEFFREY, Brenda, 9, SE9
358 KEEN, William, 5, N16
359 LEWIS, John, 6, W. Kensington
363 MILLS, Teresa, 13, Blackwall
364 NOAH, Rachel, 12, W. Kensington
365 PALLIS, Elsie, 11, Dalston, E8 *
366 PALLIS, Patricia, 9, Dalston, E8
367 POTTER, Theresa, 14, SE18
368 RANDALL, June, 13 N16 *
369 RANDALL, Howard, 10, N16
371 SCHULTZ, Jean, 10, E1
372 STEVENSON, Cyril, 14, W6
373 STROUD, Joan, 10, SW7
374 WATERS, Kenneth, 8, SW1
377 AUSTIN, Laura, 13, Newcastle-on-Tyne
378 GRAHAM, Dorothy, 13, Newcastle-on-Tyne
379 HUDSON, Valerie, 5, Newcastle-on-Tyne
380 QUINN, Robert, 13, Newcastle-on-Tyne
381 SMITH, Joan, 6, Newcastle-on-Tyne
382 STEPHENSON, Robert, 9, Belford, Northumberland
383 TRIGG, Charles, 13, Newcastle-on-Tyne *
384 TRIGG, William, 12, Newcastle-on-Tyne
385 BARRETT, George, 13, Dereham *
386 BARRETT, John, 12, Dereham
394 BROWNE, Ann, 8, Norwich
395 KNIGHTS, Ronald, 12, Norwich

396 POWELL, Elizabeth, 11, Merthyr Tydfil
397 BARRETT, Norman, 13, Plymouth
401 HOOK, Laura, 13, Port Talbot *
402 HOOK, Trevor, 11, Port Talbot
403 DWYER, Patrick, 11, Romford
404 KERSHAW, Rosemary, 7, Romford *
405 KERSHAW, Judith, 6, Romford *
406 KERSHAW, Anna, 5, Romford *
407 PROCTOR, Elizabeth, 13, Gidea Park, Essex *
408 PROCTOR, Andrew, 5, Gidea Park, Essex
413 DINGWALL, George, 14, Sheffield *
414 DINGWALL, Audrey, 12, Sheffield *
415 DINGWALL, Kenneth, 8, Sheffield *
416 DINGWALL, Yvonne, 6, Sheffield
417 LOWE, Kathleen, 11, Sheffield
418 SLINGSBY, Joseph, 9, Sheffield *
419 SLINGSBY, Sheila, 6, Sheffield
420 STACEY, Jack, 14, Sheffield
421 STEVENS, Geoffrey, 11, Sheffield
423 FUDGE, Judith, 6, Southampton
424 HOLWAY, Eileen, 10, Portsmouth
427 WILLIAMS, John, 9, Southampton *
428 WILLIAMS, Jean, 7, Southampton
430 DUFF, Irene, 14, South Shields *
431 DUFF, Laura, 12, South Shields
432 STAFF, Denis, 11, South Shields *
433 STAFF, Heather, 9, South Shields

434 THOMPSON, Gordon, 14, South Shields

435 CLAMPS, Stanley, 11, Stockton

436 COLLINS, George, 15, Stockton

437 DAWSON, Theresa, 8, Stockton *

438 DAWSON, Marie, 7, Stockton *

439 DAWSON, Peter, 6, Stockton

441 WALTERS, Vera, 10, Liverpool

442 HANDYSIDE, Sylvia, 10, Stockton

443 HARVEY, Ronald, 15, Stockton

444 MACAULAY, John, 12, Stockton

445 RILEY, William, 8, Stockton

446 SHUTE, Charles, 9, Sheffield

451 BOARD, Joyce, 13, Swansea

452 BUDGEN, Gerald, 12, London

456 PERKINS, Rosina, 12, Tottenham *

457 PERKINS, Albert, 10, Tottenham

458 WHEATLEY, Eileen, 8, Tottenham

459 GREGORY, Kenneth, 10, Willesden

460 TWEED, Leonard, 11, NW10

461 ASH, Douglas, 14, Wimbledon

462 HEATH, Patricia, 13, Wimbledon *

463 HEATH, Derek, 12, Wimbledon

464 JUDD, Arthur, 8, Wimbledon *

465 JUDD, Douglas, 10, Wimbledon

466 McCAPPIN, Joan, 14, Wimbledon

467 SHARPE, David, 12, Wimbledon

470 LOCKWOOD, Roger, 12, York

471 RICHARDSON, Terence, 11, York

472 VARLEY, Robert, 10, York

473 EVANS, Muriel, 10, York

474 SPELLER, John, 8, York

475 STOUT, Freda, 13, York

476 YOUNG, Raymond, 14, Hessle *

477 YOUNG, Julia, 12, Hessle *

478 YOUNG, Albert, 7, Hessle

480 PAGE, Jean, 14, Middlesborough

481 RUSSON, Christine, 11, Redcar *

482 RUSSON, Doreen, 7, Redcar

483 SKINNER, James, 13, Thornaby *

484 SKINNER, Rhoda, 11, Thornaby *

485 SKINNER, William, 9, Thornaby

486 WILSON, Ruth, 13, Sunderland

487 FOGGAN, Blanche, 12, Blyth *

488 FOGGAN, Joseph, 10, Blyth *

489 FOGGAN, June, 8, Blyth

490 LAST, Hetty, 12, Brightlingsea

491 DOMMERSON, Kenneth, 13, Rayleigh

492 CHAMBERS, Kathleen, 12, Liverpool

493 STONE, Geoffrey, 14, Manningtree *

494 STONE, Michael, 12, Manningtree *

495 STONE, Philip, 9, Manningtree

496 BISHOP, Ronald, 10, Hornchurch

497 DRAKE, Pauline, 15, Tollesbury

498 HUMBER, Leslie, 13, Romford *

499 HUMBER, Geoffrey, 10, Romford

500 HARE, Peggy, 13, Hornchurch *

501 HARE, Betty, 12, Hornchurch *

502 HARE, Joan, 10, Hornchurch *

503 HARE, John, 7, Hornchurch

504 BUNDOCK, Trevor, 8, Thundersley

505 BLAKEMAN, Charles, 13, Birmingham

506 ROBINSON, Philip, 14, Birmingham

509 DONALD, George, 13, Bishop Auckland *

510 DONALD, Barbara, 11, Bishop Auckland *

511 DONALD, Harry, 10, Bishop Auckland (see no. 514)

512 HARDING, Elsie, 12, Billingham *

513 HARDING, George, 10, Billingham

514 DONALD, Martha, 13, Bishop Auckland

515 WEEKS, Leslie, 14, Durham

516 RUDGE, Raymond, 13, Gateshead *

517 RUDGE, Alan, 8, Gateshead

518 MUNRO, Joseph, 14, Tyneside *

519 MUNRO, Charles, 9, Tyneside

520 WINDER, Terence, 10, Bristol

522 WALKER, David, 13, N21

524 HIBBERT, Edwin, 9, Teddington

525 LANG, Benedict, 12, Ashington

526 DIXON, Charles, 12, Whitton, Middlesex

527 LE GROS, Daphne, 14, Teddington

528 EDWARDS, Eileen, 12, Hampton

529 VINCENT, Ann, 11, Hampton

531 RUMENS, Terence, 10, Wembley *

532 RUMENS, Geoffrey, 10, Wembley

533 EDKINS, Peter, 11, Hayes, Middlesex

534 DOUGHTY, John, 15, Holloway

535 URSELL, Marjory, 11, Hampton

536 PALMER, Pamela, 14, Harrow

537 BURROW, Enid, 7, Salford (see no. 552)

538 TONGE, James, 13, Wembley *

539 TONGE, Anthony, 10, Wembley *

540 TONGE, Michael, 6, Wembley

541 PLENTY, Anthony, 7, Wembley

542 BULLARD, Robert, 8, Wembley

544 WIX, Dennis, 13, Teddington

545 STOREY, Roy, 15, Teddington *

547 STOREY, Michael, 8, Teddington

548 TOFT, Philip, 6, Ruislip

549 FARQUHARSON, Paul, 12, Ashford *

550 FARQUHARSON, Reginald, 10, Ashford

552 BURROW, Marion, 11, Salford

554 PIPER, Kenneth, 9, Edgeware

555 ROGERS, Anthony, 9, Twickenham *

556 ROGERS, David, 6, Twickenham

563 DAVIES, Cyril, 12, Walsall *

564 DAVIES, Philip, 10, Walsall

565 COOPER, Douglas, 11, Walsall

566 MITCHELL, Albert, 13, Walsall

567 COCKER, Donald, 9, Oldham

733 MALLETT, Brenda, 9, Raynes Park

1982 VOS, Kenneth, 12, Harrow *

1983 VOS, Theodora, 14, Harrow

1984 FREEBORN, Mary, 13, Wimbledon *

1985 FREEBORN, John, 9, Wimbledon

1986 GUTHRIE, Donald, 13, Liverpool

1987 MACLAGAN, Robert, 9, Chertsey *

1988 MACLAGAN, Ian, 10, Chertsey *

1989 MACLAGAN, Catherine, 12, Chertsey*

1990 MACLAGAN, Sheila, 14, Chertsey

1991 BIRTWISTLE, Shirley, 5, Stockport

1992 HIGGINS, John, 8, Stockport

1993 FAGEN, William, 8, Cheadle Hulme *

1994 FAGEN, Arthur, 5, Cheadle Hulme

1995 HUME, Peter, 11, Manchester

1996 CHADWICK, David, 10, Stockport

1997 WILLIS, John, 13, Stockport

1998 GARNER, Jack, 12, Manchester *

1999 GARNER, Ann, 6, Manchester

2000 KENYON, Charles, 10, Stockport

2001 SCOTT, Florence, 13, Stockport

2002 ELLIS, Leonard, 13, Manchester *

2003 ELLIS, Alan, 9, Manchester

2004 ORWIN, Joan, 11, Cheadle

2005 JAMES, Geoffrey, 9, Stockport

2006 ECCLES, George, 12, Stockport

2007 JONES, Janet, 6, Stockport

2008 EMBLING, Barbara, 15, Stockton

2010 MANNING, Dulcie, 9, London

2011 VICKERY, John, 5, Tiverton

2012 BESWICK, Audrey, 14, Oldham

2013 BARNARD, Ernest, 13, Ealing *

2014 BARNARD, Margaret, 9, Ealing

2016 JENKINS, Gwyneth, 12, Bury St Edmunds

2017 BOOCOCK, Joan, 10, Bradford *

2018 BOOCOCK, Clarice, 13, Bradford

2021 WATKINSON, Roger, 10, Thornton Heath

2022 REED, Martin, 11, Banstead *

2023 REED, Derek, 9, Banstead

2024 O'DOWD, Pamela, 15, Surbiton

2025 CLEWES, Mary, 13, Orpington

2027 HAMMOND, Sheila, 11, Tolworth

2028 TILLMAN, Robert, 13, Mortlake

2029 STANDAGE, Brenda, 12, N. Cheam *

2030 STANDAGE, Norman, 9, N. Cheam

2031 MINTER, Beryl, 10, Purley

2032 EDWARDS, Derek, 11, Worcester Park

2033 LOWE, Ernest, 13, Coulsdon

2035 PAWSEY, Derek, 8, N. Cheam *

2036 PAWSEY, Sylvia, 12, N. Cheam *

2037 PAWSEY, Peter, 6, N. Cheam

2039 WATTS, Hilary, 13, Epsom

2040 MORAN, John, 10, Mitcham

2041 HEDGECOE, Kathleen, 12, Cheam

2044 DUBERY, Mervyn, 13, Epsom

2045 BOLING, Michael, 11, Surbiton *

2046 BOLING, John, 6, Surbiton *

2047 BOLING, Geraldine, 13, Surbiton

2048 LONGWORTH, Joan, 14, Sutton *

2049 LONGWORTH, Iris, 6, Sutton

2050 ROGERS, Janet, 10, Bristol

2051 JARRITT, Frieda, 14, Bristol

2052 CASTLE, Pauline, 14, Bristol

2550 MORGAN, Maurice, 7, Liverpool *

2551 MORGAN, Freda, 12, Liverpool *

2552 MORGAN, Percy, 14, Liverpool

2553 FLETCHER, John, 7, Liverpool *

2554 FLETCHER, Geraldine, 8, Liverpool

2555 CLARKE, Thomas, 12, Liverpool *

2556 CLARKE, Gladys, 10, Liverpool *

2557 CLARKE, John, 5, Liverpool

2564 HACKETT, John, 12, Liverpool *

2565 HACKETT, Sheilagh, 9, Liverpool

2566 DUFF, Gordon, 13, Bolton

2567 GARDNER, Beryl, 9, Manchester *

2568 GARDNER, William, 6, Manchester

2569 PRINCE, Marjorie, 5, Manchester

2570 HODGSON, Margaret, 13, Prestwich *

2571 HODGSON, Joan, 8, Prestwich

2572 CLIPSTONE, Patricia, 11, Nottingham

2573 CRAWSHAW, Nellie, 12, Bolton

3129 MILLINGTON, Kenneth, 12, Warrington

3130 HOUGHTON, Tony, 14, Warrington *

3131 HOUGHTON, Donald, 11, Warrington

3132 NAYLOR, Stuart, 11, Warrington

3133 SMITH, Gordon, 12, Southport

3134 RIMMER, Henry, 13, Southport

3137 WILSON, Harry, 13, Rochdale

3138 GARFAT, Frank, 12, Rochdale

3140 RILEY Leslie, 11, Manchester

3141 THOMPSON, Gordon, 13, Manchester

3142 MASSEY, David, 11, Liverpool

3143 CARDY, John, 12, Lancaster

3144 BEECH, Arthur, 13, Oldham

3145 HUMPHREYS, Clifford, 12, Oldham

3146 TOMLINSON, Jess, 12, Blackburn

3148 EASTHAM, Alan, 13, Foulridge

3149 MITCHELL, Donald, 13, Colne

3150 PHILLIPS, Anthony, 13, Colne

3501 FERN, Lloyd, 12, Dundee

3502 HERD, Ian, 11, Methil *

3503 HERD, Andrew, 9, Methil

3504 KILPATRICK, George, 10, Burnbank *

3505 KILPATRICK, Emerson, 8, Burnbank (see no. 3563)

3506 LAUGHLAN, Samuel, 11, Bellshill *

3507 LAUGHLAN, Duncan, 8, Bellshill

3510 RUNDLE, Douglas, 8, Motherwell *

3511 RUNDLE, Gregor, 12, Motherwell

3512 SCOTT, John, 14, Ayr

3513 BARCLAY, Robert, 13, Edinburgh

3514 BRALSFORD, David, 7, Edinburgh

3515 CRUDDAS, John, 13, Enfield

3516 GLASIER, William, 8, Edinburgh (see no. 3545)

3517 MACKIE, David, 8, Edinburgh *

3518 MACKIE, Walter, 9, Edinburgh

3519 McINTYRE, Peter, 13, Edinburgh

3520 NICHOLSON, William, 13, Edinburgh

3521 ROBERTSON, George, 12, Edinburgh *

3522 ROBERTSON, William, 10, Edinburgh

3523 ROBERTSON, William, 10, Leith (see no. 3553)

3524 SMITH, David, 12, Edinburgh

3525 VALVONA, Ralph, 9, Edinburgh

3526 AITCHISON, Thomas, 14, Dumbarton

3530 HILL, Ian, 9, Glasgow

3531 HOOPER, Brian, 9, Johnstone

3532 LAIRD, John, 8, Glasgow

3533 MILLAN, William, 11, Glasgow

3534 McDONALD, Ramsay, 10, Glasgow (see nos 3578, 3579)

3535 McNEIL, Thomas, 11, Glasgow

3536 PATERSON, Samuel, 12, Baillieston

3537 TIERNEY, Albert, 11, Glasgow

3538 TURNBULL, Robert, 12, Glasgow

3539 WIGG, Arthur, 9, Glasgow (see no. 3599)

3540 YOUNG, Andrew, 10, Glasgow

3541 BLANCHE, Adina, 11, Edinburgh *

3542 BLANCHE, William, 7, Edinburgh

3543 CAMERON, Sheila, 14, Edinburgh

3545 GLASIER, Dorothy, 11, Edinburgh

3546 LAW, Annie, 14, West Calder

3547 PATERSON, John, 5, Glasgow *

3548 PATERSON, Margaret, 9, Glasgow

3549 RENNY, Mabel, 7, Arbroath *

3550 RENNY, Maureen, 8, Arbroath

3551 RICHARDSON, Elizabeth, Edinburgh

3552 ROBERTSON, Constance, 12, Edinburgh *

3553 ROBERTSON, George D., 5, Leith

3554 SINCLAIR, Margaret, 7, Edinburgh

3555 TROTTER, Margaret, 11, Edinburgh

3556 CUTHBERT, Helen, 9, Glasgow *

3557 CUTHBERT, Katherine, 7, Glasgow

3558 FARMAN, Harriet, 12, Bridge of Don

3559 GOUGH, Christopher, 6, Edinburgh

3560 HOOPER, Kathleen, 11, Johnstone (see no. 3531) *

3561 HOOPER, Winifred, 5, Johnstone

3562 HOWE, Ethel, 12, Glasgow

3563 KILPATRICK, Margaret, 7, Burnbank

3564 LOW, Helen, 5, Dundee

3566 MILLAN, Terence, 7, Glasgow (see no. 3533)

3568 SOMERVILLE, Isabella, 12, Ruthenglen

3569 TIERNEY, Joseph, 6, Glasgow (see no. 3537)

3570 WYLLIE, Jessie, 10, Mauchline

3578 McDONALD, Mary, 14, Glasgow

3579 McDONALD, Margaret, 12, Glasgow

3580 McINTYRE, Mary, 11, Edinburgh (see no. 3519)

3581 SWAN, Ruby, 9, Leith

3583 VALVONA, Caroline, 6, Edinburgh (see no. 3525) *

3584 VALVONA, Doreen, 13, Edinburgh

3585 WALKER, Janet, 8, Edinburgh

3586 BARTON, Roberta, Glasgow

3587 CUNNINGHAM, Annie, 10, Glasgow *

3588 CUNNINGHAM, Esther, 7, Glasgow *

3589 CUNNINGHAM, Isabella, 12, Glasgow

3590 LAUGHLAN, Jeanie, 10, Bellshill (see nos 3506, 3507) *

3591 LAUGHLAN, Jessie, 14, Bellshill

3592 MACKIE, Lois, 10, Glasgow

3593 MILLER, Mary, 13, Glasgow

3595 McINTYRE, Rachel, 10, Glasgow

3596 McNEIL, Jessie, 12, Glasgow (see no. 3535)

3597 ROSS, Irene, 12, Cambuslang

3598 TIERNEY, Agnes, 12, Glasgow (see nos 3537, 3569)

3599 WIGG, Elizabeth, 7, Glasgow

3600 WILLIAMSON, Nessie, 11, Glasgow

3601 WHITE, Margaret, 10, Bonnybridge

3602 FULLERTON, Jack, 9, Glasgow *

3603 FULLERTON, Marion, 14, Glasgow *

3605 DAVIDSON, Annie, 13, Glasgow *

3606 DAVIDSON, Margaret, ?, Glasgow

3607 GAIRDNER, William, 12, Glasgow

3610 OSWALD, John, 6, Edinburgh

3611 YOUNG, Grace, 11, Edinburgh

3612 CREEVY, Charles, 8, Glasgow *

3613 CREEVY, Mary, 11, Glasgow

3614 GRAVIL, Sydney, 14, Glasgow

3720 BOYD, Ross, 12, High Burnside

Bibliography

The following books provided useful background to the CORB scheme and other Second World War evacuation programmes, insights into the impact of evacuation on children, accounts of wartime air and sea operations, and details of other child migration schemes involving Australia. Michael Fethney's The Absurd and the Brave, *the overall account of CORB evacuation to the four Dominions, was invaluable— especially regarding the politics behind the scheme, the convoys' various fates and the children's experiences with host families. Australian city newspapers were a useful source of comments and photographs, especially concerning the evacuees' arrival in October and November 1940.*

Bailey, A. 1981, *America Lost and Found*, Faber & Faber, London
Barker, R. 1987, *Children of the Benares*, Methuen, London
Barnett, C. 1991, *Engage the Enemy More Closely*, Hodder & Stoughton, London
Bean, P. and Melville, J. 1989, *Lost Children of the Empire*, Unwin Hyman, London
Bowyer, M.J.F. 1990, *The Battle of Britain*, Patrick Stephens, Wellingborough
Calder, A. 1969, *The People's War,* Jonathan Cape, London
Fethney, M. 1990, *The Absurd and the Brave*, The Book Guild, Sussex
Gelb, N. 1990, *Dunkirk, the Incredible Escape*, Michael Joseph, London
Inglis, R. 1989, *The Children's War*, Collins, London
Johnson, B.S. 1968, *The Evacuees*, Gollancz, London
Lin, P. 1991, 'Perils Awaiting Those Rising Above Their Allotted Status', Princeton University, New Jersey (unpublished thesis)
Oats, W. 1986, *Headmaster by Chance*, Aguerremendi Press, Hobart
Pertek, J. 1975, *Krolewski Statek Batory* (*The King's Ship Batory*), Wydawnictwo Morskie, Gdansk
Priestley, J.B. 1940, *Postscripts*, Heinemann, London
Shakespeare, G. 1949, *Let Candles be Brought In*, Macdonald, London
Wagner, G. 1982, *Children of the Empire*, Weidenfeld & Nicholson, London
Wicks, B. 1988, *No Time to Wave Goodbye*, Bloomsbury, London

The following books are dated and generally eulogistic. However, they include some interesting details of the CORB evacuation to Australia. M. Maclean was the Batory *escort who inspired the ships' community singing. B. Sandbach recounts the sinking of the* Rangitane *in November 1940, when some ex-*Batory *escorts were killed. J. Lorimer includes letters sent from evacuees and their Australian hosts to the children's parents.*

Lorimer, J. 1942, *Pilgrim Children*, Frederick Muller, London
Maclean, M. 1941, *The Singing Ship*, Angus & Robertson, Sydney
Sandbach, B. 1941, *Prison Life on a Pacific Raider*, Hodder & Stoughton, Sydney

Photographic acknowledgements

About half of the photographs in the book are from evacuees' personal albums. I am most grateful to the many 'CORBs' who showed me their photographs, and particularly to those who later lent photographs for inclusion in this book, despite their being mostly irreplaceable and of great sentimental value.

Thirty four of the photographs are from the collection of the Imperial War Museum, London. The Imperial War Museum's generosity in waiving its usual reproduction fees, so allowing inclusion of these fine photographs, is very much appreciated, and is acknowledged in the Preface. Imperial War Museum photographs appear on the following pages:

xi, xii (and cover), 9, 11, 12, 15, 17, 19, 22, 24, 26, 29, 31, 33, 37, 39, 42, 45, 57, 61, 64 (both), 67, 72, 75, 87, 88, 114 (both), 171, 174, 177, 196, 205.

One photograph has been provided by the *West Australian* newspaper. This appears on page 105.